Other Materials by Lucia Capacchione

BOOKS
Recovery of Your Inner Child
The Creative Journal
The Power of Your Other Hand
The Creative Journal for Children
The Creative Journal for Teens
The Well-Being Journal
The Picture of Health
Lighten Up Your Body, Lighten Up Your Life
   (co-authored with Elizabeth Johnson and James Strohecker)

AUDIOTAPES
The Picture of Health (Meditation, Drawing, and Writing)
The Wisdom of Your Other Hand (set of 5 tapes)

For a catalog of lectures, workshops, books, and tapes contact:
   Lucia Capacchione
   P.O. Box 1355
   Cambria, CA 93428
   (310) 281-7495 or (805) 546-1424

Other Materials by Sandra Bardsley

Birth Journaling Guide (a booklet for childbirth classes)
Audiotape: Birth Cave Imagery

For Co-Creations workshops, lectures, consultations, and materials contact:
   Sandra Bardsley
   Co-Creations
   P.O. Box 3204
   Ashland, OR 97520
   (503) 488-3446 FAX: (503) 482-8295

Creating a Joyful Birth Experience

by

Lucia Capacchione, Ph.D.

and

Sandra Bardsley,
R.N., F.A.C.C.E.

A FIRESIDE BOOK
Published by Simon & Schuster
New York   London   Toronto   Sydney   Tokyo   Singapore

FIRESIDE
Rockefeller Center
1230 Avenue of the Americas
New York, New York 10020

FIRESIDE and colophon are registered trademarks
of Simon & Schuster Inc.

Manufactured in the United States of America
1   3   5   7   9   8   6   4   2

Library of Congress Cataloging-in-Publication Data is available.

ISBN: 0-671-87027-0

Material on page 195 from *The Prophet* by Kahlil Gibran,
copyright 1923 by Kahlil Gibran and renewed 1951 by
Administrators C.T.A. of Kahlil Gibran Estate and Mary G.
Gibran, reprinted by permission of Alfred A. Knopf, Inc.

"If you truly respect life, you will learn to preserve it."
—*Chin Li*

Dedicated to:
the unborn children
and the families
who are lovingly
welcoming them
into the world.

With gratitude

To our teachers who brought us to these insights.

To our ancestors, especially our grandparents and our parents.

To our children, grandchildren, and future generations.

Contents

Susannah Dintzis

Acknowledgments

Thanks to our students and clients who generously provided us with illustrations for this book.

Thanks to:

Our personal editor, Aleta Pearce, for her tireless work, clear thinking, and invaluable input

Our researcher, Celia Pearce, for her painstaking attention to detail in compiling the resource guide

Our assistant and proofreader, Francesca Nemko, for her technical and moral support

Kathi Wheeler, of Nordesign, for the graphic charts and Alison Gunn for editorial assistance at Co-Creations

David Chamberlain for his support in reading the manuscript and making valuable suggestions that made this book more useful

Lynn Moen, of Birth and Life Bookstore, for coaching us in the beginning stages and for being such a general resource person

William Emerson, Gayle Peterson, Penny Simkin, Mariellen O'Hara, Karen Beesley, and Elizabeth Hallett for their encouragement and professional input

We thank Futsu Francis Treon for his continuous spiritual and emotional guidance throughout the information gathering and final writing of this book

Our editor at Simon and Schuster, Sheila M. Curry, for her patience, support, and guidance during the final stages of labor

Marilyn Abraham and Sheridan Hay, whose initial enthusiasm helped make our dream a reality

Authors' Note

Introduction

When I began writing self-help books, it was a lonely process. I felt like I was writing to people I had never met and would probably never know. After the publication of my first book, *The Creative Journal: The Art of Finding Yourself*, I was pleasantly surprised. Beautiful, heartfelt letters came from readers, who told me their stories. They wrote about how Creative Journaling had touched their lives, and thanked me for my courage and hard work. I also heard from professionals who were applying the method with great success in their work as therapists, teachers, doctors, and nurses.

One of these correspondents was Sandra Bardsley, a nurse, childbirth educator, and mother of five. She expressed great enthusiasm for Creative Journaling and asked if she could use it in her childbirth classes. From my experiences as a therapist I had already concluded that my method belonged in the childbirth field. My sixth sense told me that Sandra could be trusted to apply my work creatively, so I readily agreed.

Early in my private practice (working mostly with women and families), I learned how powerfully the birth experience affects a person's entire life. Using art and movement therapy in combination with role-playing, clients regressed to early childhood or infancy and recounted emotional wounds that needed to be healed. Sometimes my client regressed to a time before birth *in utero*. Nothing in my professional training had prepared me for this, and the first time it happened, I was utterly amazed. This was in the seventies, before David Chamberlain, Thomas Verny, and other psychologists showed us that babies remember their *in utero* and birth experiences and that, as adults, they have access to these memories.

During one session Gloria drew a fetus and instantly flashed back to being in the womb. She sensed that she had been unwanted. In the regressed state she could *feel* her mother's anxiety over being pregnant with her. In a powerful moment she realized that she had spent her entire life trying to "not be here" (being shy, unassertive, agreeing with what everyone else wanted of her). After her regression Gloria had a heart-to-heart talk with her mother and found out that her mother had been horrified when she learned she was pregnant. There were other children in the family, times were hard, and Gloria's mother was extremely apprehensive about having another mouth to feed. Gloria's birth had been torturous: slow, difficult, and injurious to the baby. Although Gloria had never been told about the family situation when she was conceived, her *in utero* experiences remained in her unconscious and became conscious only when she was in a regressed state.

Much to my surprise other clients had similar regression experiences. After these sessions I gave assignments to them such as journal writing and, when appropriate, I suggested that the client ask family members about their birth. There was an amazing correlation between the *in utero* regression experience and the actual birth.

The most dramatic experience I had with this phenomenon of fetal flashbacks was my own. During a session of bodywork therapy I regressed to the *in utero* state. I felt myself clinging desperately to a wall. Sheets of red liquid were pouring down over me, threatening to dislodge me and wash me out. I knew that my survival depended upon my holding on for dear life. After I shared this imagery with my therapist, we both agreed that this was an *in utero* experience. We concluded that I should find out about my conception and gestation period.

My mother told me that, using traditional methods, the doctor had timed conception from her first missed menstrual period. According to their calculations I was to have been born in late December. When I was born in early November, a healthy, full-term baby, the doctor concluded that my mother had had a period during her first month of pregnancy.

In reflecting on my *in utero* experience, I thought about my own two pregnancies. The first time my doctor told me I was pregnant, an urge came over me somehow to communicate with the baby *in utero*. An artist and closet poet, the first thing I did was address my unborn child by writing a poem:

Who are you
who shall call me mother
placing on my head
that joyful crown
tied with the love knot?

Next I created a mural on a large sheet of white paper. I integrated the poem into a collage, a wreath of flowers cut out of magazines. The mural hung in the hallway that opened onto our kitchen. Those images caught my eye every day. They fed my soul. Intuitively I knew what pregnant women have probably always known: We can indeed communicate with the unborn child.

What I did not know then was that the unborn child can communicate with us—in words. I discovered this by observing the journal dialogues of expectant mothers in my classes and art therapy practice. Their work convinced me that Creative Journaling was a powerful tool for communicating with the unborn child. In their journal entries and artwork these women revealed their true wants and needs and those of the unborn child. They were then able to share these desires with their partners. Sometimes the expectant father kept a journal as well. It became clear to me that these techniques could help in creating a joyful birth experience for the whole family.

My busy schedule made it impossible for me to research and apply Creative Journaling to childbirth education. I realized that this would have to be done by an experienced professional in the childbirth-education field. I waited until it was time for the idea to be born.

—*Lucia Capacchione*

In 1979 I returned to the U.S.A. from Central America, where I had been living with my husband and five children for several years. I was recuperating from a serious car accident that had resulted in severe head and spinal-cord injuries. Miraculously, following years of intense therapy, I had regained the ability to think, talk, and walk.

Prior to my accident I had been a nurse in maternal and child health care. I wanted to stay in that field. As my health prevented me from resuming my nursing career, I decided to return to school and become a childbirth educator. Following my training I began teaching pregnant women and their partners about birth and early parenting.

I was teaching traditional childbirth preparation skills: breathing, focusing, physical exercises, and so forth. Although this practical information was valuable, it was obvious to me that there was something missing. Many women in my classes wanted to get in touch with their feelings and understand the emotional aspects of pregnancy and birth. They were leaving my classes still feeling unsure of themselves and unable to trust their innate ability to give birth. They didn't know what kind of birth they wanted or how to go about creating it. These women, and their support persons, were not learning how to maintain their power during pregnancy and delivery. Even though they were thrilled with the safe birth of their babies, they later admitted to me that they were somehow dissatisfied.

My heart went out to my students. I wondered, *How can I emphasize emotional and relationship awareness in my classes?* As the mother of five children I knew how important feelings and relationships were during pregnancy and birth, and I wanted to address these issues in my classes.

Searching for more teaching ideas, I saw that the majority of childbirth classes focused primarily on physical and intellectual preparation. In the field of childbirth education I could find no techniques for exploring feelings during pregnancy. In an attempt to meet this need I incorporated traditional journal-keeping methods into my classes.

Although they made some effort at journaling, it was difficult for students to explore on their own time. We had limited time to do journaling in class, and the majority of students were not doing it at home. Some women even experienced additional stress because they saw journaling as one more thing they "had to do." They told me they wanted to write in their journals but couldn't and ended up feeling guilty. I also noticed that the support person often felt left out, and family bonding was not occurring. Traditional journal keeping excluded men, who saw it as unmanly.

While I was teaching these classes, I discovered the importance of the right hemisphere of the brain for accessing feelings. I already knew that the right hemisphere specialized in visual and spatial perception. What I hadn't known was that emotional expression and intuition are also associated with the right side of the brain. I also learned that memory of physical and emotional trauma (such as child abuse and sexual abuse) that has been stored in the body is more accessible through right-brain techniques.

I concluded that right-brain activities would help my students deal with the fear of pain and other emotions typical of pregnancy. Hopefully such techniques would also build a strong emotional bond between the mother, baby, and support person. But where would I find such a method? It had to be fast, fun, and easy to do.

I didn't know of any way to fulfill these requirements until I discovered Lucia Capacchione's book, *The Creative Journal: The Art of Finding Yourself*. First I used it for self-discovery. Her technique of writing with the non-dominant hand produced extraordinary results. As I gained deeper insight into my own feelings, I knew the Creative Journal method was what I had been searching for.

I integrated Lucia's method into my classes as the Creative Birth Journal and found that my students responded enthusiastically. It provided an enjoyable way to look at feelings as well as at outmoded values and beliefs that needed to be changed. The techniques for replacing negative beliefs with positive ones enhanced my students' self-esteem. My classes now incorporated emotional and relationship issues along with physical and intellectual preparation.

My students and I felt satisfied. However, this new method was not greeted with much interest from either my childbirth colleagues or the hospital where I taught. In spite of this poor response I decided to press on. In 1985 I started my own business, Co-Creations, teaching private childbirth classes using my new technique. My goal and motto were "to awaken joy, creativity, and inner guidance" in each woman and her partner.

Later I discovered the Association for Pre- and Perinatal Psychology and Health (APPPH). This organization supports scientific exploration in the mind-body connection of prebirth, birth, and early parenting. I was glad to find fellow professionals speaking about some of the same concerns I had surrounding childbirth preparation. This organization acted as an anchor and support system for Co-Creations.

Over the next eight years my classes focused on welcoming the baby and strengthening the family bond. This included the crucial periods of pregnancy, birth, and the first two years of life. Women and their partners were now leaving my classes feeling empowered and ready for birth and early parenting.

—*Sandra Bardsley*

The method presented in this book grew out of many years of field-testing. It includes the physical, emotional, intellectual, and relationship aspects of pregnancy, labor, and birth. Our results show that this approach is highly effective because it bridges the gap that presently exists between the strictly medical approach to childbirth and the very real emotional-psychological needs of pregnant women and their partners.

Our approach helps you to:

- Understand how you really feel

- Define what you want and learn to ask for it clearly

- Create a cohesive birth plan and support team

- Strengthen family bonding

- Welcome your baby into the world

Our goal is to assist the expectant mother, her birth partner, and support team to create a joyful pregnancy, birth, and early parenting experience. We do this with:

- Food for thought (information and guidance)

- Creative activities (illustrated with writing and artwork by expectant parents)

- True stories about parents who have empowered themselves

- Checklists

- Resources

- Bibliography

In addition this book has special relevance for those who have suffered traumatic experiences in childhood, such as physical, emotional, or sexual abuse or serious illness. Many exercises in this book have proven successful with survivors of such trauma. These parents use their pregnancy as an opportunity to heal the past. As they learn to nurture and protect themselves through Inner Child work, they move past fear and anxiety about having and caring for a baby. Instead of replaying the painful past, parenting becomes an empowering and fulfilling experience.

This book is also for medical and mental health professionals working in the fields of childbirth and early parenting. It provides new methods and techniques for use in classes or individual sessions. It can also be recommended for direct client use as follow-up at home.

Throughout this book we have done our best to keep the techniques simple and fun. Our suggestions are both practical and easy to blend into everyday life. As mothers we know from experience that during pregnancy parents are confronted with many challenges. There are preparations, decisions, new demands, and financial responsibilities. The last thing you need is a long list of "have-tos" added to your already full menu. Please accept our ideas and resources as suggestions. Use these techniques to learn how to listen to yourself. Become the expert and write the book about *your* pregnancy, labor, delivery, and early parenting.

—*Lucia Capacchione and Sandra Bardsley*

1

So You're Going to Have a Baby

Becoming a parent is one of the most powerful and enlightening of all human experiences. It changes our lives forever, and it affects the lives of others. There are certain mysteries of life and love that can only be experienced through conceiving and having a baby. That is why parenting is such a gift. However, we do not suddenly become parents when we conceive or give birth. Parenting begins long before the baby is born, long before conception. The roots of how we feel and behave as parents go back to our own birth and childhood. They are based on *beliefs* both conscious and unconscious. We develop these beliefs firsthand from our own experience and secondhand from what others have said.

Our beliefs and feelings about having a baby powerfully influence how we experience pregnancy, labor, and birth. With this in mind our approach to childbirth preparation focuses on four levels of awareness:

Physical Awareness: Hearing and trusting messages from your body and caring for yourself

Emotional Awareness: Listening to your feelings and expressing them

Intellectual Awareness: Examining your thoughts and beliefs; choosing and creating what you want through the power of imagination

Relationship Awareness: Communicating your needs and wants; creating a team (family, friends, co-workers, health professionals) for a strong personal support system

Physical Awareness

During pregnancy a woman's body goes through more changes than at any other time in her life. Her size and shape, her weight and distribution of weight, are altered dramatically. A pregnant woman feels sensations she has never had before. She may crave certain foods and her energy level may fluctuate. She may feel awkward in a body that is changing so rapidly. Pregnancy challenges a woman's feelings about her body and herself.

It is extremely important that the expectant mother be aware of her body and all of its messages. One early realization she has is that she is never truly alone because her body is now supporting another being. This can feel overwhelming and invasive at times. She also has to cope with the media's attitude toward the female body and notions of the ideal "look." Seldom does the expectant mother see the pregnant body held up as an image of beauty. Instead pictures of ultra-thin, flat-tummied models and actresses surround her. This may cause her to feel conflict about the physical changes she is undergoing.

Learning to listen to your body is probably one of the most important skills you can learn during pregnancy. Sensitivity to your physical needs will help you to nurture yourself. In taking good care of yourself you are also taking good care of your unborn child.

Emotional Awareness

Knowing how you feel emotionally is an important part of pregnancy, birth, and parenting. When you are clear about your emotions, your mind can function more effectively. If emotions remain unacknowledged and unexpressed, you lose mental focus and clarity. Also, pent-up emotions can get trapped in your body, causing stress-related conditions (stomach upset, back pain, headache) that can complicate your pregnancy. Understanding and valuing your own emotions gives you a stronger sense of self.

A woman who has not established a strong sense of self may find it difficult to bond with her baby. Once she has decided to go through with the pregnancy, the woman cannot *physically* abandon the fetus. However, it is possible for her to check out *emotionally*. All childbirth professionals have seen women who are not emotionally present during pregnancy, labor, or birth. Sadly these women don't believe they are capable of handling childbirth. They do not know what they want or need, and they avoid planning the kind of birth they want. They become passive and want others to take charge of the delivery. Overwhelmed, they easily succumb to medical authority or the uninformed opinions of others. Out of fear these women often end up asking for drugs and maximum medical intervention. As a result they miss the power and joy of birth.

Intellectual Awareness

One of the great causes of stress for expectant mothers is negative beliefs about pregnancy and birth. Many doubts, fears, and worries come to the surface ("Will I get sick during pregnancy? Will the baby develop normally? How painful will delivery be? Will I have a healthy baby?" and so on). Negative beliefs about pregnancy and birth that are not addressed can cause fear and anxiety that go unexpressed. However, these fears don't disappear. Instead they are likely to get stored in the body and to cause discomfort, fatigue, or pain. Pregnancy is a very good time to reduce the stress that results from negative beliefs and unexpressed feelings. Practicing the art of listening to yourself and changing negative beliefs can remove unwanted stress from your life.

Intellectual awareness gives you the ability to recognize and honor your feelings and values. During this incredible period of transition you can achieve profound insights and learn to communicate your values and needs clearly.

Relationship Awareness

At no time in a woman's life are her relationships and support system more important than during pregnancy and birth. Communication becomes essential. As a relationship skill, communication involves two people sharing themselves with each other. Clear communication is an art. It takes time and is not always easy. Sometimes people do not know how to share their true feelings and needs. One couple, authors Gerald Jampolsky and Diane Cirincione, have said that the word *intimacy*, when broken down, means "in-to-me-see." Revealing ourselves makes real intimacy possible. Being in a marriage or partnership develops relationship awareness. It provides many opportunities to explore and express feelings. It prepares a woman for sharing her life with her baby.

Some expectant mothers do not have a partner or supportive relationship with anyone. Many teenage mothers fall into this category. Often the baby's father has abandoned the pregnant girl, and her family may be unsupportive or downright abusive toward her. Still other women are survivors of past sexual, emotional, or physical abuse and have a great fear of intimacy. In all these cases some training in relationship awareness is crucial during pregnancy. Relationship awareness helps a woman strengthen her sense of self, bond with her unborn child, and develop a strong support system.

Throughout this book you will learn about and work with three important concepts:

- Claiming the territory

- Re-parenting your Inner Child

- Clearing a space

Claiming the territory means taking charge of your pregnancy by:

- Listening to your body

- Honoring your feelings

- Knowing your needs and wants

- Communicating your desires to others

- Devising a birth plan

- Asserting your right to have the kind of birth you want

- Forming a support team

Re-parenting your Inner Child is a process of recognizing the child who lives within you by:

- Listening to your deepest emotional needs

- Learning to be a nurturing and protective parent to yourself

- Communicating your needs to your partner or other support persons in your life

- Clearing the way to being a better parent to your child

For individuals with a history of abuse, re-parenting the Inner Child is a powerful tool for healing the pain of the past, allowing for an easier pregnancy and birth, and breaking the cycle of abuse.

Clearing a space refers to the practice of changing negative thoughts and beliefs by:

- Discovering negative attitudes about pregnancy, labor, and birth

- Recognizing and changing negative expectations about parenting

- Focusing on what kind of pregnancy, birth, and early parenting you really want

- Using positive images to create a healthy pregnancy, joyful birth, and fulfilling early parenting experiences

Techniques

The methods you will be using to create the birth experience you want are based on the latest body-mind research. Our techniques include imagery, art, and Creative Birth Journaling (using both drawing and writing). These activities use and develop right-brain skills and integrate both the right and the left hemispheres of the brain. To help you understand how and why these methods work so effectively, here is a brief explanation of how the brain functions:

The human brain is divided into two halves, or hemispheres. Each side of the brain specializes in certain functions. In most people the left hemisphere contains language centers and excels in verbal, analytical, and rational processes. When we speak (using rules of grammar and syntax) or solve logical mathematical problems, our left hemisphere is functioning. Setting objectives, following schedules, proceeding in a sequential manner are all typical left-brain activities. By contrast the right hemisphere governs visual/spatial perception, intuition, emotional expression, and sensory awareness. It is holistic, recognizes patterns, and is integrative. Right-brain processes allow for inspiration, which does not come from logic. The right brain excels in creative breakthroughs, new solutions, innovation, and artistic expression. (See the diagram on page 24 for a list of common characteristics of each brain hemisphere.)

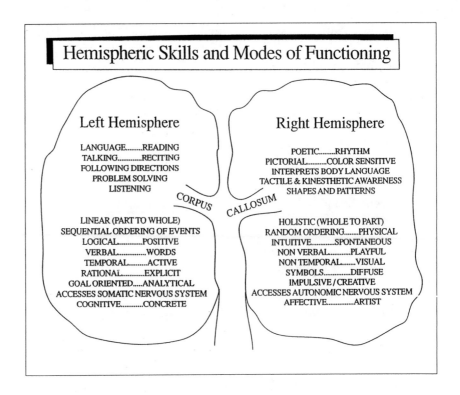

Hemispheric Skills and Modes of Functioning

Left Hemisphere

LANGUAGE.........READING
TALKING............RECITING
FOLLOWING DIRECTIONS
PROBLEM SOLVING
LISTENING

LINEAR (PART TO WHOLE)
SEQUENTIAL ORDERING OF EVENTS
LOGICAL............POSITIVE
VERBAL..............WORDS
TEMPORAL.........ACTIVE
RATIONAL..........EXPLICIT
GOAL ORIENTED.....ANALYTICAL
ACCESSES SOMATIC NERVOUS SYSTEM
COGNITIVE...........CONCRETE

Right Hemisphere

POETIC.........RHYTHM
PICTORIAL..........COLOR SENSITIVE
INTERPRETS BODY LANGUAGE
TACTILE & KINESTHETIC AWARENESS
SHAPES AND PATTERNS

HOLISTIC (WHOLE TO PART)
RANDOM ORDERING........PHYSICAL
INTUITIVE............SPONTANEOUS
NON VERBAL..........PLAYFUL
NON TEMPORAL.......VISUAL
SYMBOLS.............DIFFUSE
IMPULSIVE / CREATIVE
ACCESSES AUTONOMIC NERVOUS SYSTEM
AFFECTIVE..............ARTIST

CORPUS CALLOSUM

Although the two sides of the brain appear to speak different languages, there is a bridge between them. The corpus callosum, a bundle of nerve fibers, connects the brain hemispheres. This is how the two halves of the brain communicate with each other. Ideally we would use both sides of the brain in a balanced and integrated way, letting each side do what it does best. However, our educational system relies heavily on left-brain analytical and logical thinking, so right-brain processes, such as emotional expression and intuition, are generally ignored in the curriculum. Some people are naturally more right-brain dominant. They may be highly intuitive or artistic but may have difficulty with left-brain subjects, such as math. Most people tend to favor one type of thinking over the other. Whether a person is right- or left-brain dominant, the fact remains that our culture does not foster a balanced development of both sides of the brain, nor does it offer training in how to integrate both sides of the brain.

Drawing and Writing with the Non-dominant Hand

Because *sensory* awareness and *emotional* communication are so important in pregnancy, these right-brain abilities play a key role. One technique that opens up the right hemisphere is drawing and writing with the non-dominant hand (the hand you do not normally write with). Lucia's research shows that this activity taps directly into the right, non-verbal side of the brain. This is true even for left-handed people. (They use their right hand when doing non-dominant hand exercises.) Throughout this book you will be doing exercises that call for writing and drawing with your non-dominant hand, accessing your emotions, (senses), intuitions, and imagination. You will also be exploring imagery, drawing, doodling, and sculpting for stimulating the right brain. A talent in art is not required.

Right/Left-Hand Dialogues

Some of the exercises in this book link both hemispheres of the brain through written conversations using both hands. These dialogues between the dominant and non-dominant hand allow the rational, verbal left brain to know what the emotional right brain is feeling and sensing. In addition they create an interplay between the physical and the emotional experiences. For more in-depth information about the research on writing and drawing with the non-dominant hand we recommend Lucia's earlier book, *The Power of Your Other Hand* (see Bibliography).

Communication between hemispheres is especially important in pregnancy, which is often a very emotional time. By putting our true feelings into words we are better prepared to communicate our needs to others. Pregnancy is also a time when we can develop intuition and find our own inner wisdom. Powerful feelings and instincts flow through the non-dominant hand with ease, simplicity, and the straightforwardness of truth. Try it now! Get a pen and piece of paper. Put the pen in your non-dominant (non-writing) hand and allow it to write your feelings about this pregnancy. Don't worry about penmanship or spelling. Just write freely. This activity can be done by expectant mothers, partners, and support persons.

Imagery

What you can imagine, you can create. This is a fact that artists and inventors have always known. We harness the power of imagination by using imagery. Imagery is the practice of creating mental representations of an experience or fantasy. It includes all the senses: sight, sound, smell, touch, taste. Everyone uses imagery. For instance, the phrase "beautiful sunset at the ocean" probably evokes multisensory images from your own personal memory bank. Maybe your favorite sunset was on a beach in Hawaii, or over San Francisco Bay, or on a Caribbean island. Imagery comes from sensory impressions—sights, sounds, tastes, fragrances, tactile sensations—that we have experienced. Imagery also makes fantasy and imagination possible.

Some people think imagery is the same as visualization. This is not so. Imagery involves all the senses. Visualization is *mental picturing*. Perhaps it is difficult for you to visualize. If so, then you probably use another mode of imaging, such as auditory (sounds) or tactile (the sense of touch).

Imagery is an integral part of life. Our ability to remember or describe an experience depends upon the use of imagery. Our dreams (whether we are asleep or awake) manifest themselves in the form of imagery. We use imagery to imagine experiences we have not had. Without imagery we could not communicate in language, plan new projects, or dream of new possibilities.

Imagery plays a crucial role in health and is an important aspect of childbirth preparation. For instance, negative imagery can contribute to poor health. If you think pregnancy is a time for feeling ill and uncomfortable and you keep imagining such a condition in your mind, you will likely experience it. Positive imagery strengthens the body and immune system. Expectant mothers who anticipate pregnancy as a time of health and well-being tend to have a more fulfilling pregnancy experience. When asked to free-associate on the word *pregnancy*, these women describe positive images (such as feeling contented, happy, fulfilled, strong, womanly, creative, nurturing, etc.). Imagery combined with intellectual awareness allows us to change our negative thoughts to positive ones.

Imagery does not require "special talent." However, it does require a little practice to help it come naturally. Try the following to strengthen your imaging abilities:

Close your eyes and re-experience the last time you were out in nature. Consider the following questions:

- Where were you?
- Can you remember what you were wearing?

- Who were you with?

- What were you doing?

- How did you feel there?

- What did you see?

- What objects or textures do you remember touching?

- What was the temperature?

- What fragrances did you smell?

- What kind of environment was it? Hilly or flat? Forest or meadow?

- What time of year was it?

- Were there trees or plants?

- Was there a body of water?

- How did it feel to move around in this environment? Were you walking, riding, sitting still?

- Think about the sounds you heard while you were there. Did *you* make any sounds?

Now imagine going to a place you have never visited. Perhaps you've seen it in a film or on TV. Maybe you've read or heard about it. Where is this place? What would you experience with your senses if you were there? Pause for a moment and imagine taking a trip there.

You can discover your own style of imaging by observing how you approached this imaginary trip. Did you *see* the setting in detail in your mind's eye, with all its colors and visual details? Or did you recall *tactile sensations*, such as the temperature, smells, and textures? Was it easier for you to remember the *sounds* you heard or any conversations you were having? Knowing the way you use imagery will help you in your birth preparation.

People who rely on *auditory* impressions easily recall what they *hear*. One pregnant woman might say, "I *heard* people talking about how huge I was." Those whose *visual* sense predominates tend to *see* experiences in their mind's eye. The expectant mom might say, "I *look* so huge!" *Kinesthetically* aware people rely on *physical sensations* of movement, texture, and the feel of things. Such a woman would probably say, "I *feel* so huge!"

You may also have noticed that it was easier for you to imagine the past experience (what *was*), rather than imagine an as-yet-unreal future experience (what *might be.*) In this book there will be techniques that help you develop your skills of imagining the future and what you want.

Imagery Through Art

In many of the exercises in this book you will be asked to draw. Many people are uncomfortable with this idea. When you were younger, someone may have told you your art was "ugly" or "dumb." Maybe an early attempt at artistic expressions was laughed at or simply thrown in the trash. If this happened to you, you may have concluded, *People ridicule my art. I don't have any talent. I can't draw.*

Creative expression is an innate human ability. This includes drawing. The belief that you can't draw is simply that: a belief. Like all beliefs it can be changed. We once thought it impossible for humans to walk on the moon. That belief was disproven when Neil Armstrong took the first lunar walk. Centuries ago people assumed the world was flat and immovable and that the sun revolved around it. Later we learned differently. Beliefs about your ability to draw can also change.

The kind of art you will be asked to do in this book is private and personal. Its purpose is to help you recognize your true thoughts and feelings. It is not art for exhibition. The techniques come from art therapy, a form of psychotherapy in which the client creates spontaneous drawings (or other artwork) and then interprets the symbols and messages found there. It is like having a dream on paper. This kind of artwork comes from your heart and your guts instead of from your head.

You may find that your artwork looks quite primitive and childlike. Sometimes you may wonder what your picture means. At other times you may find yourself knowing intuitively. By drawing first and then writing down your thoughts and feelings, sooner or later the meaning usually emerges.

Dancing on Paper

Get a pencil or pen and some blank paper. If you have some crayons or felt-tip markers around, you might try using those. Turn on your favorite music. Now doodle or draw in rhythm to what you hear. Don't try to make a picture of anything. Just let your arm and hand respond to the music. It's like "dancing on paper." Do as many of these drawings to music as you like. If you find yourself being critical of what you are drawing, just bring your focus back to the music and to your "dance on paper." Relax and enjoy yourself.

"A Dance on Paper"

Full of Feelings

Have you ever experienced a time when you were "speechless"? Perhaps you were full of feelings but couldn't "put a name" on them. Do you remember ever feeling angry, hurt, or fearful, but unable to say anything to anyone? Unexpressed feelings remain inside us. They don't disappear. If they are not expressed in a healthy, creative way, they get bottled up inside and can contribute to stress and tension in the body. Many people experience music as a wonderful way to express feelings. Drawing has the same effect and is a wonderful way to release pent-up feelings.

Express Yourself

With the same materials you just used for Dancing on Paper, try expressing the way you feel right now on paper.

- Tune in to your feelings about this pregnancy.

- If your feelings had a color, what would it be?

- Draw that color. Perhaps there are many colors.

- What is the shape of your feelings?

- See if you can express that on paper.

- Do your feelings have a texture or a pattern to them?

- Can you show that with your drawing?

Allow yourself to be free in the way you express yourself. Don't think in terms of making your drawing look a certain way. Have fun, explore, and experiment. Scribble, doodle, make abstract shapes, lines, dots, and patterns. Try switching hands and doing another drawing of feelings with your non-dominant (non-writing) hand.

Later in this book you will see how spontaneous drawing can help you with difficult emotions, such as sadness, anger, frustration, or confusion. Expressing yourself through art helps identify and release your thoughts and feelings. You can observe them without judging them or yourself. This will help you understand and accept yourself more fully.

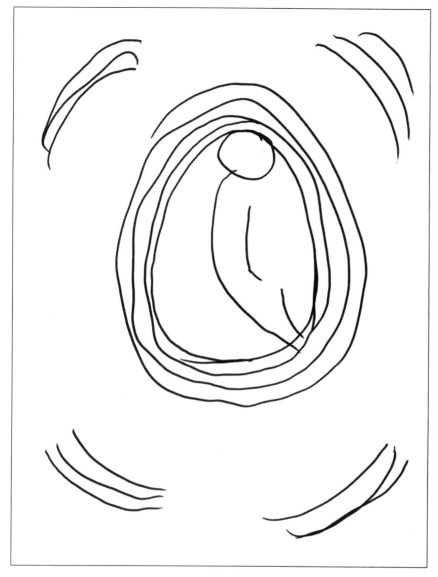

"How I Feel"

Creative Birth Journaling

The Creative Birth Journal is a private place to discover your feelings, thoughts, and experiences. Unlike a traditional diary it is not merely for recording events. Rather it emphasizes feelings, sensory awareness, beliefs, and relationships. What sets this method apart is that it uses drawing as well as writing. Furthermore, you will be journaling with both the dominant and the non-dominant hand, which stimulates both sides of the brain. You'll learn how to "think and feel on paper." These journal activities invite communication between your body, mind, and emotions. They address themes and concerns that have special relevance during pregnancy.

In order to do Creative Birth Journaling, you need no special talent or training in art. If you do not consider yourself an artist, you may have an advantage. Professional artists or writers are often preoccupied with the art product. In Creative Birth Journaling we concern ourselves only with the *process*. *You* are the product, not your artwork. *The goal is self-discovery through writing and art.* No one will criticize you, so relax and enjoy yourself. These techniques are easy, fun, and creative. They are intended for the expectant mother, her partner, and her support persons.

Creative Birth Journaling can help you:

1. Explore and express your feelings and needs
2. Become more aware of your body and your unborn child
3. Understand your feelings and beliefs about various aspects of pregnancy, labor, birth, and early parenting
4. Re-parent your Inner Child by learning to nurture and protect yourself
5. Transform negative and limiting beliefs into positive and creative ones
6. Discover your own innate creativity
7. Celebrate the sacred moments of parenting through art and writing
8. Empower yourself by creating a happy, healthy pregnancy, birth, and early parenthood

Guidelines for Creative Birth Journaling

Each journal activity includes a title, list of materials, purpose, and simple steps to follow. It is advisable to do the exercises in the order given. Once you've become familiar with this method, we encourage you to go back and repeat specific journal exercises as the need arises. For instance, closer to your due date you can repeat exercises that prepare you for your labor. We also urge you to invite any or all members of your birth support team to keep a Creative Birth Journal of their own.

Examples from the Creative Birth Journals of others are used to illustrate journal activities. Please don't compare your work with the samples shown. *There is no right or wrong way to do journal work. Your* way is best. Be creative. Draw and doodle, make shapes and colors, experiment and explore in words and pictures. Whatever you do, have fun!

You don't have to make journal entries every day. Most journal keepers report that the more they do it, the greater the benefits. You may want to set aside a certain time of day or evening to use your journal. If it is difficult to find journal time, try making a regular appointment with yourself. Put it on your calendar as you would any other appointment. You can also take it with you during the day and use it while "killing time" (waiting for appointments, while "on hold" on the telephone, etc.). The important thing is to make it easy for yourself by fitting journaling into your normal day. Date the first page of each entry and keep your entries in chronological sequence.

Privacy

We recommend that you keep your journal confidential. Privacy helps you feel safe enough to be *honest* with yourself. To ensure privacy, keep your journal in a safe place. Don't leave it lying around for anyone to pick up and browse through. These are intimate sharings with yourself. They need to be respected and honored. You may wish to share certain journal entries with people you trust. For instance, partners often share journal excerpts with each other. This often promotes greater intimacy. Choose when and how much to share with each other. It's *your* journal. Own it! Safeguard it!

If you and your partner or support persons are keeping Creative Birth Journals, we suggest you each keep your own. Also, if you already have a personal journal or diary, you might want a separate one that is devoted exclusively to your pregnancy and birth experience. Someday in years to come you may want to share parts of your Creative Birth Journal with your child.

Materials for Creative Birth Journaling

1. *Journal:*
    A bound blank journal book with unlined white paper, preferably 8½ by 11 inches or larger, or

(continued on next page)

A large three-ring folder with lots of plain white unlined paper
Optional: A pocket-size blank book that is easily portable

2. **Drawing materials:**
Felt markers in assorted colors (non-toxic)
Crayons
Optional: Colored pencils, oil pastels, or chalk pastels
Note: If you use a fixative to prevent chalk pastels from smearing, *be careful that it's non-toxic.*

3. **Writing materials:**
Colored felt-tip pens with fine points for writing and printing

Materials for Art Activities

1. **Collage and painting materials**
Art paper (18 × 24-inch newsprint, drawing, or watercolor paper)
Note: Newsprint end rolls can often be obtained free from local newspaper publishers.
Optional: Colored construction paper, colored tissue paper
Old magazines with lots of photos
Cardboard or posterboard (any size you wish, preferably 11 by 14 inches, 18 by 24 inches, or larger)
Inexpensive set of watercolors or tempera paints
Brushes
Scissors
Glue (white glue or glue stick; be cautious choosing adhesives because many of them are toxic)
Optional: Yarn, string, found objects, old jewelry, dried pasta, beans, and so on

2. **Sculpting Materials**
Ceramic clay (terra-cotta) (This is available inexpensively in large plastic bags from art supply stores. It is nontoxic. *If you use any other type of sculpting material, be absolutely sure it is nontoxic.*)
Work surface (wood, Masonite, or heavy plastic drop cloth)
An apron or smock
A bucket of water

3. **Cleanup supplies (paper towels, old rags, or sponges)**

As you embark on this journey, we hope that you awaken the innate creativity Friedrich von Schiller described in his "Ode to Joy":

> Joy, divine spark of the Gods
> . . . we enter your sanctuary . . .
> Your magic reunites
> What custom has sternly parted.

May this pregnancy and birth be "an exultation of the spirit." This is your birthright. Claim it!

2

Claiming the Territory

Taking charge of your entire birth process is an essential part of a joyful birth. We refer to it as *claiming the territory*. The territory includes every element and every phase of pregnancy, labor, delivery, and early parenting. This is your body, your baby, and your birth experience.

Claiming the territory starts with your body. To *claim the territory*, you need to understand and respect your body's needs, for your own sake as well as your baby's. Every pregnant woman has needs that are unique and personal to her. Taking the time to discover and communicate those needs is extremely important. *Claiming the territory* is valuing yourself through good nutrition, exercise, rest, and stress reduction. It includes everything necessary to stay physically and mentally healthy throughout pregnancy. It also means telling others what you need so that they can show respect for you and your baby.

Claiming the territory by choosing the kind of pregnancy and birth you want is one of the greatest gifts you can give your unborn baby. In the last decade science has discovered immense amounts of new information about life in the womb. New technology, such as ultrasound, electron microscopes, and fiber optics, have enabled science to enter the world of the unborn baby. We now know that babies have amazing sensory abilities. For instance, by the fourth month your baby has a well-developed sense of touch and taste. At that developmental stage he can also react to light and sound. By five months your baby can perceive patterns of sound and speech—including your voice. Thus, interacting with your unborn baby is another way you can claim the territory and begin building a strong family unit.

Contrary to popular belief, your baby is conscious in the womb and has some awareness of himself and the world outside. Psychotherapists who do regression therapy attest to this. In this type of therapy the client re-experiences feelings he or she had in the womb or at birth. These individuals frequently express profound grief and anger because their parents did not protect them during pregnancy and birth. They say things like: "My mother was completely drugged and unconscious when I was born. Why wasn't she awake and there to greet me?" Or they might cry about their father not being around at the time of birth. They often experience rage about their treatment by professionals, with comments such as: "The doctors and nurses were acting like auto mechanics. They handled me as if I was an object and had no feelings."

Birth psychologists agree that traumatic experiences *in utero* or at birth leave lasting impressions and memories. This kind of entry into the world can result in deep-rooted feelings of unworthiness and fear of abandonment that last a lifetime. These traumas can be healed later on through regression counseling, hypnotherapy, or birth re-facilitation. However, much of your child's birth trauma can be prevented when you claim the territory of pregnancy and birth.

Let's start the process by focusing on your body and your feelings. During pregnancy many thoughts, feelings, and needs arise. If you are not aware of them, they will communicate through your body. When Sheila met Dr. Larson for the first prenatal visit, she felt uneasy. He seemed cold and distant. The staff appeared overworked and were impersonal. Sheila ignored her feelings by talking herself out of them. She told herself, "He has good credentials and came highly recommended by my friends."

Before each prenatal visit Sheila's stomach would tighten up and she would get a headache. Sheila did the following exercise in her journal and discovered that Dr. Larson's manner was the cause of her upset. She decided to find different prenatal care. Upon finding a doctor and staff she liked, Sheila's symptoms disappeared.

This exercise has two sections, each one in its own box. If you have time, you can do them all in one sitting. If not, do them in separate journal sessions.

Developing Body Awareness: *Talking with Your Body*

Materials: Journal and felt-tip pens
Optional: Large sheets of newsprint, 18 by 24 inches; crayons; oil pastels; large felt-tip markers

Purpose: To acknowledge and express your thoughts, feelings, and needs on paper. To develop body-mind awareness. Especially helpful when you are experiencing discomfort or stress.

Technique:

1. *Relaxing*

Find a comfortable, quiet spot where you can be alone without interruptions or distractions. Start by paying attention to your breathing. Don't try to change it, just be aware of its flow. Observe the rhythm of your breath going in and out. For a few minutes allow your breathing to become slower and deeper. Do this naturally without forcing anything. Close your eyes and shut out any visual distractions. Relax completely.

Note: For parts 2 and 3 of this exercise it is advisable to have your eyes closed. You may want to record the narration of this guided tour through your body and play it back while you relax and follow along. An audiotape of Lucia leading you through a similar exercise may be of some use. It is entitled *The Picture of Health* (see "Audio Recordings" in Bibliography).

---

2. *Body Imagery*

Now focus your attention on your body. Starting at your toes and the soles of your feet, slowly go through each part of your body and check in to see how that part is feeling right now. Gradually move up your feet and legs—first the left, then the right.

Then move your awareness up through your pelvic area. For a moment focus on your baby, paying very close attention to all the sensations you feel. Is there any discomfort, pressure, or stress? Does this part of your body feel fine? Then move up through your torso, your abdominal area: stomach and other internal organs. How does it feel? Then move up through the upper torso: chest, lungs, heart.

Check out your back as well, moving up your spine from your lower back up to your neck. What sensations do you feel there? Now focus your attention on your shoulders, arms, and hands, down to the fingers. Check out your left arm and hand and then your right arm and hand.

Now become aware of your neck, front and back. Is there any stiffness or tension there? Does it feel okay? Then continue up into your head: back of the head, left side and left ear, right side and right ear. Now tune in to your face: mouth, chin, and jaw. Is your jaw clenched or relaxed? Be aware of your cheeks, nose, and eyes. Check out your forehead and then the whole crown of your head. Is there tightness or tension in these areas? Or do they feel relaxed?

Take a moment to review your body journey. Remember any sensations you felt as you focused on each part at a time. Don't try to change anything. Be aware of how your body is feeling now.

Note: For this part of the exercise you will need your journal, colored pens, and white paper, 8½ × 11 inches or larger.

---

3. *Body Picturing*

With your non-dominant hand draw a simple outline of your body. Don't worry about accuracy or artistic merit. Let yourself draw like a child. On your picture color in any areas of your body that feel uncomfortable or painful at this moment. Also draw in the areas that feel good. With your intuition choose colors, shapes, textures, symbols, or images that express how you feel about those areas of your body.

Still using your non-dominant hand, around your body drawing write in any words or phrases that express the feelings in each part of your body. This can include physical sensations as well as emotions. Write them in near the corresponding body part in your drawing.

4. *Body Chat*

On a new page write a conversation with your body. You will be interviewing each part of your body that may need extra attention because of stress or discomfort. Ask the following questions by writing them down with your dominant hand. Your body responds with your non-dominant hand. Use a color that seems right for that body part. The body part often writes with the same color used in the body picture.

- What part of my body are you?

- How do you feel right now?

- What caused you to feel this way?

- How can I help you?

5. *Body Re-picturing*

What would your body picture look like if you were free of pain, discomfort, stress, or fatigue? On a piece of paper, with your non-dominant hand draw a new picture of yourself feeling comfortable, peaceful, relaxed, and energetic. Then write a positive statement on your picture. Use the first person, present tense. For example, "I feel relaxed and peaceful." Put this picture up where you can see it and keep reinforcing this positive image of yourself.

"Body Talk"

Vitality Blocks

Unacknowledged feelings create vitality blocks. These blocks usually appear in the form of physical pain or low energy. For instance, during pregnancy women often have backaches, fatigue, or other physical discomforts. Often treating the symptoms doesn't alleviate the problem because they are simply emotions trying to guide the woman toward needed changes in her life. Rather than see the symptom as something to be removed, listen to what it might be telling you.

For instance, during pregnancy Betty experienced pains shooting into her thighs and legs. She dialogued with her legs (using the "Body Chat" exercise) and found that they were telling her to "stand up for herself." She thought about this and realized that it was true. There were areas in her life where Betty needed to be more assertive. She did this and the pain soon dissolved. Acknowledging and acting upon her feelings created a change in Betty's body.

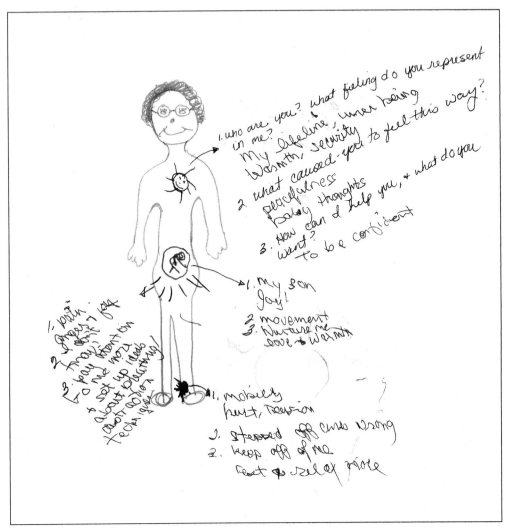

"BODY CHAT"

Warning Signs During Pregnancy

Pay close attention to signs from your body during pregnancy. Your body will let you know that there might be a physical or emotional problem. It is important that you learn to listen to and trust your body's signals.

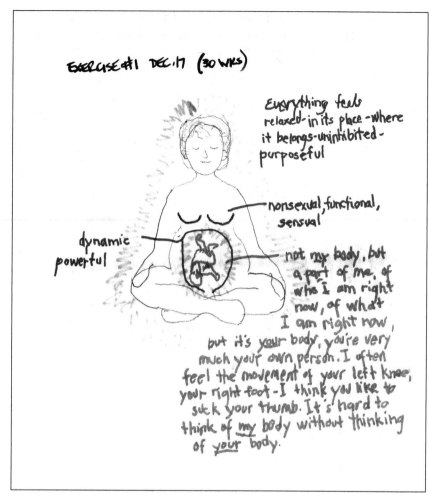

"TALKING WITH MY BODY"

If any of the following warning signs occur, notify your health care professional immediately:

- Vaginal bleeding

- Abdominal pain

- Leaking or gushing of fluid from the vagina

- Sudden puffiness or swelling of the hands, feet, or face

- Severe, persistent headache

- Disturbance of vision—spots, flashes, or blind spots

- Dizziness, light-headedness

- Pain or burning sensation on urination

- Irritating vaginal discharge, genital sores, or itching

- Fever—oral temperature of 100 degrees F or higher

- Persistent nausea or vomiting

- Noticeable reduction in fetal activity

After you've informed your health care professional and taken whatever action he or she recommends, do a journal dialogue with the symptoms. Write out questions with your dominant hand. Let the symptom or body part respond with the non-dominant hand. Use the exercise on page 39, "Body Chat," part 4.

Honoring Your Pregnant Body

All of us go through life being bombarded with images of the "ideal" female body. To fit the image of a woman, we're supposed to look a certain way. No matter how hard we try—with diets, girdles, cinches, strenuous exercise, cosmetic surgery, anorexia, and bulimia—we don't measure up, and we often damage our health in the process. Sometimes we achieve our goal for a short time, only to lose it again. Tyrannized by the media and multibillion-dollar diet, exercise, and fashion industries, we have been made to feel inadequate.

If you have a negative body image coming into pregnancy, chances are it will get worse. That can be changed. Your body wants you to appreciate it NOW, this very moment, for *what it is* (not what you or anybody else WANTS it to look like). Your body wants you to honor it for what it does for you and the experiences it allows you to have. Now that you're pregnant, acknowledge your body for that magical, mysterious, treasure trove that it is: a vessel for co-creating new life.

To help you claim your birthright, we've included some suggestions, activities, and journal exercises. For inspiration we're sharing some stories of expectant mothers who discovered a "new woman" inside their pregnant body, a new sense of selfhood, sovereignty, and beauty.

Katarina's story demonstrates how one woman came to terms with her body image during pregnancy:

As a teenager I had a negative attitude about my body. I was shorter and a little heavier than my friends and used to compare myself to them. When I went away to college, I stopped worrying so much about not looking like a fashion model or movie star. I was too busy enjoying my freedom and all the excitement of new classes. I lost weight without trying and suddenly found that I liked my body. I developed a kind of self-confidence I had never experienced before.

I was married shortly after college graduation and got pregnant right away. Although I wanted children, I started getting panicky. People started warning me that women get fat when they're pregnant and I shouldn't let it happen to me. I wondered, what if my "hormones went crazy" (the way they had in my teen years)? Would I gain a lot of weight? Would I lose my looks? Would my husband stop being attracted to me? Would I get my figure back after the baby was born? I don't remember talking to anyone about these feelings, but I worried about them.

Then my mother did two wonderful things for me. First she took me shopping for maternity clothes. We didn't go to the typical maternity shops. Instead we found some great-looking A-line dresses and jumpers in a boutique. They made great maternity clothes.

Then we selected some fabric, and she made me dresses patterned after the ones we bought. They were really classy. With her help I developed my own pregnancy style. I felt and looked good. Dressing for pregnancy became a form of creative expression for me. I can honestly say that I felt like a queen when I was pregnant. I seemed to become more attractive, not less. It also helped greatly that my husband really loved my pregnant body.

Another woman, Patrice, described having very positive feelings about her body throughout pregnancy:

I felt really great during both of my pregnancies. I'm grateful that I was already very active before getting pregnant. I didn't plan it as a preparation for pregnancy. I just was active; I danced and walked a lot. I felt good about my body. Getting fat was not my main concern. The baby's health and well-being were forefront in my mind.

In my second pregnancy I had an office job and was less active. The work was very stressful and involved long hours. I worked all the way until I went into labor. Before I knew it, I had gained sixty-five pounds (compared with the twenty-five pounds I gained in my first pregnancy).

After the birth I weighed in at 185 pounds. It really surprised me that I had gained all that weight. Displeased with my body and upset with myself, I was determined to change. I lost the weight in a year's time by cultivating better eating and exercise habits.

Now, after having two children, my body is in the best shape that it's ever been. I'm healthier than ever. I discovered all kinds of creative ways to stay in shape. When I go someplace in the car, I don't worry about parking near the place I am going. I park a distance away and then walk. This increases my exercise during the day.

Mirror Work: *Body Image / Self-image*

Materials: Journal and crayons or felt-tip pens; full-length or large mirror
               Optional: Large art paper; drawing and/or painting materials.
Purpose: To explore how you feel about your body now that you are pregnant. To identify any negative attitudes about your pregnant body and change them if you wish.

Technique:

1. In a quiet, private place, look at your unclothed body in a mirror. Take plenty of time and observe yourself from all angles. How do you feel about your reflection in the mirror? What thoughts come to mind as you observe your pregnant body? What changes have you noticed? Are there any new changes you hadn't seen before?
2. Draw a picture of yourself showing your entire body. Remember, this drawing is only for you. If your Inner Art Critic starts putting you down for having "no talent" or for wasting time making "stupid, ugly art," observe what is said, but continue drawing anyway.

Note: You can do this and the next drawing in your journal or on large sheets of paper, if you wish.
Optional: Make a drawing of yourself in X-ray fashion showing the baby inside.

---

3. In your journal write down your reactions to the drawing(s) that you just did. Just write your thoughts and feelings freely without editing or worrying about grammar, spelling, or syntax.
4. Using two different-colored pens, write a conversation between you and your body. You write with your dominant hand. Your body writes with the non-dominant hand. Ask your body to tell you how it feels right now. What is its reaction to the things you just wrote in step 3? What does your body want you to do so that it feels appreciated, cared for, and loved? What does your body want you to do so that the *baby* will feel nurtured and loved?

Comfort in Pregnancy

When your body changes shape, your center of gravity shifts. You may need to adjust your posture so that performing everyday activities will require less strain and effort. This can also help prevent many symptoms common in pregnancy, such as back pain and leg cramps. Increase your comfort by paying attention to how you stand and move.

The following books provide particularly helpful information on movement and posture during pregnancy:

Positive Pregnancy Fitness, by Sylvia Klein Olkin

Guide to Moving Through Pregnancy, by Elisabeth D. Bing

Mirror Work: *Standing Tall*

Materials: Journal; paper and felt-tip pens; full-length or large mirror
Purpose: To become aware of your changing posture so that you can improve it if necessary. To develop good posture, which will reduce fatigue and common aches and pains.
Technique:

1. Look at your body in a full-length mirror or in a window: front view and side view. Notice how you are standing. Observe the position of your feet and knees. Look at your tummy, your butt, your back and shoulders. Now notice the position of your head, your chin, your neck.
2. Write the following chart in your journal:

Good Posture	Poor Posture	My Present Posture
Head: Up	Hanging down	
Chin: Level	Jutting out	
Shoulders: Back, down, and relaxed	Slouched or pulled back	
Tummy: Firm	Bulging and loose, hanging out	
Back: Upright, in a gentle **S**	Swayed, or hollowed	
Buttocks: Tucked under	Jutting out	
Knees: Slightly bent	Locked or held stiffly	

Feet: Shoulder width apart, parallel	Too close or far apart, turned inward or outward,
Weight: Centered	Off center

3. In your journal record your present posture.
4. Do a drawing of the posture you would like to have during this time in your pregnancy. Hang your drawing in a place where you can frequently see it. Focus on your posture during this stage of your pregnancy. (Hang it on the bathroom mirror, bedroom wall, or closet door.)
5. Repeat this exercise monthly, or more frequently during your pregnancy.

Self-image

Many women believe pregnancy means becoming frumpy, dumpy, old, and unattractive. Some think they have to endure this condition until after the baby is born. Others think that with motherhood, youth, beauty, and vitality fly out the window, never to return again.

You probably know some women who have fallen into this trap because of their attitude. Fortunately attitudes and beliefs can be changed. Cultivating a positive attitude about your body will help you feel good about your pregnancy.

Inner and Outer Selves: *Discovering the Real Me*

Materials: Journal and felt-tip pens or crayons
Purpose: To identify and examine attitudes and beliefs about your internal self-image and your external body image. To look at how you feel about your body. To gain perspective and awareness about your whole self.
Technique:

1. Close your eyes and allow an image of your body to come to mind.
2. Using your dominant hand, draw a picture of how you see your *outer self* (the "you" that is seen by the outside world). This includes how you express yourself: your behaviors, accomplishments, appearance, and body.

3. With your non-dominant hand draw an image or symbol of how you see your *inner self.* This is your internal, private world of thoughts, feelings, fantasies, memories, and wishes.
4. Reflect upon your drawings. Near each one, write a comment with your non-dominant hand that states your feelings.

INSIDE
Happy, Happy, Happy!
I WISH EVERYONE KNEW
I LOVE BEING PREGNANT
OUTSIDE
I CAN'T TELL HARDLY ANYONE
YET BECAUSE I'M AFRAID
THEY WON'T LOVE ME ANYMORE
AND WON'T HELP ME.

"Inner and Outer Selves"

Cluster Writing: *Pregnant Body*

Materials: Journal and felt-tip pens or crayons
Purpose: Put your feelings about your pregnant body into words.
Technique:

1. Using your dominant hand, write the words *Pregnant Body* in the center of your page. Then draw a circle around it.
2. With your non-dominant hand write five words around the circle that reflect your feelings about your pregnant body.
3. Think about each feeling and circle them one at a time. Connect them to your central phrase. (See example below.)
4. Focus on each of your five words, and around each one write feeling words that relate to it. Circle these and connect them with straight lines to the words that evoked those feelings. Continue this process with each word until you have filled the page.
5. Now read all the words you've written. On another page, with your dominant hand, write a poem using the feeling words from your cluster exercise. (See example on page 50.)
6. Is there anything you want to do about those feelings? If so, write down what action you would like to take.

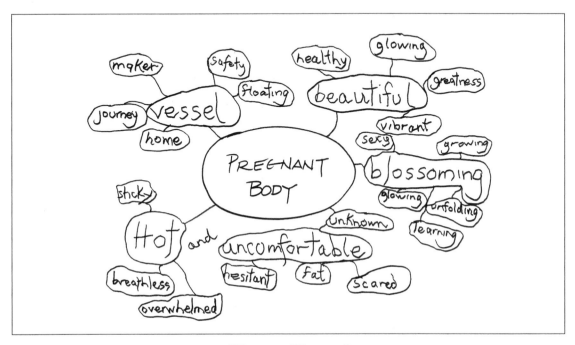

The pregnant body unfolds as it grows —
energy flows from the unknown, nurturing
and loving this spark of a being, safe
in its vessel as it journeys home.
Suspending, breathless, a glowing, healthy
sacred being, sometimes hesitant...
wanting to stay with the maker in the
safe, vibrant warmth. Emerging
through sacred passages to the unknown.

1. Support and encouragement for other
pregnant women and womankind.
2. Open lines of female energy and
allow that flow, working on what
makes me hesitate.

Choosing Health Care

One of the first challenges you will face during pregnancy is choosing health care. The process of making these decisions is part of claiming the territory. There are many options: obstetricians, gynecologists, physicians, midwives, nurse practitioners, chiropractors, acupuncturists, osteopaths, counselors, and so on. Choosing the care you want also includes selecting who will assist you throughout your pregnancy, and deciding where the birth will occur and who will be there to assist you. Deciding what is right for you can be very time-consuming and confusing.

If you were going to buy an expensive item such as a car, you would not buy just any car. First you would decide what features you want.

Then you would begin looking at cars. You would get some well-informed advice. You might choose to talk with friends or others whose cars have the features you're looking for. Or you might talk with professionals.

Choosing your health care should be no different. Be a good consumer and approach health care as you would when buying any other expensive item or service. You are dealing with your body and the well-being of your unborn baby. *It is for you to decide exactly what kinds of health care you want and need.* This is where skill in claiming the territory becomes crucial. Prepare by carefully looking at all your options. Learn to weigh the benefits against the risks.

In seeking health care it is important to consider the location in which the birth will take place. It is important to do research and know your alternatives well in advance of labor and delivery. Whether you have your baby in a hospital, in an alternative birth center, or at home should be your choice. While interviewing health care professionals ask where the caregiver delivers babies. For instance, most OB/GYNs do deliveries only in hospitals. Many midwives do both hospital and home births. If you select a particular location or method of birth, this will probably determine your selection of a caregiver. For example, if you want to deliver at home, you'll need a midwife or doctor who does home births.

Find out what each method or approach offers and make an informed decision. Some important considerations are:

- The birth options available in your community

- The feeling of personal safety and comfort in the birthplace (consider your baby, yourself, and your partner)

- Your financial status at the time of your pregnancy and your baby's birth, including health insurance coverage

- Your health and the baby's welfare during pregnancy and at the time of the birth

- Your past birth experiences and what you needed at that time

Note: Regarding midwives, insurance companies are increasingly willing to pay for direct-entry midwife services (home birth). Third-party payment may be determined by the state you live in. Check with your insurance company or care provider.

Olivia wanted to give birth at home. Her husband wanted to go to a hospital. Together they explored their options. They met with a local midwife, who explained the safety factors of home birth. She pointed out that home birth enhances support for the emotional aspect of labor and delivery. For comparison they visited their local hospital, researching information about the medical caregivers in their area. They also considered the wishes of their unborn baby by doing a dialogue with the baby through Creative Birth Journaling. Finally they considered that they lived in the country forty-five minutes away from any hospital. By weighing the benefits against the risks, they came to a mutual agreement in favor of home birth with a midwife.

Marina wanted her husband to be her labor coach and to attend prenatal classes. Her husband, however, wanted to support her at the birth but did not want to go to the classes. Together they came to the decision that Marina would have a friend attend classes with her. Then she would share the information with her husband. We cannot overemphasize the value of weighing the benefits against the risks. By doing this you will always find a solution.

People often bombard expectant parents with opinions and theories. Experts have written hundreds of books, all claiming that their way is best. Many of their theories contradict each other. What's a parent to do? Well-meaning family members or friends suddenly become experts on pregnancy, labor, and birth. They have many stories to tell and often relish replaying their experiences in giving birth. Some of these may be helpful while others may be horror stories. These stories are usually followed by advice, warnings, and recommendations. Take the good, supportive information and leave the horror stories behind. Remember, your pregnancy and your baby's birth is entirely your own. YOU are the expert on this particular pregnancy, the only one who truly knows what you need and want. It's as simple as that.

You will inevitably come across many opinions and ideas. Listen to them. Some of the information might apply. In the final analysis you will need to pay attention to your own experience, needs, and desires. Listening to yourself is a skill you will practice throughout this book. It is also a skill you can use for the rest of your life. Inner wisdom is a natural human ability. Don't let anyone try to take it away from you. By all means reseach, gather information, be open to new ideas, but know that ultimately the decisions are yours. That's how you can empower yourself and welcome your baby into the world. You can find out what you want by keeping a journal and writing down your feelings, reactions, and needs on a regular basis.

Inform yourself about all your health care options regarding pregnancy and childbirth. There are many good books on the subject. At the back of this book you will find a Bibliography and a Resource Guide. The following books offer a general summary of health care options:

Midwife Means with Woman, by Elizabeth Hallett and Karen Ehrlich

The Experience of Childbirth, by Sheila Kitzinger

Pregnancy, Childbirth and the Newborn, by Penny Simkin, Janet Whalley, and Ann Keppler

A Good Birth, A Safe Birth, by Diane Korte and Roberta Scaer

Your first choice involves deciding what kind of prenatal care you want and from whom. This may not be as easy as it sounds. We've interviewed many women and heard their stories about the challenge of finding compassionate, helpful health care professionals.

Look around, do your homework, and select carefully. In this section we offer guidelines on how to do this. Once you've made your selection, be sure to speak up if you are not receiving the kind of treatment you want. If you are still unsatisfied, don't be afraid to change to another health care professional.

Guidelines for Choosing Health Care

When a productive, vital company makes major choices in hiring, they do not do it randomly. These decisions are *never* left to chance. Management does not assume things will happen in their favor. They create a job description for the position, make a list of requirements, and begin the interviewing process. Following the interviews, two key factors are considered: the person's qualifications and his or her ability to support the existing staff or team. An educated and well-informed decision is made once these steps are complete. Take the same approach to finding a health care provider. Don't forget to factor in your emotional and gut responses.

Remember, you are the client. You are *hiring* the provider and paying for prenatal care. You have the right to get what you pay for and receive the kind of care you want. However, like any intelligent employer, you need to know what you want and to communicate it clearly to others.

Pregnancy is a very emotional time. It can be the time in a woman's life when she is the most vulnerable. When you are feeling emotional, it is difficult to be assertive with professionals who use intimidating technical language. To make informed choices, it is crucial to work through feelings of inadequacy. This is especially true when confronted with medical routines and procedures. We advise doing journal exercises that help you get in touch with your feelings, such as "Express Yourself" (Chapter One).

Interviews

One way to research prenatal care is to interview health professionals before making a commitment. Since there is usually a fee for face-to-face interviews, you can start by doing initial screening over the phone. Before you can effectively do your phone interview, you will want to be familiar with your options and to set some of your goals. The books listed on page 53 of this chapter have useful information concerning how to choose your health care providers. In addition to those sources, you may want to consider the following:

- Do I feel comfortable with this person and his or her staff?

- Is their birth philosophy compatible with mine?

- Do I agree with their methods of childbirth and early infant care?

- Do their fees fit my budget?

- What services do they offer (lab facilities, ultrasound, bilingual ability)?

- How many health care professionals are in this service, and do they have nurse-midwives on their staff?

The medical statistics to consider are:

- C-section rate

- Episiotomy rate

- Types of interventions commonly used (vacuum extractor, forceps, internal fetal monitor, internal uterine catheter, routine I.V.'s)

Types of Interviews

PHONE INTERVIEW
When you make your initial screening calls, make sure you find out about:

- The type of services offered

- How many care providers are in this practice

- Methods of labor and delivery available with this practice

- Options regarding the location of the birth, such as hospital, birth center, home, and so on

- Percentage of cesarean-section deliveries

Write your own list before doing telephone interviews. Organize your thoughts and be aware of your priorities. This will help you focus and remember to discuss areas of special concern to you. You may want to use the telephone checklist on page 56 as a point of reference.

OFFICE INTERVIEW
When you go to your first office interview, take your list of questions. Most office visits are fairly short. Because of this, preparation becomes very important. Highlight the concerns that are most important to you at this time. During the interview write down any further questions that come to mind. If any go unanswered, you can address them at your next appointment.

Medical Professional Telephone Checklist

Care Provider	Issues	Interventions		Office Services	Staff	Credentials	Birth Place	Costs
Rate potential caregiver on a scale of 1–10 or write information in each square. Your information will be based on the quality of the answer you receive during your telephone interview.	Attentive, Compatible birth philosophy	% of interventions	Reason for intervention	Lab, ultrasound, other tests	Staff seems warm and caring	Care provider has good recommendation/ credentials	Home, Hospital, Freestanding birth center	Insurance coverage, Medicare

After you've decided which care providers you want to interview, use this chart to keep track of the information.

Write the questions and concerns that are important to you. The following sample list may give you some ideas.

Interview Topics

GENERAL PRACTICE (POLICIES)

1. What services do you offer?
2. How many partners are in this practice?
3. Will I be seen by all of them?
4. Approximately what percentage of the women in your practice have unmedicated births?
5. What percentage of your clients have undergone the following: early artificial rupture of membranes, continuous electronic fetal monitoring, episiotomy, cesarean section, and other interventions.

SELF-CARE/PREGNANCY

1. What is your policy about my partner, family, or friends participating in my prenatal appointments?
2. What about childbirth classes? Who sponsors them and where are they held?
3. Do you recommend a certain method of childbirth preparation?
4. Do you do all the birth counseling?
5. Do you refer clients to a birth counselor, or is there someone on your staff who will counsel me if I want it?
6. How do you feel about a Birth Plan—a written list of my preferences for care during labor, birth, and postpartum?
7. Are you willing to participate in creating a Birth Plan?
8. When you sign our Birth Plan, will it be honored by the staff as your orders?
9. What are your dietary recommendations during pregnancy?
10. What do you consider normal weight gain during pregnancy?
11. How do you feel about medication during pregnancy, such as cold and cough medications, aspirin, pain relievers, and so on?
12. What types of exercise do you recommend? What should I avoid?
13. What do you advise concerning sex during pregnancy?

14. If I develop complications during pregnancy, will you still take care of me? If not, who will be my caregiver?

LABOR AND BIRTH

1. What methods of labor and delivery are available in your practice (unmedicated, birth center, VBAC, underwater)?
2. What is your definition of "natural" childbirth? (This question determines if their definition matches yours.)
3. What is your policy about my partner, family, or friends participating in my labor and delivery?
4. How do you feel about our other child (or children) being present at the birth?
5. What is your philosophy about medication in labor?
6. What are your beliefs about eating and drinking during labor?
7. What kind of interventions do you routinely require during labor? (I.V., continuous electronic fetal monitor—external or internal, complete bed rest, etc.)
8. I've heard that some caregivers say a woman has to dilate a specific number of centimeters per hour. If my body doesn't follow this schedule, what would you do? (Use pitocin, forceps, vacuum extraction, or cesarean birth?) What percentage of your clients have these?
9. If I develop complications during labor, will you still take care of me? If not, who will be my caregiver?
10. Where do you deliver babies?
11. Will I be able to deliver in a birthing room? Will the baby stay there with me?
12. At the place of birth do you have to follow specific procedures of that institution? Can you override their rules and dictate what you want for your patient?
13. How do you feel about professional childbirth assistants (doulas)? How do you feel about my having one at the birth?
14. Does the location where you deliver have a childbirth assistant (doula) service, or do you know of one in the community?
15. (If there are several physicians and midwives in the practice) what are the chances you will be present when I deliver? What happens if you aren't available?
16. If you're not present at the birth but you've signed my Birth Plan, will the person attending me respect the decisions that we have made?

17. Will the hospital staff honor our Birth Plan in your absence? Will they follow your orders rather than those of the attending caregiver?
18. Are you familiar with methods of natural childbirth (such as the Leboyer method) and do you incorporate them into your practice?

POSTPARTUM

1. What are your beliefs about a baby's perceptions at birth?
2. Who will examine our baby immediately following birth? Do you recommend that we select our own pediatrician before the birth?
3. Do you have recommendations for a pediatrician? (This is a question for those who are interviewing a physician who does not perform newborn care.)
4. Can our baby stay with us the whole time? Does he or she have to go to the hospital nursery for "routine observation" for a time after birth?
5. What is your policy about my leaving the birth place within hours of my delivery? What about staying longer if I wish to?
6. What is your policy regarding follow-up care after delivery?
7. What care will my baby receive if he or she is ill? How can we participate in his or her care?
8. What if our baby is premature? How do you handle the situation?

Take someone along for the initial office interview if possible. Sharing the experience with a partner or friend who knows your needs and desires can be extremely helpful. Having another person with whom to discuss the interviews provides moral support and can broaden your perspective.

Birth Location

A key aspect of finding health care is determining where you will give birth. You may want to give birth at home. If so, you will have to find a midwife or doctor who does home births. If you prefer a hospital or other birth facility, the health care professional you are considering may work at a particular location. Visit the facilities and make sure you feel comfortable there. Take a tour, observe the staff, and inquire about hospital policies and procedures. Consider asking the following questions:

- How many babies do you deliver every month?

- What are your birthing-room options (traditional labor and delivery, alternative birth center)?

- Do you have bathtubs or a spa for use during labor?

- Do you have rocking chairs for use during labor?

- Do you have battery-operated fetal monitors (to allow for movement during labor)?

- How many people may I have in the room during delivery? May my other children be present?

- Do you have rooming-in (baby stays in my room with me after the birth)?

- Who can visit me and my baby (age limits, number of people at one time, visitation hours)?

While touring the birth location observe the staff. Are they helpful and courteous? Visit the nursery and observe the staff. How do they handle newborns? Notice if the nursery is nearly empty or full. If it is empty, that may mean that the babies are rooming in with their mothers. The quality of your birth experience will depend largely on the people who surround you. Is there a sense of peace and calm there? Do you feel comfortable there?

Changing Prenatal Care

You can change your mind about your prenatal care at any time during pregnancy, but it is easier to do this early in your pregnancy. If, later, you come across any serious problems, make every effort to improve the situation. If nothing works, find another health care provider. Develop the habit of consulting your feelings, your body, and your inner self. Here is one woman's experience:

It was my first pregnancy, and I wasn't certain I was pregnant, but I thought I was. We had wanted a child, and I'd missed a couple of periods but had no other symptoms. I went to an OB/GYN listed with the insurance provider that we had through work. He was the closest one to our house. Geographical convenience won out in this case. My best girlfriend (who later turned out to be my labor coach) went with me to the doctor's office. I went for a urine test, which came out positive. Until then we hadn't met the doctor, we had dealt only with the nurses. After getting the results we made an appointment to return in a few days to meet the doctor.

Cost wasn't a big issue in our decision making because we had good insurance. The main concern was the birth itself and the philosophy and personality of the doctor. At this point I didn't know anything about what to expect. I knew nothing about the different approaches to pregnancy and childbirth, about medical intervention or anything else. I was going strictly by instinct. I did know that I wanted a natural childbirth with as little pain as possible. I also knew that I wanted to do more research about the different options, different methods and approaches.

I was concerned about the "what ifs": what if I needed any medical intervention, what if there were complications. I wanted a general understanding of what kinds of problems could occur. With a good understanding of how they are typically handled, I could be an active decision maker along with the doctors.

It was very important for me to have a support person as a backup throughout pregnancy, labor, and birth. This person would know my philosophy and wishes in case any complications did arise and would know my thinking well enough to make decisions if I were unable to. I chose my best friend because she was available and motivated to join me in the research. Our philosophy about health was the same, so I trusted her in this role.

We returned for the appointment with Dr. McKay. After the pelvic exam we met with him in his office. The first thing on his agenda was the discussion of money, so we let him go on about costs, and so on. I told him that this was not a top priority on my list because we had good insurance. Then he examined me. He said that because he hadn't heard a heartbeat, he was recommending an amniocentesis. I thought this was usually recommended for older women or those with high-risk pregnancies. I had misgivings because, at twenty-four years of age, I was in better health than I'd ever been before. I saw no reason for such a test. However, I wasn't certain. We left the office with his test prescription in hand and told the nurse we'd call back for an appointment.

We went home and discussed the meeting. We both had the same gut reactions to the doctor and his support staff (all of whom looked like identical fashion models and exuded an air of aloofness). We also noticed the doctor's preoccupation with financial matters. On the subject of his approach to birth he seemed to want to tell us as *little* as possible. We, on the other hand, wanted to know as much as possible. There was very little dialogue.

We were also concerned about his insistence on the amniocentesis. It is an expensive procedure and, as we later found in our research, is not without risk. This left us both with a feeling of alarm. At the same time our instincts were saying that his reason for doing the test was questionable. After all, I was only about ten or eleven weeks pregnant. It occurred to us that it might be a little early to insist on hearing a heartbeat.

This was on a Friday, and we couldn't get any second opinions until Monday. I recall having feelings of anxiety because we really didn't know for sure and wanted more information. On Monday we called another doctor for a second opinion. As we had suspected, we were told that not hearing a heartbeat this early in pregnancy was not a cause for alarm. We were also told that such a test was totally inappropriate considering my age and the fact that I had no other symptoms and was in perfect health. Needless to say, Dr. McKay had disqualified himself.

The next step was to call local doctors at random using the health-care-provider book from the insurance company. We couldn't afford a lot of appointments with different doctors, so our goal was to have brief phone conversations with some in order to find one that sounded reasonable and supportive. This was frustrating because the doctors were never available to talk on the phone (the nurse or bookkeeper called back to explain costs). After trying this with twelve or fourteen doctors, I realized that this strategy wasn't working at all. My pregnancy was progressing without the prenatal care I was seeking.

Then I decided to stop my search for a while, as I was getting too stressed out about it. At this point a woman I knew called some friends of hers who were midwives. They recommended Dr. Brandeis. I called his office in the morning and left a message (as I had done so many times before). That night at eight I received a call. It was Dr. Brandeis. In view of my prior experiences I was completely surprised. He never did bring up the subject of money. All he wanted to talk about was childbirth, his philosophy about pregnancy, birth, and the postpartum period. When I got off the phone, I realized that forty-five minutes had gone by. I knew I had found my doctor. It just so happened that Dr. Brandeis was in my health provider's directory as well. I immediately called my best friend to let her know the good news. I was four months' pregnant by this time.

We went to his office for the first appointment. Again he was very easy to talk to. He wanted me to know as much as I wanted to know. We agreed about this being a team effort. The basic team consisted of myself, the doctor, my best friend, and my husband. My husband and my best friend both attended the Lamaze classes with me and they both participated in the labor and delivery (along with my mother, sister, and another friend). My chiropractor came to the hospital and did an adjustment on me while I was in labor. It was definitely a team effort. I followed my instincts and my feelings, and they did not let me down. I had the birth experience I wanted: natural childbirth, a team effort, feeling supported and empowered.

Consulting the Inner Self: *What's Right for Me?*

Materials: Journal and felt-tip pens
Purpose: To help you determine whether you feel totally comfortable, trusting, and safe with the health care provider you have chosen
Technique:

1. Sit quietly and get in touch with your Inner Self or Higher Power. This is the part of you that contains all the wisdom and guidance you need to make the best choices for yourself and your baby.
2. Write a dialogue with your Inner Self. This is your own internal sage or wise person who knows what is healthy for you—physically, emotionally, mentally, and spiritually. Use two different-colored pens. Write the questions with the dominant hand. Let the Inner Self respond with the nondominant hand. The following sample dialogue offers ideas about what questions to ask:

> Dear Inner Self: What about Dr. L., is she trustworthy?
>
> **I like her a lot. She smiles—genuinely—and pays attention when you speak. She wants to know how you really feel and what you want. I like her philosophy. She believes in the body's natural wisdom and healing powers.**
>
> Do you think she has good training and experience?
>
> **Yes. I liked her answers to your questions at the interview. She seemed to understand you right away. She questioned the use of medication and medical interventions that can do more harm than good.**
>
> What about her staff and the environment?
>
> **Her office is beautiful. It feels very warm and homelike because of all those floral bouquets and the artwork. It's peaceful there. Also, they didn't keep you waiting a long time like they do in so many doctors' offices. That shows they respect your time. The office people were very friendly and helpful. They seemed relaxed and like they enjoyed working there.**

(continued on next page)

3. Write a dialogue like the one above, but this time interview your body. Ask the questions with your dominant hand and let your body respond with the non-dominant hand. Find out how your body feels about any particular health care professional, method of childbirth, hospital or other facility, and so forth.

Special Tests

Dealing with exams and special tests during pregnancy is another aspect of *claiming the territory*. In this section we will introduce several of these tests and exams. If such tests are recommended, often conflicting or confusing emotions may arise. If this occurs, we invite you to redo "Consulting the Inner Self: What's Right for Me?" on the previous page to assess how you're feeling about taking the test.

Some tests are standard procedure. At the first or second prenatal exam the following are commonly done:

- Complete medical history

- Physical examination

- Pelvic (vaginal) examination

- Blood test

- Urine test

If you are feeling uneasy just reading about this, it may be helpful to explore these feelings in your journal. Express all of your worries, doubts, and fears. Just releasing these emotions can help you feel more relaxed and self-confident.

As your pregnancy continues, visits to your caregiver will become more frequent: monthly (until your seventh or eighth month), then twice a month, and finally (the month before delivery) you will go weekly. The purpose of each visit is to determine the health and well-being of both you and your baby. Some of the procedures done at those visits are:

- Weight check

- Blood pressure test

- Urine test

- Abdominal exams to measure the growth of your uterus and to feel the position of your baby and estimate its size

- Discussing your questions with your caregiver

- Recommendations about nutrition, exercise, and any other concerns

- Occasional vaginal exam (if your caregiver deems it necessary)

We encourage you to explore your feelings about medical procedures and tests in your journal. Draw, dialogue, or simply write your observations and reactions.

Other exams that may be done during pregnancy are as follows:

Amniocentesis

Purpose: This test is generally done to provide information about certain diseases. The age, sex, and lung maturity of your baby and genetic characteristics such as chromosomal abnormalities can also be determined.

Considerations: This test is costly. It has many risks, such as miscarriage; injury to the baby, placenta, or cord; and possible complications for the rest of your pregnancy. There can be pain or discomfort both during and after the procedure. Women report that the procedure often feels "quite invasive" and "frightening."

This test is accurate for genetic defects only from the fourteenth to the sixteenth week of pregnancy. The results are then not available for an additional four to six weeks. This can be a trying time for expectant parents waiting to find out if they have a healthy baby. Be certain that it is truly necessary before having it done. If an amniocentesis is ordered for you, we suggest that you journal your feelings about it both before and after the exam.

Ultrasound

Purpose: To determine accuracy of estimated due date, size, and position of baby, amount of fluid surrounding the baby, and fetal well-being. Like an X ray it shows a picture of your insides. It is used to determine age and size of your baby, accuracy of your due date, position of your baby, placement of the placenta, amount of amniotic fluid, and the size of your pelvis. This test is often done at least once during your pregnancy.

Considerations: There is still some question as to the long-term effects of an ultrasound on your baby. Although some authorities claim that it is probably safer than X ray, it is a relatively new test, and medical authorities do not have long-term studies on its physical and psychological effects. We suggest that you approach this test with some caution. Ultrasound is relatively simple and *appears* to be harmless, but we do not advise having it done repeatedly. Have a journal dialogue with your baby before this test is done and find out how he or she feels about it. If you take the test, have another dialogue with your baby afterward.

Vaginal-Probe Ultrasound

Purpose: This procedure has the same purpose as described under "Ultrasound."

Considerations: This is a new test, and medical authorities do not have long-term studies on its physical or psychological effects. The most difficult part of this test is the psychological effect on the expectant mother and her partner. It is both physically uncomfortable, frightening, and embarrassing for many women. We suggest that you approach this test with some caution. We encourage you to have a journal dialogue with your inner self and with your baby before and after having this test. It is important that you confront your feelings about it.

Non-stress Test

Purpose: This test is generally done late in pregnancy, or after the "due date" to determine that all is well with your baby.

Considerations: The non-stress test and the oxytocin challenge test often bring up a number of worries and fears for the woman, and even for her partner. Following this test we suggest that you take your journal and have a dialogue with your baby. When Jan was "overdue," she was a bit worried about the well-being of her baby. After the non-stress test she did a dialogue with her unborn child, and her child told her not to worry, all was well.

Oxytocin-Challenge Test

Purpose: The oxytocin-challenge test shows how your baby handles a contraction.

Considerations: Women tell us the only uncomfortable part of this test is having the electronic fetal monitor belts strapped to the abdomen and having to stimulate their nipples in front of the nurse (usually a stranger). Following the exam, we suggest that you take a few minutes and journal about your emotions. Many women find that doing journal writing after medical tests or other procedures helps sort out their feelings. Write down all your feelings about test procedures and your fears of negative outcomes just as you wrote out your feelings in Chapter One ("Express Yourself," page 30).

Biophysical Profile

Purpose: To determine fetal well-being during late pregnancy and past the due date. This test has five aspects. It includes a non-stress test to determine fetal movement and fetal heart rate and an ultrasound for determining muscle tone, fetal breathing movements, and amniotic-fluid volume.

Considerations: This is an expensive test. Feelings of inner unrest may occur. Feelings of inner unrest generally occur when the woman is past her due date. Doing a Creative Birth Journal dialogue with your baby provides an opportunity to awaken awareness and inner guidance. (See example on page 68.)

Throughout your pregnancy other tests may be suggested to you. We encourage you to weigh the pros and cons. Just as you research your options concerning health care, do the same for all tests prescribed. Use your journal to help you to make informed decisions.

I'm scared about whether you're O.K.

I'm fine, don't worry. I just like feeling you squeeze me. It feels like hugs.

Well hurry and be born and I'll give you lots more hugs. And Daddy will hug you too.

O.K. I'm ready, but I've been waiting for you to be ready. You still seem pretty scared. I don't want to hurt you.

You won't — & I'm ready. I can't wait to see you & hold you.

"DIALOGUE WITH UNBORN CHILD"

Birth Plan

In *claiming the territory* of the actual labor and delivery of your baby, a Birth Plan will be essential. A well-thought-out, written plan of what you want helps you to communicate to your health care professionals, as well as your partner or support team. In Chapter Five you will be given clear guidelines on how to develop your own Birth Plan.

3

Awakening Feelings:

Parenting the Inner Child

Pregnancy can be an emotional time for the expectant mother. There are many reasons for this: hormonal changes, lifestyle adjustments, new responsibilities, and financial concerns, to name a few. Emotions may run high, not only for the pregnant woman but for everyone else around her. Western society has placed many conditions on pregnancy and birth. We expect childbirth to be a certain way and are disapproving of any variations from the standard. Therefore having a baby pushes many people's emotional buttons. They are confronted with their attitudes about children, aging, responsibility, relationship, immortality, and the meaning of life.

In the film *Terms of Endearment* we see an example of emotional reactions to pregnancy. Shirley MacLaine plays a vain, self-centered woman. When her daughter (Debra Winger) becomes pregnant, the grandmother-to-be has a fit. Having a grandchild means she is growing older, a fact that she doesn't want to admit. The daughter has to deal with her own feelings in addition to her mother's reaction. This puts a great deal of stress on the daughter.

Cultural bans on certain emotions complicate how a woman handles the many feelings that arise during pregnancy. In some families specific feelings, such as fear, anger, or sadness, are taboo. For instance, expressing fear was forbidden in the Kramer family. Ridicule and harsh criticism were used to enforce this ban on fear. It was not okay ever to admit feeling scared, anxious, or nervous. These feelings went underground and showed up as chronic psychosomatic symptoms or in addictive behavior.

The Kramers' teenage daughter, Jennifer, became pregnant. She was afraid and could tell no one in the family about the pregnancy or how she was feeling.

She hid her pregnancy and her emotions, putting her and the baby's health at risk. After several months of hiding her pregnancy from the family, Jennifer finally received prenatal care. Unfortunately it was too late. The baby had not developed normally, was ill at birth, and required expensive medical care. The whole experience was a disaster for Jennifer, her baby, and the family.

Suppression of certain feelings puts an added stress on the pregnant woman. Being trapped in an emotional pressure cooker is not only debilitating, it robs her of energy and a sense of well-being. Withheld feelings also undermine relationships. Intimacy is not possible when feelings are being hidden. The healthiest thing you can do for yourself and your loved ones is to *acknowledge and share your feelings.*

Carla was pregnant with her second child. Her toddler, Alicia, was a year and a half old. When Carla was in her seventh month of pregnancy, her in-laws came to town. What followed was a huge conflict between the two grandmothers. Carla's mother had a set routine for visiting with Alicia. Now that Carla's mother-in-law was on the scene, rivalry broke out over who would spend time with the granddaughter.

Carla got caught in the crossfire. Her body started sending out loud signals of distress in the form of excruciating low-back pains. Carla's husband, Raoul, didn't want to hear about the conflict. He chalked it up to "women's stuff" and wanted nothing to do with the situation.

In Carla's next office visit she talked about her back pain and asked if it might indicate some problem with the pregnancy. After examining her and finding no physiological cause, Dr. Maurice suspected that it might be stress-related. Dr. Maurice, Carla's OB/GYN, was also a trained hypnotherapist. He suggested doing some hypnotherapy. During the session Carla shared the domestic problems she was facing. Breaking into tears, she acknowledged feeling totally unsupported by her family. "They're all caught up in what they want. No one cares that their arguing really gets to me. I'm the one who's pregnant, but it's as if that doesn't matter at all."

After receiving support from Dr. Maurice, Carla worked up the courage to confront her mother and mother-in-law. She expressed her feelings clearly and without blame by simply telling them how this behavior was affecting her. They became very sympathetic and realized how immature they had been. The older women worked out their differences. Carla's symptoms were relieved almost immediately. The whole situation changed because Carla discovered the source of her discomfort and spoke up.

The next activities explore feelings and how to express them.

Drawing the Inside Out: *Full of Feelings*

Materials: Journal or large sheets of paper and drawing tools
Purpose: To become aware of how you really feel without judgment or self-criticism. To reduce stress by releasing pent-up emotions.
Technique:

1. With your non-dominant hand draw a picture of how you feel right now. Don't try to make "art." Scribble, doodle, make abstract shapes of color and texture. Let yourself become like a little child, and draw like a little child. This is just for your eyes. If your Inner Art Critic starts nagging at you about not having talent or making stupid art, just notice that voice and continue drawing anyway. Let yourself play on the paper. If you wish, do more than one drawing of feelings.
2. With your non-dominant hand, on another page write down any words that express the feelings represented in your picture. Don't worry about grammar, spelling, penmanship, or complete sentences. Just let the words flow.

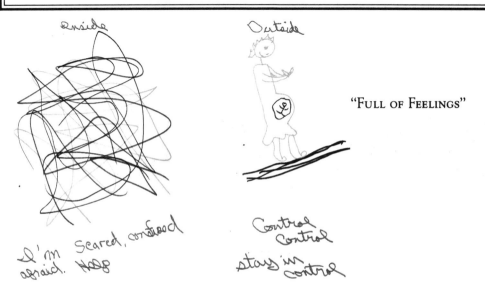

"FULL OF FEELINGS"

Cluster Writing: *A Quick Look at Feelings*

Materials: Journal and felt-tip pens

Purpose: To explore your feelings about an emotionally charged word. To learn more about yourself and what is important to you.

Technique:

1. Using your dominant hand, in the center of your page write down the first feeling that comes to mind (e.g., fear, anger, excitement, joy, grief, tenderness, love). Then draw a circle around it.

2. With your non-dominant hand write five words around the circle. Use words that reflect your feelings about the original word.

3. Think about the five additional words or phrases you have written and circle them one at a time. Connect them to your central phrase. (See examples below.)

4. Take these five words and write your feelings about each one. Circle these and connect them with straight lines to the words that evoked those feelings. Continue this process with each word until you have filled the page.

5. Now read all the words you've written and reflect on them. On another page, using your dominant hand, write a poem with the words from your cluster exercise.

6. Is there anything you want to do about those feelings? If so, write down what action you would like to take.

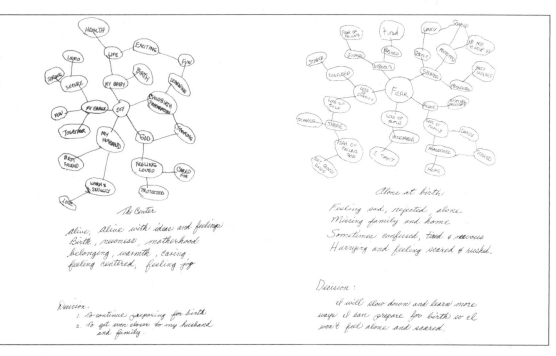

The Center

Alive, alive with ideas and feelings
Birth, newness, motherhood
belonging, warmth, caring,
feeling centered, feeling joy

Decision.
1. To continue preparing for birth
2. To get even closer to my husband and family.

Alone at birth

Feeling sad, rejected, alone
Missing family and home
Sometimes confused, tired & nervous
Hurrying and feeling scared & rushed.

Decision:
I will slow down and learn more
ways I can prepare for birth so I
won't feel alone and scared.

Like Carla, you may sometimes feel overwhelmed during your pregnancy. This can be stressful, both physically and emotionally. The following activity can help you regain a sense of well-being in a situation that might otherwise feel disturbing or even chaotic.

Venting Inner Feelings: *Talk Back*

Materials: Journal and felt-tip pens
              Optional: large paper, crayons, markers
Purpose: To regain composure by expressing your upset feelings
Technique:

1. Focus on a situation or a person that is currently upsetting you or causing concern or worry.
2. Use your dominant hand and write down all the things that are troubling you about that situation or person.
3. With your non-dominant hand draw a symbol or image of what is troubling you. Write a caption that describes it.
4. Using your non-dominant hand, in your journal write a letter expressing your true feelings. This letter is not to be sent. It's just for you. It's a way of getting things off your chest and clearing your body of trapped emotions. Express any feelings of anger, hurt, or disappointment you may have. Don't hold back. You need not be polite.
5. Continue until you feel better. It may take a while, and you may want to write more than one letter.

The Inner Child During Pregnancy and Birth

In every adult there is a childlike part of the personality. This is called the *Inner Child. It is the emotional, physical, and intuitive part of you.* The Inner Child is alive in you today and will never grow up. It's the part of you that is emotionally sensitive, physically active, spontaneous, playful, and creative. She lives in your body, your feelings, and your gut instincts. She knows what is healthy and safe for you and what isn't.

To know your Inner Child is to know yourself. If you ignore your Inner Child (feelings, body, intuition), you will have difficulty communicating what is in your heart. A healthy Inner Child gives us energy, creativity, and honesty in relationships.

Your Inner Child plays an important part in pregnancy, birth, and parenting. In fact the Inner Child can help you to be a better parent. By allowing your Inner Child to speak to you *well before* labor and delivery, you can clear a space for a happier, healthier birth experience. Your Inner Child is an important inner resource in pregnancy and parenting both.

In our clinical work we have discovered a phenomenon that we call the *Inner Child Sibling Rivalry Syndrome.* By this we mean that the Inner Child of the parent competes with the new baby for attention. When the expectant mother does not care for her own emotional and physical needs, the woman's Inner Child may feel abandoned. It has no recourse but to make itself heard through physical discomfort or emotional upset. These symptoms may indicate that your Inner Child is trying to talk to you. Being on good terms with your Inner Child will help you to have a healthier and happier pregnancy and prevent conflict with your unborn baby.

The Inner Child Sibling Rivalry Syndrome affects all aspects of pregnancy, birth, and early parenting. It can actually contribute to infertility. Beyond physical problems and emotionally challenging issues such as an unhappy relationship, financial insecurity, or unsafe living conditions, a woman's relationship with her Inner Child definitely plays a part in her ability to conceive and carry her baby to term. Getting on good terms with your Inner Child can resolve conflict between your unconcious feelings and your conscious desires. Through written journal conversations with the Inner Child, our clients have uncovered their psychological blocks to getting and staying pregnant.

Valerie and her husband, Ken, wanted to have a baby but were unable to do so. Their physician could find no physical reason for their infertility. Valerie and Ken suspected that psychological factors might be contributing to her inability to conceive. Because of this, she came to Lucia for counseling.

In one of Valerie's therapy sessions her Inner Child spoke out in a role-play activity. When asked about the subject of having a baby, her Inner Child (Little Valerie) said the following: "I don't want a kid around here. She [meaning the adult Valerie] doesn't pay any attention to me as it is now. If she has a kid, I'll be *totally* left out. All she does is work, worry, and act like a serious grown-up. We *never* have any do-nothing time, never any fun."

Valerie asked her Inner Child if she was responsible for preventing Big Valerie from getting pregnant. She responded, "Yes, I don't want her to have a kid. *No way.* I know her. She'll go into being a parent to this kid and get really serious and overworked about it. I'll be *completely* out of the picture."

Valerie realized that she needed to learn how to take care of herself and her Inner child. She took time off from work, played the piano for her own enjoyment, took walks every day with Ken, got facials, and generally pampered herself. Six months later she conceived. Valerie and Ken had a healthy baby. Valerie is learning to have fun as she and Ken enjoy parenting.

Lisa also experienced Inner Child Sibling Rivalry Syndrome. Her first baby was delivered by C-section. As an incest survivor, Lisa found that becoming a parent evoked tremendous fear and difficulty in bonding with her newborn. In counseling, Lisa found an Inner Child who was very wounded because of early childhood sexual abuse. When she became pregnant for the second time, Lisa's Inner Child panicked. Her physician and counselor referred her to Co-Creations. They felt that her Inner Child needed extra support. Lisa did journal dialogues with her Inner Child. She also brought her husband in for some of the counseling sessions. Lisa was finally able to help her Inner Child feel safe, loved, and ready to be part of the birth. Her second child was delivered vaginally and without drugs.

Knowing how your Inner Child thinks and feels prepares you to be a better parent. Listening to your body and emotions throughout pregnancy will prepare you to better understand your baby when it's born.

Following are some Inner Child activities appropriate for pregnancy. These exercises are simple and enjoyable. They will help you *experience* your Inner Child. Sometimes unresolved feelings from the past may arise as you do these exercises. *If at any time you feel overwhelmed with emotions, we urge you to seek professional help.*

Inner Child Chat: *How Do You Feel?*

Materials: Journal, felt-tip pens, and crayons

Purpose: To experience the Inner Child state firsthand. To express feelings, wants, and needs through the language of the child: creative expression.

Technique:

1. With your non-dominant hand let your Inner Child draw a picture of itself. Let the image appear spontaneously on the page without planning it.
2. Write out a dialogue between yourself and the Child who appeared in your drawing. It doesn't matter what the child looks like or what age it appears to be. Your adult self writes with your dominant hand. Your child self writes with your non-dominant hand. The Inner Child may wish to print, and the printing may be very awkward. If so, just be patient and allow it to write as slowly as it needs to. Ask your Inner Child to tell you about himself or herself:

   • Name and age

   • How it feels

   • How it feels about your pregnancy

   • What it wants from you

Do this dialogue on a regular basis (every few days or so) throughout pregnancy and after your baby's birth. We strongly recommend that you and your partner (or other support persons) write "Inner Child Chats" in your journals. When members of a family group embrace their own Inner Children, they enjoy welcoming the newborn baby into the world even more.

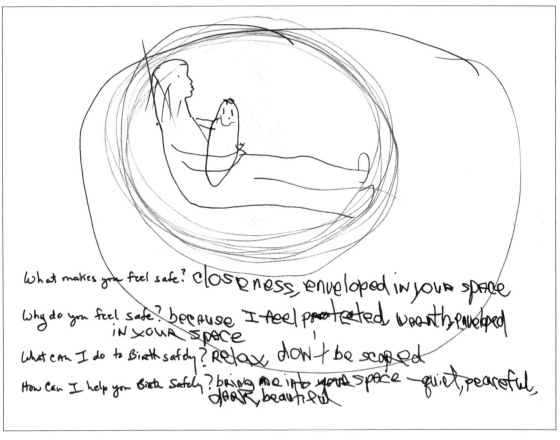

What makes you feel safe? closeness, enveloped in your space

Why do you feel safe? because I feel protected, warmth enveloped in your space

What can I do to Birth safely? Relax, don't be scared

How can I help you Birth Safely? bring me into your space — quiet, peaceful, dark, beautiful

"INNER CHILD CHAT"

Healing the Pain of the Past

Inner Child work is crucial for pregnant women who have experienced physical, emotional, or sexual abuse. Sometimes survivors of abuse have forgotten these experiences. The experience of being abused is simply too traumatic, too overwhelming, and blocking the memories or the severity of abuse are understandable reactions, necessary for self-protection and survival.

The body stores blocked memories and unexpressed feelings of past abuse. When survivors of abuse (especially sexual abuse) become pregnant, the body may start "speaking out" non-verbally. Pain, discomfort, and physical problems often surface. Some women experience anxiety attacks, or constant worries and fears. These emotions may have little to do with any current situation.

Awakening Feelings:
Parenting the
Inner Child

"Pelvic Freeze" during labor is a common phenomenon for women who have been abused. The pelvic area, often the focus of attack during abuse, can go into paralysis. This interrupts the natural progress of labor and can lead to medical interventions.

Recent research and documentation regarding sexual abuse of women has revealed that anywhere from one in three women to one in five have been abused. Sexual abuse is common, and addressing this type of abuse is an important part of childbirth preparation.

If you know or suspect that you are a survivor of physical or sexual abuse, we strongly recommend that you do Inner Child work during pregnancy. The Creative Birth Journal provides a gentle way to begin your healing process. Lucia's earlier book, *Recovery of Your Inner Child*, can lead you to further healing.

Again, please seek professional help if emotions and memories of past trauma become overwhelming. There are counselors and licensed therapists with training and clinical experience working with survivors of abuse. This is a time to find loving and compassionate support. Recovering from abuse is something that needs time and care. Don't expect to be able to complete this work during pregnancy. However, you *can* get started before the birth of your baby.

Healing the Past: *Taking Care of Unfinished Business*

Materials: Journal, fel-tip pens, and crayons
Purpose: To become your Inner Child's own loving parent or understanding counselor
Technique:

1. Find a location where you feel safe to do this exercise. Be sure that there will be no interruptions. Sit quietly and imagine a bubble of protection surrounding you. The bubble can be made of any material you wish. Focus on your breathing and relax your body. Recall a time when you were physically or emotionally hurt. Allow an image of the scene to appear in your mind.
2. With your non-dominant hand draw the emotions associated with this experience. Let your feelings come out in your drawing. Remember, you're not being asked to produce art, but rather to allow your Inner Child to express

feelings. If a critical voice judges your artwork, tell it to be quiet, and continue drawing.

3. With your non-dominant hand, on another page allow your Inner Child to express these feelings *in words.*

   • How did your Inner Child want to be treated in that situation?

   • What does your Inner Child want now in order to feel comforted?

4. With your dominant hand write your Inner Child a love letter. (*Optional:* Make a tape recording of this letter and play it back to yourself, or have someone you trust read your letter to you.)

The following journal drawing and writing was done by Roberta, a woman who had regressed during a therapy session. She remembered her *in utero* experience of abandonment and rejection by her parents. Here is her non-dominant-hand drawing of herself as a fetus:

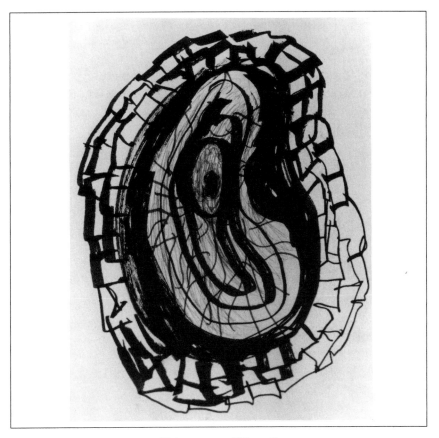

"Me in the Womb"

On the page facing her drawing, Roberta wrote the following (also done with her non-dominant hand):

> I'm a girl fetus. A girl baby. I'm all walled in. I want someone to touch me deeply, but I'm barricaded in here. I'm afraid. If someone touches or sees me and is disappointed, they'll leave. I won't live up to their expectations & it's bleak & dark. I just want to fold up & sleep & block it all out.
>
> I'm shut away in here. I can't get out. I was wrong—the wrong kind. I don't deserve to be loved. I wasn't what they ordered.

As she was growing up, Roberta remembered her mother telling others that "This child was supposed to have been a boy with black hair and blue eyes." Roberta disappointed her mother by being a girl with fair hair and hazel eyes.

Roberta cried as she did the fetus drawing and writing. The feeling of having disappointed her parents by simply *being* who she was had left a deep scar in Roberta's psyche. As a result she tried to *earn* their acceptance through accomplishment. Although she became a high-achiever there was still a lingering feeling of having disappointed her parents.

After doing the fetus drawing, Roberta drew a picture of how she would have liked things to be. In contrast to the black, frightened fetus, she now drew a bright red woman dancing on a yellow background (below).

Through this work Roberta learned to *accept herself.* She then wrote the following words in orange with her non-dominant hand:

> I am a woman who contains many women & children . . . Who pulses with life . . . I am a child of the earth and also of the sky.

More Unfinished Business: Losses from the Past

During pregnancy memories of past losses often come to the surface. Delayed mourning related to a past abortion, miscarriage, stillbirth, or death of a child is common. For instance, many women have kept their abortion experiences secret due to feelings of shame and guilt. Regardless of the reason for the abortion, they have never really mourned their loss.

While Barbara was pregnant, she frequently broke out in uncontrollable tears. She was baffled by her tears because she and her husband wanted a baby very much. She sought counseling and discovered the cause was her unexpressed grief about an abortion she'd had as a teenager. Unprepared for motherhood at that time, Barbara had terminated the pregnancy. Since then she had harbored feelings of self-blame and remorse. What's more, she never mourned the loss. After being guided through grieving and self-forgiveness, Barbara was able to embrace her pregnancy with joy. Her crying spells stopped.

To clear an emotional space for pregnancy, it is important to heal pain from past losses. Three processes that are particularly helpful are the following:

- Writing a journal letter to or dialoguing with the baby or person you have lost. *Use both hands: The dominant hand speaks for you, and the non-dominant hand speaks for the other (baby, loved one, etc.).*

- Drawing your feelings about the loss.

- Sharing your experience with a trustworthy person who is non-judgmental and supportive.

If you decide to share this information please be cautious. Share only with someone you really trust and feel safe with such as a counselor, good friend, or spouse. If you sense any criticism or blame from the other person, stop. Don't worsen the situation by forcing yourself to deal with someone else's negative reaction. What you need is compassion, support, and love, not criticism.

Following her abortion Katie poured her heart out in a letter to her unborn baby (whom she called David). By expressing herself on paper she was able to sort through her feelings.

New Moon

Letter to David

I woke up crying last night and couldn't stop. I cried all night. I'm not usually the crying type; demonstrations of emotions tend to embarrass me. I didn't even have the emotional strength to be mad at any Higher Power, my usual style. Instead I floundered, begging for help and willing to actually listen for guidance. A quiet voice in my head spoke, "Write him a letter." I asked for better guidance. The voice was irritatingly calm as it repeated, "Write him a letter." Okay I thought, we're in for some major resistance here. I don't want to. I don't WANT TO!! Because . . . I know that once I put it down on paper, I'd be letting it go; and realizing that, I'd have to face how I hate to let you go . . .

. . . Maybe someday, maybe now, the joy will stand on its own without the watery shadows of tears of the pain that sometimes tears at me, or stabs, or sometimes just lingers throughout the day and long into the night. But that pain is another of your incredible gifts, and I promise you I will never keep it secret from myself. It reminds me that I can feel. Already it makes my happiness happier, my gratitude deeper, my compassion stronger and more complete. I think of it like your mark on my body. Just like the silvery signature your sister left on my breasts and belly. I see now that in letting you go I am free to love you. I will treasure that pain and I am willing to watch it transform or allow it to hollow a permanent groove in my heart. I am so grateful to you and I will love you always.

Love, Mother

Clearing a Space

Earlier we described *clearing a space*. *Clearing a space includes getting rid of what you don't want to make room for what you do want.* For example, pregnant women frequently get the urge to "nest." They become very domestic: cleaning out closets and drawers, redecorating, painting, and generally reorganizing the environment. They do this to *clear a space* for the new arrival.

Clearing a space also includes cleaning out thoughts and beliefs that are not productive. Call it a mental spring cleaning. The mind stores beliefs and attitudes as *self-talk:* the internal chatter that we direct to ourselves constantly. Some self-talk is positive, some is negative. Negative self-talk is usually self-criticism. Some common *negative* self-talk in pregnancy is as follows: "I'm fat as a cow." "I waddle like a duck." "I'm as big as a barn." "I look like a beached whale."

Self-criticism is incessant and all-pervasive. Often we aren't even aware of it. Like background music to our everyday experiences, we don't even realize how pervasive and powerful negative self-talk is. It colors our emotional moods and affects our bodies.

The good news is that you can get the upper hand. When you identify negative self-talk, you can *clear a space* for more positive beliefs. The following exercise focuses on your inner reaction to external events and gives you tools for choosing more positive self-talk.

Self-Talk: *What I Say to Myself—What Others Say About Me*

Materials: Journal and felt-tip pens
Purpose: To explore your beliefs, attitudes, and moods. To develop positive self-talk.
Technique:

1. Divide the page vertically into three columns. Label them *Comment, Reaction,* and *Action.* With your dominant hand, in the *Comment* column write some of the things that people say to you regarding this pregnancy. Include some of the things you say to yourself as well.
2. Using your non-dominant hand, in the *Reaction* column respond to each item listed.
3. Look over your responses. Do you want to keep these feelings, attitudes, and beliefs? Are there any you want to change? If so, circle them.
4. Using your dominant hand, in the *Action* column write positive actions you can take to respond to each item in the *Reaction* column.

(continued on next page)

Comment	Reaction	Action
"She's not very big for eight months."	I feel real worried	I need to deal with these comments in a more positive manner. Because I know the baby is fine and that I need not worry.
"She looks cute pregnant."	Embarrassed, good/happy, sometimes degraded	I like to have this feeling. It makes me smile.
"Looks like she's carrying a basketball."	Angry, worried	I've gotten to the point where I laugh at this comment because of its silliness.
"I'm fat."	Embarrassed, depressed, sad	I have to realize why I'm larger. Since realizing this, I can look at myself and say, "I look good."
"I'm content."	Feeling of fulfillment	I like this feeling the best and become more content as time passes.

Sharing Self-talk

During the first couple of months, even with a planned pregnancy, it is quite normal for a woman (and her partner) to feel some ambivalence about the pregnancy. Having a baby brings big changes and responsibility for both partners. Some fear, anxiety, and misgivings are perfectly normal and understandable. Fully accepting the pregnancy takes time. Exploring feelings through journaling and sharing helps clear the air. It also strengthens your relationship.

Sharing Feelings: *Baby Talk*

Materials: Time and quiet location, drawing materials
Purpose: To explore your partner's or support persons' feelings and share your own. To cultivate communication skills and strengthen your relationship.

Technique:

1. Get together with your partner or support person. Find a quiet place to spend some uninterrupted time together. Taking turns, interview each other using the following questions. One person asks while the other one answers.

   - How did you feel when you first found out about this pregnancy?

   - What did you think others (such as your mate, your parents, his parents, your friends) would say or feel? How did that affect you?

   - Do you have any concerns about this pregnancy? What are they?

   - What are some of the things you feel good about regarding this pregnancy?

   - How do you feel about your body at this time? How do you feel about your partner's body?

   - Is there anything you would like me to do for you at this time?

2. Using your non-dominant hand, draw a picture of how you can support the mother.

slow walks
talking, connecting
getting clear
how Ann is
feeling And
what she's
wanting

sharing
how I
feel And
what I
can give

talking
And laughing

holding Anns hand
or rubbing her
back through the
sad times
making the time
slide by

"SUPPORTING EACH OTHER"

Cultivating Your Mental Garden

The mind is a garden; our thoughts are like plant life. Some thoughts are negative and deadly. Like weeds and parasites, they sap our energy. Positive thoughts are creative and life-affirming. They can be compared to majestic trees, beautiful flowers, delicious fruits and vegetables. Positive thoughts build our confidence and lead to productive action and inner peace. One feels good simply strolling around amid such thoughts. When a woman is expecting a baby, creating positive thoughts contributes to a healthy pregnancy.

Jocelyn thought of herself as "an unlucky person." As a result her efforts to accomplish her goals often failed. She believed that an "unlucky person" doesn't succeed in life. The belief was like a weed choking her energy. Thinking of herself as a victim, Jocelyn lacked liveliness and enthusiasm.

When Jocelyn became pregnant, the chronic depression she experienced concerned her doctor. He referred her to Co-Creations for counseling and childbirth-education classes. There she discovered her pattern of expecting the worst. Her negative expectations were a self-fulfilling prophecy. Through journaling she learned to monitor her thoughts and redirect her focus in a more positive direction. She began to experience herself as a capable and successful person. By preparing for and having a joyful birth experience Jocelyn proved to herself that she could attract good fortune.

There is a big difference between *experiencing* misfortune and *classifying oneself* as "an unlucky person." The first has to do with events and situations. The second has to do with assuming the role of a victim. Even though a pregnant woman may encounter difficult situations, it is very important that she not think of herself as a victim and perpetuate negative thinking. Negative thoughts are toxic to her and her baby.

Where there is a garden, there is always a gardener. A good gardener cultivates the plants of her choice. She recognizes the weeds and removes them. She nourishes the flowers and allows them to flourish and gathers them in full bloom. It takes love, time, patience, and the right tools. This section contains guidance for cultivating your most beautiful and creative thoughts.

A New View: *Changing Your Beliefs*

Materials: Journal and felt-tip pens
Purpose: To identify your beliefs and where they came from. To keep your positive beliefs and let go of negative ones.
Technique:

1. Divide the page in half vertically. Label the left column *Beliefs About Labor and Delivery.* Label the right column *Where This Belief Came From.*
2. In the left column, using your dominant hand, without stopping to think, make a list of your beliefs about labor and delivery.
3. In the right-hand column, using your non-dominant hand, respond to each belief with who told you this and when the belief started.
4. After completing both lists, sit quietly and review them, thinking about which beliefs make sense to you now and which you need to let go of.
5. On a separate page, using your non-dominant hand, list the beliefs about labor and delivery you want to keep.
(See example on page 88.)

Beliefs about labor & delivery	Where they came from
1. It always seems to go on for days & days.	1. My grandma, my aunt Harriett (when I was little & her telling Mom about her birth)
2. It's horrible — very painful	2. It seems like everyone has "horror stories to tell
3. Almost everyone has trouble	3. " " "
4. Trust your doctor and the nurses.	4. My mom
5. That I can't trust the Drs. & nurses — I can't trust anyone.	5. Some of my friends — like Jennifer
6. That I'll "know" when I'm in labor.	6. My mom, my aunt Hattie my friends.
7. That my bottom will be sore for months from delivering	7. Sue (she had a big cut & then she tore besides)
8. That sex will always hurt after delivery	8. Sue.
9. I've heard some good things too like — that it's a wonderful "high."	9. Reading now that I'm pregnant, my midwife, my mom.
10. That seeing the baby right after birth makes everything O.K.	10. My mom
11. That I can do it!	11. My midwife, my mom, my childbirth teacher
12. That my body was built for birth.	12. My midwife, my mom, my Lamaze teacher
13. That God will help me.	13. My minister
14. That Bob can stay with me.	14. My midwife, my teacher.

Turning Worries Around

Worry and Fear

There is a difference between worry and fear. Fear can be a healthy indicator that motivates you to change. It alerts your body and mind to take action. Taking action produces results and dissipates fear, such as in the following example: The unborn baby doesn't move for a few hours, and you are afraid. Your fear motivates you to take the action of *calling* your caregiver and *getting an exam.* By taking this action your fear will dissipate. Another example: Your caregiver prescribes a particular test to be done, and you feel afraid. Your questions automatically arise. What is this particular test normally given for? How is it administered? How will it affect my baby and me? Your questions motivate you to take action by *talking* with your caregiver and other informed people about the test, by *reading* about it, and by *journaling* with your baby and your body. When you take action and increase your knowledge, your fear begins to leave.

It is good to be afraid sometimes because fear may be a sign that something is wrong. In pregnancy some fears are natural and justifiable, and it is important to listen to them. With the increase of complicated childbirth technology, pregnant women have more things to be afraid of than ever before. It is easy to feel intimidated by high-tech equipment, terminology, and procedures that are often unexplained. However, instead of allowing yourself to feel fear, become informed and take action.

Worry is imagination used self-destructively. It is an endless cycle of negative thoughts leading nowhere. Worry clutters up the mind with negative images, leaving little room for positive ones. Chronic worry eats away at your vitality and self-confidence. "What if" questions nag at you and lead into a non-productive loop. "What if the baby isn't in the right position? What if that means the baby won't come out? What if I can't have a vaginal birth? What if I have to have a C-section? What if? . . . What if? . . ." As these feelings go on and on, your panic rises.

When your feelings of fear threaten to overwhelm you and you catch yourself beginning the endless-worry loop, we recommend that you stop and journal with your fear. Your Inner Child can be a valuable asset in determining when fear needs your attention and what action to take. Once you discover what you want and work toward having it, your worry and negative thinking will diminish.

In the next exercise practice uncovering your worries and fears. From there you can *clear a space* for a positive mental picture to emerge. This may seem difficult at first, especially if you have a habit of looking at the worst-case scenario. This is more common than you might think. Many people can describe in great detail what they don't want or what they are afraid will happen. However, clearly describing what they *do want* in life can be a very difficult task. By imaging what you *want*, you can convert worries into wishes and take charge of your life.

Positive Imagery: *From Worries to Wishes*

Materials: Three pieces of paper and felt-tip pens
Purpose: To learn to identify your worries and replace them with positive images of your desired results
Technique:

1. With your dominant hand, on your first piece of paper draw a picture of some aspect of your pregnancy that you fear. Perhaps you're afraid of having a C-section or maybe a miscarriage. You may have more than one fear. Choose the one that is uppermost in your mind.
2. Reflect on the situation you pictured above. Divide your second page in half vertically. Label the left-hand column *Worries* and the right-hand column *Action*.
3. In the left-hand column, using your dominant hand, write all the worries you associate with your present fear.
4. Sit quietly and feel your fear. Notice where the fear resides in your body. Is it a knot in your stomach? Do you feel like you have the weight of the world on your shoulders? Using your non-dominant hand, write in the "Action" column. Contest each worry with an action statement: What action are you going to take?
5. Again sit quietly. Contemplate each action you have just written. How does it feel in your body when you think about taking action? Using your non-dominant hand, create a drawing of what your ideal outcome is to each action. This might feel unfamiliar at first. If you keep trying, it will become more comfortable. Remember not to judge yourself. Let the imagination of the Inner Child show you the way.
6. Place your picture where you can see it daily. Whenever you begin to worry, stop yourself and replace your negative mental image with your new positive image.

Kathy's midwife sent her to Co-Creations for counseling a month before her due date. She was full of fear and worry. Here's what she told us about the counseling she received:

No one ever talks about fear. I remember how scared I was at the birth of my first child. I thought that the second birth would be the same. I worried about being overwhelmed by fear and that I wouldn't be able to listen to my body. That's how it was when I had my first baby.

I did some journal exercises about fear and worry and dialogued with the Birth Energy. What came up seemed to be answers from God. They were rather like prayers. That's what the Birth Energy is . . ."Energy from God." It told me not to be afraid. That birth was a natural process. . . . It was giving me a blessing.

Sandra suggested that Kathy continue journaling with the Birth Energy and her unborn baby during the remainder of the pregnancy. She also suggested that Kathy do an exercise called "Fear Busters," identifying her resources for breaking through fear. Kathy reflected on the result of having done these exercises:

I felt much more confident when I focused on the positive. I grew stronger and less fearful. Despite the sudden onset of labor and rapid delivery, our beautiful little daughter was born safely. My husband, Bruce, and I felt calm and competent throughout the delivery. It was a very fulfilling and rewarding experience.

Here is the exercise that helped Kathy face her fears:

Imagery: *Fear Busters*

Materials: Journal and felt-tip pens; separate piece of paper
Purpose: To break through the worry cycle by learning how to focus on your inner resources while confronting fear. To regain energy and a sense of control when feeling the debilitating effects of fear.

Technique:

1. Close your eyes and get in touch with the feelings in your body. Consider any fears you have about pregnancy, delivery, and birth. Where do those fears occur in your body? (Examples: a knot in your stomach, feeling of nausea, lower-back pain, cold hands or feet, tightness in your pelvic area, a tension in your shoulders or neck, etc.)
2. More than one fear may be revealing itself this time. Choose the one that is foremost in your mind. Imagine that fear as a symbol. With your non-dominant hand, draw your fear in the center of your journal page.
3. Draw a box around the symbol of your fear. Leave the four corners of your box open (see illustration on page 92). Now your fear is somewhat contained. The fact that the corners of your box are open means that the fear can get

(continued on next page)

out. You have the power to contain this fear by using your resources to seal those exits through which fear can sneak out and take over.

4. Think of an inner strength or outer resource you have that can help you to contain this particular fear. Using your non-dominant hand, draw a symbol that represents that strength or resource.

5. Continue this process until all four corners of your box are closed. Now your fear is fully contained.

6. If you still feel afraid and that you cannot yet control this fear, continue adding other symbols around the walls of your box until you feel strong.

7. On a separate piece of paper complete the following sentence as often as you like: "I feel safe and secure because . . ." (Make this an affirmation statement using the three P's: Positive, Personal, and Present tense.) Put it up in a place where you can see it every day.

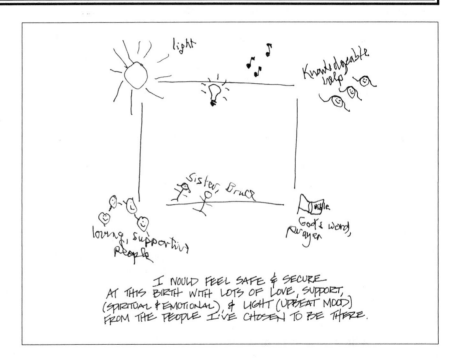

Affirmations

Verbal affirmations are short sentences that state exactly what you want. It is crucial that you speak or write your affirmations *in the first-person present tense.* If you use the future tense, then your desired goal will remain *in the future* and never become a living reality. For example, Jean's affirmation "I will enjoy a healthy pregnancy" did not help her attain her goal. Her pregnancy was fraught with physical discomfort that made it anything but enjoyable. Instead of "I will" a more effective affirmation would have been, "I AM enjoying a healthy pregnancy."

An effective affirmation allows you to act as if you have already achieved the goal. A woman who is actually experiencing a healthy pregnancy speaks in the present tense, saying, "Yes, I feel great and *I am enjoying* a healthy pregnancy."

Verbal affirmations use words to turn negative thoughts into positive attitudes. To be able to do this, you need to know exactly what your negative thoughts are. Unconscious negative thoughts block you from creating your new belief. For example, Len was nervous about finances when he learned his wife, Patty, was pregnant. He had been experimenting with affirmations in his business, so he decided to try it in his personal life to clear his financial worries. Len wrote down his affirmation: "We have everything we need financially for this pregnancy and birth." Immediately he could hear a voice in his head saying, "Who are you kidding? You don't really believe that. Medical bills will be astronomical. Everybody knows that. Get serious," and so on and so forth. These negative statements used up Len's energy, drowned out his affirmations, and his worry persisted. It wasn't until Len identified his negative voices and got rid of them that he could attain success with his affirmation.

Like weeds, negative thoughts choke the growth of your new affirmations. Your negative thoughts may have been around a long time. They may have formed a well-worn groove in your mind. In the next activity you will learn how to "change your mind" by clearing those negative thoughts. To clear them, you've got to hear them. Like tuning a musical instrument, it takes repeated effort. Your mind is your instrument. If you want to play beautiful music, you must "tune" it by training it. That's what the next activity will help you do.

Verbal Affirmations: *Clearing a Space*

Materials: Journal and felt-tip pens
Purpose: To affirm what you want during pregnancy and to clear away negative thoughts and expectations that block you
Technique:

1. Take two pens, each a different color, one in each hand. With your dominant hand write a strong, positive statement (a belief or behavior you want to cultivate in yourself), for example: "I'm enjoying a healthy pregnancy." Affirmations come from the three P's: keep them *Positive*, *Personal*, and in

(*continued on next page*)

the *Present* tense. See the list below for ideas if you can't think of any affirmations.

2. After you have written your affirmation, pause and notice your *feelings* about it. Be totally honest. With your non-dominant hand (using the other colored pen), write the first reaction that comes to mind, whatever it is.

3. Continue writing the affirmation with your dominant hand. Each time you write out your affirmation, let the non-dominant hand write your reaction. The reactions will probably change. Allow them to be whatever they are. Be honest with yourself. (See examples below and on the next page.)

4. Continue this "call and response" dialogue, until you observe that your reaction has become neutral or positive. At that point you may choose to stop. Always end with the affirmation or positive statement. Doing so will help you re-program the "cleared space" in your unsconscious mind.

Affirmations List:

1. I love being pregnant.
2. My body looks beautiful, or I look great.
3. I am full of energy and confidence.
4. I feel organized and ready for this birth.
5. I love who I am.
6. My needs are important.
7. I can trust my inner wisdom.
8. I feel safe and protected.
9. I can say no and still be respected.
10. I can think and feel at the same time.
11. I feel good being pregnant.
12. I have time for this pregnancy in my life.

I AM CONFIDENT ABOUT LABOR

NO I'M NOT

I AM CONFIDENT ABOUT LABOR

I'M INSECURE ABOUT SHOWING MY SENSITIVITY.

I AM CONFIDENT ABOUT LABOR

EVERYTHING WILL BE JUST FINE.

I AM CONFIDENT ABOUT LABOR

Visual affirmations are one of the most powerful ways to make wishes and dreams come true. They create a tangible image of what you want. Seeing what you want leads you to your goal. The old adages "Seeing is believing" and "A picture is worth a thousand words" are true. Drawings, photo collages, paintings, or sculptures are excellent ways to create visual affirmations. Displaying the art where you can look at it repeatedly reinforces the images for your visual right brain.

Like verbal affirmations, you can use visual affirmations to clear a space and focus on your goal. If you have difficulty visualizing, creating art is a hands-on way to develop this skill. Visual imagery brings what you want into view.

Visual affirmations are "seed thoughts." You plant them in your imagination. You *cultivate* them by looking at the image frequently. Before a gardener plants flowers, she goes to the nursery and looks at the pictures on the seed packets. The pictures tell her what will grow if she plants and cultivates those seeds. Visual affirmations work the same way as pictures on seed packets. By picturing what you want, you select what will grow in the garden of your mind.

For more powerful affirmations, combine words and pictures. In this way you are using both sides of the brain—verbal and visual. It's easy, fun, and gets results.

I am confident about labor

No your not. You feel scared
I am confident about labor
I am scared of the unknown
I am confident about labor

Maybe with support & love
I can feel confident
I am confident about labor

I know with Greg's support
& encouragement I am confident
about labor
I am confident about labor

Awakening Feelings:
Parenting the
Inner Child

As George Bernard Shaw once said,

> Imagination is the beginning of creation:
> You imagine what you desire;
> you will what you imagine;
> and at last you create what you will.

Here's Loretta's experience. It is typical of the comments we get from people who do visual affirmations on a regular basis.

> Since I started doing visual-affirmation collages of my goals, I have realized all my desires. It's amazing! I had made New Year's resolutions for several years about settling down in the right house and getting pregnant. I still had no house and no baby. I was feeling really frustrated. About five years ago we were ready to begin house hunting. We made a collage of the home we wanted using magazine photos. We also did a drawing of the floor plan.
>
> Wow, what a miracle! We found the house we wanted right away (within days). Right after we moved in, I did a collage of pregnant women, mothers, and babies. Before long I was pregnant.
>
> One thing I learned was that I didn't have to *do* anything but listen to my desire and get clear about it. Putting it on paper helped me get clear. Then I just kept looking at my picture, which I had hanging on our bedroom wall. I saw it when I woke up and when I went to sleep and any other time I was there (reading in bed or getting dressed or talking on the phone). It was like a billboard advertising to me what I wanted. I figured, It works for the advertising industry, why not for me?

Here's an exercise that is especially effective for expectant mothers and fathers in creating a joyful pregnancy, labor, and birth.

Visual Affirmations: *Picture Perfect*

Materials: Large sheets of drawing paper (construction paper or poster board), drawing materials, glue, scissors, magazines with lots of photos of the topic you are focusing on

Purpose: To affirm what it is you want to experience in reality. To create a blue-print of your heart's desire and program it into your unconscious mind.

Technique:

1. Relax and think about something you want to realize in your pregnancy. Allow images to come into your mind. For example: a healthy mother, happy baby, contented family, financial security, and so on.

2. Find or draw an image or symbol of your Higher Power. For you this might be your Creative Self, Inner Self, Holy Spirit, the Birth Energy. Whatever you call your Higher Power, place this image in the center of your paper.

3. Go through your magazine(s) and cut out all the photos that express what it is you want to manifest. Don't glue anything down yet, just gather your materials. In choosing images, *follow your heart, follow your impulse.* Don't analyze whether the pictures you like are practical or possible. Just select the ones that attract your attention, that make you feel good. Also be on the lookout for captions, words, or phrases that make good affirmations for your specific theme. Cut them out and set them in a separate pile to be used later.

4. When you feel you have done enough research, go through all the photos you've chosen and select your favorites. Then place them around that central image of your Higher Power or Creative Self on your paper. Let this be a process of discovery. Using your intuition, feel your way as to which photo goes where.

5. Glue the photos down when you're satisifed with their placement. Remember, there are no right or wrong ways to do this kind of art, only *your* way.

6. Then write in affirmations or glue down phrases you found in the magazines (positive statements that apply to your desired goal).

7. Display your collage in a place where you can look at it frequently. Use it to visually reinforce your desired goal.
(See example on pages 98–99.)

Conclusion

Tuning in to your feelings and focusing on what you want is a way to practice claiming the territory of your pregnancy. It also is a powerful gesture of self-nurturing and an expression of self-love. You deserve to have a fulfilling childbirth experience—and your baby deserves to be welcomed into an atmosphere of tender, loving care.

Happy Family
Good Start be gentle
Get in on the Action
Our baby
protect your greatest creation.
FIRST-TIME DAD

Joy

LIFE AFTER BIRTH

Contented &
Secure

Involved

4

Nurturing Yourself,
Nurturing Your Baby

Caring for yourself during pregnancy is more than just physical. Of course eating right, exercising, getting enough rest, and receiving good prenatal care are essential for your health and the health of your baby. However, there are other things that are just as important. Self-care includes your emotional, mental, and spiritual as well as your physical health. Every choice you make and every aspect of your lifestyle affects you and your unborn child. What you do, how you relate to others, and the atmosphere at home and work influence your baby's health. You are important. Pregnancy is a time to take yourself seriously and to respond to your own needs. We say this not to place a burden on you but to support you in nurturing and protecting yourself.

You were born into the world with two innate qualities: You are *Totally Lovable* and *Capable (T.L.C.)*. During pregnancy you can reconnect with your *Totally Lovable* and *Capable* self with Tender, Loving Care (T.L.C.). Unfortunately this is not as easy as it may seem. An obstacle to self-care is society's attitude. It is considered selfish for parents to nurture themselves. The problem is that unnurtured parents find that they do not have enough to give. This leads to feelings of martyrdom and frustration, which in turn are negatively expressed to children in parental statements like "We're sacrificing so you can have all the things we didn't have." "After all we've done, how could you do this?" "If it weren't for you we could have _____ ."

Excessive sacrifice for others leads to exhaustion, anger, and resentment. This is not a healthy gift to give your unborn baby. So let's get rid of the "selfless parent" mystique. Parents are human beings just like everybody else. They have needs too. As a parent, if you aren't feeling nurtured yourself, then you cannot nurture your baby.

The Nurturing Parent Within

As mentioned in Chapter Three, you nurture and protect your Inner Child and your unborn baby by responding to your own needs. The part of you that can listen and respond to your Inner Child's feelings, needs, and desires is called the Nurturing Parent Within. The process of finding the Nurturing Parent Within is called re-parenting yourself.

It's never too late to re-parent yourself. How do you do it? By nurturing *yourself* physically, emotionally, mentally, spiritually. During pregnancy self-parenting is good for you, and it's good for your unborn child. You will find that you will be able to nurture and protect your baby in ways that feel right, creative, and comfortable for you. Self-parenting also helps you be a better parent to the children you already have.

We recommend the books of Jean Illsley-Clarke for guidance on self-parenting: *Growing Up Again* and *Self-Esteem: A Family Affair.* Also Chapters Four and Five of Lucia's book *Recovery of Your Inner Child* contain exercises for developing a strong Inner Parent (see Bibliography).

The following exercise helps you develop an awareness of the Nurturing Parent Within and the ability to respond to your Inner Child's needs:

More Inner Child Chats: *What Do You Need?*

Materials: Journal and felt-tip pens
Purpose: To find out what your Inner Child needs in order to feel loved and cared for
Technique:

1. Using two different colored pens, do a written dialogue with your Inner Child asking what it needs right now. The Nurturing Parent asks the questions with your dominant hand and the Inner Child responds with your

(continued on next page)

non-dominant hand. Ask your Inner Child what it needs in order to feel loved and cared for.

2. Draw a picture of your Inner Child being cared for by your Nurturing Parent Within.

3. With your dominant hand write a letter from your Inner Nurturing Parent to your Inner Child. Think of it as a love letter in which you tell your Inner Child how you feel about her. If you haven't been taking care of your Inner Child, perhaps some apologies are in order. Tell the Child how you will take care of her.

Optional: Have your partner read your love letter to you. You can also tape-record your letter and play it back to yourself.

What do you need me to do to take care of you?

Have more fun!!

go walking in the moonlight

buy a new swimsuit so you'll go swimming

let me take a nap every day

Go dancing

Meditate more

Make me a <u>pretty</u> new dress

My dear Annie,

    I love you very much. I love how you remind me to have more fun in my life. So often I forget that. Thank you!

    I love your list of ways I can do things for you. I'm learning to really value the fun and joy I feel when I listen to my feelings. (you) I feel all giggly and excited when I think about the fun you represent in me. I'm glad you'll be around to help me with the baby.

The next journal activity helps you to discover ways to nurture yourself. It focuses on identifying particular things you already enjoy.

Dr. Teri A. Merry, a counselor and wellness consultant in Spokane, Washington, created a wonderful list of self-nurturing activities which she shared with us. We hope it inspires you to make your own list and to think of some new ways you can be good to yourself.

107 WAYS TO TAKE CARE OF YOURSELF

Give yourself a compliment.
Look at the stars.
Open up to the person closest to you.
Resolve a conflict.
Feed the ducks.
Listen to nature's sounds.
Sign up for a class.
Do something you've always wanted to do.
Contact someone you've been thinking about.
Turn off the TV.
Play a musical instrument.
Take a risk.
Simplify, simplify.
Keep a list and check off things done.
Live in the moment.
Daydream.
Doodle.
Take a trip.
Relax for fifteen minutes.
Watch aquarium fish.
Read a funny book.
Donate to a worthy cause.
Make time for solitude every day.
Watch the clouds.
Take a brisk walk.
Play like a child.
Walk to the nearest park.
Hug a child.

Throw away something you don't like.
Draw a picture, even if you can't draw.
Warm a heart.
Laugh at yourself.
Schedule time with yourself.
Value your feelings.
Talk out a problem.
Waste time without feeling guilty.
Go to bed early.
Light a candle and read by candlelight.
Follow an impulse.
Write a poem.
Volunteer some time to a good cause.
Give yourself a present.
Let someone do you a favor.
Allow yourself to make a mistake.
Watch the sunset.
Smell a flower.
Hide a love note where a loved one will find it.
Listen to music.
Dance around the living room.
Take a bubble bath.
Plant a garden.
Find something good in everyone you meet.

Face a fear.
Go for a swim.
Hold hands with someone.
Tell someone you love them.
Have breakfast in bed.
Float on an air mattress.
Call a friend.
Sing.
Follow your intuition.
Make something.
Watch the rain.
Sit in the woods.
Have a good cry.
Take ten deep breaths.
Meditate.
Begin daily stretching exercises.
Take an art class.
Don't hurry today.
Recycle your newspapers and cans.
Take a drive to the mountains.
Go to a museum.
Say no.
Finish a project.
Plant a tree.
Have someone rub your back.
Be flexible.
Read a novel.
Sit in a hot tub.

104

Take a nap.

Walk in the grass with your shoes off.

Sleep under the stars.

Call a counselor to help with difficult problems.

Make a list of your good qualities.

Hug a dog.

Talk to a cat.

Do one thing at a time.

Keep a journal.

Reward yourself for reaching a goal.

Go skinny-dipping.

Swing in a swing.

Laugh.

Go backpacking.

Receive a compliment without apology.

Throw a Frisbee.

Walk in the snow.

Go to the ocean.

Get up early and listen to the quiet.

Listen to children laugh.

Watch a funny movie.

Watch the sunrise.

Eat by candlelight.

Sit by the fire.

Love yourself.

Self-Nurturing Lists: *Taking Care of Me*

Materials: Journal and felt-tip pens
Purpose: To discover the people, places, things, and activities that nurture you
Technique:

1. Use two pages (side by side). On one page create four columns with headings as follows:

Nurturing People Nurturing Activities Nurturing Places Nurturing Things

2. With your non-dominant hand let your Inner Child fill in the columns (see example on page 106).
3. On your other pages (side by side), create two headings (one per page) as follows:

I need tender loving care when ___   **When ___ happens, I can**

4. (State the situations or times.)   (State what you'll do for yourself when you need T.L.C.)

Example:

I need T.L.C. when I feel frightened taking the oxytocin challenge test.

When I'm taking the test, I'll ask Tom to come with me, and I will ask the nurse to explain it more clearly so that I understand what's going on.

5. Complete the left-hand column with your non-dominant hand. In the right-hand column respond to each item on the left, using words created from your list of nurturing people, activities, places, and things. Do this with your dominant hand.

NUTURING PEOLE	NORTURING ACTIVITIES	NURTURING PLACES	NURTURING THINGS
Frank	reading sleeping	The mountains	foods I like
Lynn	eating & cooking	my bed	A good book
Steve		my dreams	my bed-the safe smell
Carolyn	getting a massage or footrub		my dog
Mom			my teddy Bear
Dad	A long walk		

I need Tender Loving Care When:	When......happens, I can.......
I need TLC when I'm tired	When I feel tired, I can go to bed & read get a massage from Carolyn get a footrub from Mom
I need TLC when I'm hungry	When I get hungry, I can fix a favorite food ask Mom to feed me have a snack in bed eat something I like
I need TLC when I feel lonely	When I feel lonely, I can hug my teddy bear walk my dog in the mountains talk to Lynn

Easy Does It: Rest and Relaxation

During pregnancy it is very important for you and your baby to get enough rest. If you get overtired, both of you will be under stress. Listen to your body. The amount of rest you need each day might be different. Stress, weather, diet, activity level, and hormonal changes affect your energy level. The important thing is to avoid becoming overtired. Taking little catnaps when you feel fatigued is extremely helpful.

A Place for Us

To help you get rest, finding your own comfortable place is important. It is a place to "stop the world" and get off for a while. It's not necessarily a place to sleep. In fact, it doesn't matter what you do when you're there. You don't have to DO anything except BE with yourself and your baby. Here's one woman's story of how she found a nurturing place that turned out to be very special for her during pregnancy and afterward.

> When I became pregnant with my first child, my mother (delighted with the prospect of becoming a grandmother) immediately took me shopping for what she considered a necessity: a rocking chair. Of course her thought was that I would rock the *baby* in the rocking chair. It sounded like a good idea. So off we went in my little VW bug to the part of town where there was an abundance of antique- and used-furniture stores. A wonderfully comfortable old oak rocker was waiting for us in the sidewalk display in front of one of these stores. It looked like it had held many moms, grandmothers, and kids. Somehow we miraculously stuffed it into the backseat of our tiny car and drove off happily.
>
> As soon as I had it in our apartment, it became clear that the rocking chair was really for *me*. Whenever I felt tired, stressed, or upset about anything, rocking quietly in that chair did me a world of good. The even rhythm of the movement, the sensation of being supported by its sturdy seat, arms, and high back were extremely soothing. The smooth, well-worn oak arms helped me through many ups and downs. During the years that my children were little, I used that rocker to comfort them as well as myself.

If you don't already have a peaceful place, think about finding one. It may be out in nature or in a special room or building. Perhaps your place is a park, a balcony with a pleasant view, or a garden. Maybe you feel most relaxed in a certain chair. Your special place may be in your imagination or your memory. You can go to that place by using the imagery described in Chapter One. Myrene found a special place in her memory.

> While riding home from work on the bus each day, I found that I could relax if I closed my eyes and returned to a beautiful spot along the ocean that we had visited a few years before. All the hustle and bustle of the city seemed to drop away. I was transported to that peaceful cove with smooth white sand and aquamarine water. You could see right down to the bottom, the water was so clear. I remember the sound of the surf and the warmth of the sand under my feet. Often, when it was time to get off the bus, I felt like I'd taken a nap.

The Power of Silence

There is power in silence. It enables you to leave the world behind and go inside yourself. Mastering this skill empowers you to shut out distractions during labor and focus on the birth.

When we learn to quiet the mind, the body automatically responds by relaxing. Imagery is one way to achieve that goal. Do the following imagery exercise once a day or more often until it becomes a habit. By learning the technique of the power of silence, you will condition yourself to relax automatically during labor.

Imagery: *Your Special Place*

Purpose: To develop imagery and relaxation skills
This exercise has many sections. Don't do all the sections in one sitting. Break them up into several sessions. They should be done in sequence. Move to the next section of the activity only when you feel ready. It may take days or weeks. Don't rush it! Over time this activity prepares you for labor.

Limit this activity to fifteen minutes. Find a comfortable place where you can be alone. Be sure that you will be free from interruptions and distractions. Soft music is optional. You can tape-record the following narration and play it back to yourself. If you record it, pause several seconds in the narration where you see dotted lines. Co-Creations offers a tape of this narrative (see the Resource Guide at the end of this book).

This activity is a journey through your imagination. The place where you are sitting is the starting point. It represents the left brain. You will open a door and cross through a hallway. It symbolizes the bridge of nerve fibers (corpus callosum) that connects the two hemispheres of the brain. On the other side of the hallway another door leads to your special place (right brain).

Technique:

Section A

1. Close your eyes and focus on your breathing . . . *(pause)* Don't change your breathing, just notice how it flows in and out of your body. . . .
2. Imagine a room, any room . . . The room has a door. Imagine what the door looks like. Is it tall? Narrow? Ornate? Plain? . . .

   In your mind picture yourself going toward the door and opening it. Prop the door open with something. . . .

   Beyond the door is a long hallway. Stand and look at the hallway. What does it look like? Is it cluttered? Narrow? Broad and spacious? Is there light or dark? . . .

   Cross the hallway. Notice how you are doing this. Are you crawling? Walking? Running? Floating? . . .

   Coming up in front of you is another closed door. Notice what it looks like. . . .
   Approach the door, open it, and prop it open with something. . . .

   On the other side of this door is your own special place. Take the rest of the allotted fifteen minutes to imagine what it looks like. Perhaps it is in the mountains, on the beach, or in a warm valley. Perhaps it is a special room, temple, or sanctuary. Wherever it is, it is your own special and *beautiful* place.

At first, you may feel awkward doing this exercise. Repeat the process in a safe place until you feel comfortable crossing the "hallway in your mind." Then practice doing it in other locations, such as the kitchen, the doctor's office, or the supermarket line.

Do journaling after each phase of this exercise. Express any feelings that may arise.

When you feel ready, do Section B of this exercise.

Imagery: *Your Special Place (continued)*

Section B

1. Ask your main support person to do this exercise with you. Describe your imagery; what your special place looks and feels like. Do this visualization together several times.
2. Are you comfortable allowing him or her into your special place? If not, what do you need from him or her to feel safe? Can you maintain your sense of self with this person in your special place? Notice your feelings and journal about them later.

This exercise is good preparation for labor and birth. Visiting your special place during labor is relaxing. If your support person has done this exercise with you, he or she can guide you back to your special place when necessary. Veronica and Sam discovered this during labor.

Veronica's special place was a quiet cove with ocean waves gently lapping the shore. There were huge boulders standing nearby in the water. Porpoises played, and seagulls glided overhead. It was a safe, serene environment, where Veronica readily went during early labor. However, during the intensity of the final contractions Veronica found it increasingly difficult to go into that cove. Sam felt somewhat help-less as he saw Veronica becoming more and more tense.

Veronica had shared her special place with Sam during guided-imagery sessions. During this difficult phase of labor he asked what was happening in the cove. She told him there was a huge storm. The waves were crashing on the beach, and there was no safe place in her cove anymore. Sam knew about the boulders and the porpoises. He guided her through the next contraction by having her imagine the porpoises coming and lifting her up onto the rocks. The waves continued to crash around her, but now they couldn't harm her.

As a result of doing "Your Special Place" imagery, Sam helped Veronica regain her composure. Sam's contribution calmed Veronica and helped them to share another aspect of the birth experience.

Pregnancy, Stress, and Time

In our highly industrialized society we are very conscious of time. We say, "I have no time." "Time is running out." "If I only had more hours in the day." We seem obsessed with filling time, killing time, and finding more time. We increase stress by allowing time to run our lives.

During pregnancy time is a major theme. When we speak of pregnancy, we often use terms that refer to time: "I'm expecting." "When are you due?" Your worries about time increase as you approach your due date. As one woman said recently, "The last month is the longest."

How you experience time in general will influence how you interpret time in pregnancy. How do you feel about time? Do you typically run around trying to be on time or meet deadlines? Are you anxious and apprehensive, or do you relax and surrender to nature's rhythms? Do you say things like "This baby better be on time!" If so, you may be creating unnecessary stress for yourself and your baby.

Breathing Easily: Simplify Your Life

A good way to cut back on stress is to simplify your life by dropping the things that aren't absolutely necessary. First prioritize activities, responsibilities, and projects, then eliminate all but the essentials. You can always schedule things back in. Making the effort to simplify your life is a great way to rethink your values and reshape your priorities. It is a wonderful way to prepare for parenting because having children really challenges your beliefs about what is important to you and what you have time for.

Setting Priorities: *A Slice of Life*

Materials: Art paper (two sheets), felt-tip pens, and markers
Purpose: To simplify your life and reflect upon how you relate to time
Technique:

1. On each sheet of art paper draw a large circle. Title the pages *Current* and *Revised.*
2. On the page entitled *Current* divide the circle into pie-shaped pieces. Each piece represents an activity or interest that you devote time to in a typical week. The size of each piece will be determined by *the percentage of time* you devote to that aspect of your life. Include eating, preparing for and cleaning up from meals, work, personal grooming, hobbies, social time, exercise, and so on. Don't forget to include sleep. Label or illustrate each segment of your pie so that it is clear which aspect of your life it represents.
3. Look over your *Current* pie. Now that you are pregnant, are you happy with the amount of time you spend on each of these activities or aspects of your life? Is there anything you would change, expand upon, reduce, or drop altogether?
4. On the circle entitled *Revised* create a new pie. Put greater emphasis on the things that are more important to you now that you are pregnant.
5. Using your non-dominant hand, label or illustrate each piece so that it is clear what that section of your pie stands for. Acknowledge your feelings.
6. Put the *Revised* pie where you can see it. Use it as a reminder concerning your feelings about the changes you have made or need to make.
(See examples on page 113.)

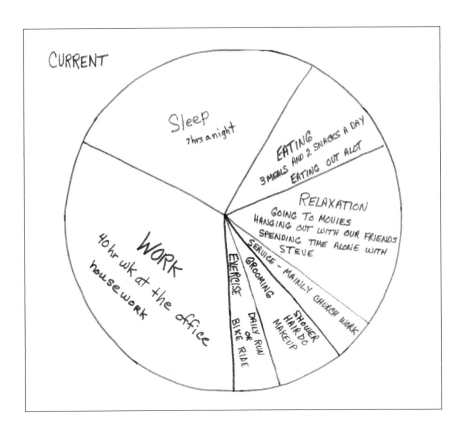

CURRENT

Sleep
7 hrs a night

EATING
3 MEALS AND 2 SNACKS A DAY
EATING OUT ALOT

RELAXATION
GOING TO MOVIES
HANGING OUT WITH OUR FRIENDS
SPENDING TIME ALONE WITH
STEVE

SERVICE - MAINLY CHURCH WORK

GROOMING
SHOWER
HAIRDO
MAKEUP

EXERCISE
DAILY RUN
or
BIKE RIDE

WORK
40 hr wk at the office
housework

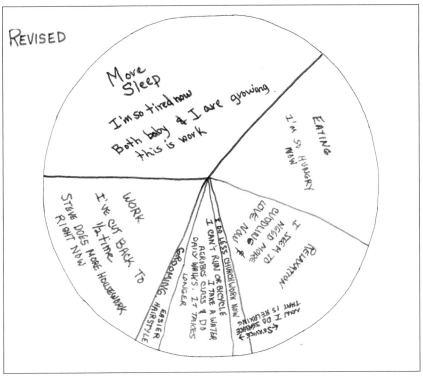

REVISED

More
Sleep
I'm so tired now
Both baby & I are growing
this is work

EATING
I'M SO HUNGRY NOW

RELAXATION
I SEEM TO
NEED MORE
CUDDLING &
LOVE NOW

I DO LESS CHURCHWORK NOW
I CAN'T RUN OR BICYCLE
I TAKE A WATER
AEROBICS CLASS & DO
DAILY WALKS. IT TAKES
LONGER

←SERVICE→
NOW I DO SERVICE
THAT IS RELAXING

GROOMING
EASIER HAIRSTYLE

WORK
I'VE CUT BACK TO
½ time
STEVE DOES MORE HOUSEWORK
RIGHT NOW

Nurturing Yourself,
Nurturing Your Baby
113

Exercise: Fitness in Pregnancy

Fitness is a multibillion-dollar business. We are bombarded with an endless stream of books, videotapes, TV shows, fitness centers, exercise equipment, and fashion. Exercise gurus abound, each one claiming to have the best way to get fit and stay fit. With this unavoidable focus on fitness a new generation of addicts has surfaced. Therapists refer to them as exercise junkies. They are addicted to the adrenaline rush of rigorous cardiovascular workouts. Like the diet industry, exercise seems to have gotten out of hand.

There are many similarities between the way we diet and the way we exercise. Often the motivations are the same: external appearance and image building. During pregnancy this attitude is totally inappropriate. We have spoken at great length about being in your body, listening to it, caring for it. This should also be applied to exercise. *Listen to your body.*

The basic rule of thumb is: If you have not been exercising regularly before becoming pregnant, now is *not* the time suddenly to embark on a regimen of strenuous routines. It is important to exercise in pregnancy, but *easy does it!* Check with your prenatal health care professional for guidance. Research shows that exercise is good for you, but it doesn't show that a lot of exercise is better than moderate exercise. In fact during pregnancy too much exercise can do more harm than good.

When you become pregnant, your body goes through many hormonal changes. One of the hormones that increases in your body is relaxin. Its purpose is to cause your ligaments, cartilage, and muscles to relax, stretch, and move more easily. Relaxin facilitates the opening of your pelvis so that your baby can grow and ultimately move down through the birth canal.

Because your pregnant body is in a much more relaxed state, this influences the type of exercise you should choose. We recommend walking, swimming, yoga, gentle stretching, tai chi chuan, expressive movement, dance therapy, and gardening. Some excellent books on exercise during pregnancy are the following:

Positive Pregnancy Fitness, by Sylvia Klein Olkin

Guide to Moving Through Pregnancy, by Elisabeth Bing

Essential Exercises for the Childbearing Years, by Elizabeth Noble

Doing strenuous or high-impact exercise can put strain on your body and cause permanent damage. Avoid high-impact aerobics, jogging, running, tennis, competitive sports, horseback riding, motorcycling, and bicycling.

During your pregnancy regular exercise is beneficial. The most important thing is to slow down and listen to your body. If in doubt, dialogue with your body and/or your baby to see if the type of exercise you are doing is healthy for both of you.

Find a form of exercise that is *enjoyable*. If you don't enjoy it, it could be harmful. *Forcing* yourself because it's "good for you" goes against everything we have said about nurturing yourself. Exercise should not cause stress or strain. Find a form of exercise that:

- You love to do

- Increases your feelings of well-being

- Exercises the specific muscles you use during pregnancy, labor, and birth

You don't have to develop a routine or join a gym. You can exercise naturally by integrating more movement into your everyday life. Chisato found that by making slight changes in how she did her normal activities she could get plenty of exercise. She walked more by intentionally parking a distance from the stores that she frequented. Inside the supermarket she chose a "less efficient," longer route to get her groceries, which provided her with a nice walk. At home she did gentle stretching exercises while watching TV or talking on the phone. She took long walks with her toddler in the stroller and played with him at the playground. She incorporated specific movements into her household chores (such as squatting to pick things up).

Nutrition

The doctor of the future will give no medicine, but will interest [teach] his patients in the care of the human frame, diet, and in the cause and prevention of disease.

THOMAS EDISON

Nutrition is usually approached from a physical point of view. Diet plans are often based on so-called objective facts. So why do diet and nutrition programs have such a high rate of failure? Because food, eating, and nourishment are charged with *emotion.* Objective facts are not enough. Counselors in the field of eating disorders know this. Anyone who has ever struggled with an eating disorder knows this too.

Nutritional programs for pregnancy are often planned by experts who focus on what you can and cannot eat. These programs often leave expectant mothers with a feeling of emotional deprivation. When you are pregnant, you need to look at nutrition from an *emotional* as well as a physical point of view. Plan a custom-made program based on *your* lifestyle, *your* body, and *your* needs. Ask your health care professional to be your personal trainer or coach who supports you in creating a custom-made nutrition plan.

It is important to be aware that as your baby grows, your nutritional needs change. During pregnancy your body uses a lot more energy, *even when resting.* At times you may find yourself feeling exhausted and weary. Intellectually you may think that food equals energy, so you may reason that you should eat more. Oftentimes when people run low on energy, they eat. They commonly try to fill their need for rest with food. Getting enough rest helps you avoid overeating.

"Eating for two" does not mean only the quantity of food, but also the quality. If you listen to your own body (as you did in Chapter Two), it will be easier to make healthy choices when eating and drinking. You won't be as likely to mistake "hunger pangs" for other needs, such as rest, exercise, and affection. Your body has a wisdom of its own. Listen to it!

Weight Gain in Pregnancy

As you observe your body expanding during pregnancy, you may be worried that you will gain too much weight. The following chart shows you *average* distribution of weight gain in full-term pregnancy.

WEIGHT DISTRIBUTION IN FULL-TERM PREGNANCY

Baby	7–8 Lb
Placenta	1–2 Lb
Uterus	2 Lb
Amniotic fluid	1½–2 Lb
Breasts	1–2 Lb
Blood volume	1½–3 Lb
Fat (minimum gained)	5 Lb
Tissue, fluid	4–7 Lb
Total	23–30 Lb

Instead of worrying about gaining weight, think of your pregnancy as an opportunity to develop healthy eating habits. What you learn can be useful for the rest of your life. Nurturing yourself emotionally and enjoying your food is the key to controlling unnecessary weight gain.

Cravings: Eating Awareness

Pregnant women often have cravings for certain foods. Emotional factors and physical changes can cause desires for particular foods. To help explain why certain cravings happen, it is helpful to understand the sense of taste and how it works.

Your sense of taste is stimulated when you eat a variety of foods that use all of the taste buds. There are six predominant tastes: sweet, sour, salty, bitter, pungent, and astringent. Some examples are as follows:

Sweet	Bread (wheat), carbohydrates (rice, pasta), milk, cream, yogurt, kefir, butter, poultry, fish, meat, honey, molasses, maple syrup, corn syrup, brown and white sugars, jam, jelly, fruit, nuts
Sour	Lemons, yogurt, cheese, cottage cheese, buttermilk, kefir, some fruits
Salty	Sea salt, soy sauce, miso, seaweed
Bitter	Green leafy vegetables, spinach, broccoli
Pungent	Most spices, mustard, horseradish, red peppers, black pepper, jalapeño
Astringent	Beans, lentils, seeds, nuts

If you don't experience all of the six tastes in your diet, your body becomes unbalanced. This results in a tendency to overeat the wrong foods in an attempt to compensate for the tastes that you are missing. The more you include the variety of six tastes in your diet, the less chance there is that you will overeat.

In American society many of us focus mainly on only three of the six taste sensations: sweet, sour, and salty. Fast food is a classic example. A burger, fries with catsup, and a soda are standard fare for many. As a result of this eating routine the body becomes nutritionally deprived. You feel unsatisfied and may eat more instead of eating better. You lose your ability to listen to internal cues and instead you may respond to external messages (such as advertising, time constraints, and peer-group pressure).

If you treat yourself to the six tastes—sweet, sour, salty, bitter, pungent, and astringent—you will get rid of many of your cravings during pregnancy and eat the amount of food your body really needs.

Food Awareness: Eats and Treats

Materials: Journal and felt-tip pens
Purpose: To monitor your eating patterns and determine your nutritional needs
Technique:

1. Divide a piece of paper in half. Above the left-hand column write *Eats and Treats*. Above the right-hand column write *Tastes*.
2. With your dominant hand, in the column *Eats and Treats* write everything you've eaten in the last twenty-four hours. Include any snacks or treats. Become still and remember the taste of the foods you ate.
3. Using your non-dominant hand, in the *Tastes* column write which taste you experienced with each item in the left-hand column.
4. Repeat this exercise monthly throughout pregnancy to assess how your sense of taste is developing. Are you including all six tastes?

Paying Attention to Eating

Many of us stuff food into our mouths while we are doing other things, without paying attention to what we are eating. For instance, we watch a television show, read the paper, drive somewhere, or talk superficially while eating. No wonder we often feel unsatisfied by what we eat. We weren't really there while we ate it. The food is gone before we even know we consumed it.

To counteract this habit, make it a rule *always* to sit down whenever you eat anything, no matter how much or how little it is. Avoid eating when you're walking around, talking on the phone, watching TV, working at a computer, or reading. Focus on tasting and enjoying your food in a leisurely manner. Doing this will help you create awareness of what you are eating. You will have a better chance of controlling what goes into your mouth if you are really tasting it. Focus on your food and get the maximum amount of *pleasure* from it. If you enjoy what you are eating, you will tend to eat less.

Snacking can help to avoid the nausea caused by an empty stomach in early pregnancy. Eating *small*, frequent meals can help prevent the heartburn and indigestion sometimes experienced in the later stages of pregnancy. However, snacking all day long is not a good idea and can definitely put on the pounds.

Helpful Hints

1. *Eat only when you are hungry.* If your stomach is full and you crave food, stop and ask, *What else would satisfy me right now?* Try drinking a large glass of water instead of eating. (Pregnant women's bodies require a great deal of water, at least eight glasses a day.)

2. *Know specifically what you are eating and how it is prepared.*

3. *Sit down when you eat and focus on your meal.* Create a pleasant environment for eating and drinking.

4. *Take small bites, eat slowly, chew thoroughly, and taste each mouthful.* This helps you avoid overeating. The slower you eat, the better your body is able to send you signals about when it has had enough. Avoid putting more food into your mouth before you have swallowed the previous bite.

5. *Pay attention to the taste of the food.* Eat what tastes good to you. Try to guess which of the six tastes you are experiencing. Discuss the tastes with the person with whom you are eating.

6. *Stop eating when you feel full.*

Nutritional Needs

How you eat and *how much* you eat are important, but *what* you eat is just as important. Many pregnant women are worried about getting the proper nutrients for themselves and the baby. There are many good books about prenatal nutrition. We recommend the following:

The Very Important Pregnancy Program, by Gail Brewer

What Every Pregnant Woman Should Know: The Truth About Diets and Drugs in Pregnancy, by Gail Brewer

Laurel's Kitchen, by Laurel Robertson, Carol Flinders, and Bronwen Godfrey

Macrobiotic Pregnancy and Care of the Newborn, by Michio Kushi and Aveline Kushi

What you eat can make you and your baby healthy and strong. Fifty to sixty percent of your total intake of food should be in the categories of fruits, fresh vegetables, and greens. These foods contain some very important nutrients.

Water

Water is the most important nutrient in your diet. Sixty to seventy percent of your body is made up of water. All nutrients and electrical impulses are carried by water molecules. Both your own body and your unborn baby's body need a great deal of water. Therefore drinking at least six to eight large glasses of water per day is absolutely crucial during pregnancy. With water pollution on the rise, pay attention to the quality of water you drink. Consider alternatives to tap water (which may be contaminated), such as bottled water and filtering systems.

Eating water-rich foods is beneficial. Foods highest in water content are:

- Leafy greens (such as iceberg lettuce)
- Vegetables (such as broccoli, carrots, beets, and potatoes)
- Fruits (such as melons, apples, and oranges)

Calcium, iron, and protein needs increase dramatically during pregnancy. It is wise to pay particular attention to these three areas of nutrition. Following is a brief discussion of each area, but please read more extensively about them in the other books that are listed in the Bibliography.

Calcium

Though most people think of milk and cheese as their primary source of calcium, it is better to fulfill your increased need from other sources.

(The calcium in milk and cheese is not easily absorbed and is high in fat.) Good sources of calcium are green vegetables, such as cabbage, kale, and broccoli; nuts, seeds (especially sunflower seeds), dried fruits, whole grains, and seaweed.

Iron

Your body has an increased need for iron because your blood volume increases as your baby grows. Iron helps your blood become rich and able to fulfill the added need for nutrients and oxygen. Iron is most easily assimilated through foods that are abundant in this mineral. Some good sources of iron-rich foods are: seaweeds (especially kelp and dulse); leafy dark green vegetables (spinach, mustard greens, chard); whole grains; dried fruits (especially prunes, raisins, and apples); nuts and seeds; blackstrap molasses (you can put one tablespoon on top of your cereal, your ice cream, or mixed into drinks and breads).

Protein

Protein is probably one of the most important nutrients during pregnancy. We highly recommend that you read up on protein needs during pregnancy and how best to add protein to your diet. Combining your foods in meals so that the essential proteins are obtained is a useful eating habit to form, for instance combining rice with legumes, or wheat with beans. Some good sources of protein are meat, fish, poultry, eggs, dried beans and peas, milk and cheese, nuts, peanut butter (and other nut butters), whole grains, natural whole-grain cereals, seeds, and soy products (miso, tamari, tempeh, tofu, soy flour, soy milk, etc.).

Carbohydrates

Eating foods that have a high carbohydrate content gives your body plenty of energy. Complex carbohydrates contain large carbohydrate molecules, which are broken down into simple sugars. Each of these simple sugars possesses chemical energy for the body. High-carbohydrate foods are:

- Vegetables
- Legumes (all beans)
- Whole grains (breads, pastas, and rice)
- Fruits

Fats

If you eat fat, you'll get fat. Avoid the following fatty foods:

- Saturated oils and chemically modified oils (such as margarine)
- Excessive amounts of dairy products (with the exception of skim milk and non-fat dairy products)
- Processed meats (salami, ham, hot dogs, bologna)
- Meat and poultry with high fat content
- Fried foods

Unhealthy Foods

The following foods are unhealthy because they are carcinogenic (cancer causing) or have a negative effect on the cell development of the fetus:

- Charcoal-cooked or burned foods
- High-sugar foods (such as candy, cake, ice cream)
- Processed foods and most chemical additives (such as artificial colors and flavors)
- Irradiated foods
- Alcohol
- Caffeine (chocolate, coffee, tea, cola)

If you have special dietary needs, such as in the case of diabetes, you may need to consult a specialist or nutritionist in addition to discussing diet with your health care practitioner.

Toxins

Toxins can be produced in the body as a result of both physical and emotional stress. It would be ideal not to produce any toxins. However, that would require living in an environment free of pollution, food additives, preservatives, and pesticides. Most of us do not have such environments, so we need to help our bodies deal with toxins.

Research shows that "free-radical scavengers" remove toxins from the body. These are natural compounds, such as vitamins C, E, and A, and riboflavin. *The most effective way to get these vitamins is by eating foods that contain them naturally.* (Many pregnant women use prenatal vitamins as a substitute for good eating habits.) Foods that are extremely rich in these free-radical scavengers are:

- Citrus fruits
- Broccoli and spinach
- Green leafy vegetables (collard greens and kale)
- Fruits

There are also many herbs or herbal tinctures that are very rich in "free radicals." Herbal compounds are like medicines. Consult a health care professional before taking them.

Nutrition and Your Baby

Many women wonder if the baby is getting the right nutrition. If you are concerned about your eating habits being in conflict with the baby's needs, check with your health professional. Also you can dialogue with the baby using the following exercise.

Baby Talk: *"Mom, Just Say No"*

Materials: Journal and felt-tip pens
Purpose: To communicate with your unborn baby and find out his or her likes and dislikes
Technique:

1. Draw a line down the center of your journal page. Using your dominant hand, on the left side of your page write a list of things you like to eat and drink (e.g., alcohol, coffee, diet cola, chocolate bar)

(continued on next page)

2. Sit quietly for a moment and focus on your baby. You may want to imagine your special place from the previous imagery exercise. When you feel calm and focused on your baby, put the pen in your non-dominant hand. Write a response from the baby concerning each one of the items on your list. Don't stop to censor or think about your responses. Write whatever comes to mind

3. After you have finished the list, contemplate your baby's responses.

If you have an eating habit that you want to overcome, we encourage you to continue with the next part of this exercise. The next part is a dialogue with the food, drink, or substance.

4. Stop and think about the things your baby said no to. Think about your cravings, the things you like to do daily or once in a while. Now take two colored pens and put one in each hand. Your dominant hand will speak for you. Your non-dominant hand will answer for the food, drink, or habit. Spend the next few moments dialoguing. Ask the following questions:

• What sensations are you satisfying in me? Describe the specific qualities each substance has (such as sweet, crunchy, smooth, or soothing)

• What need am I trying to satisfy with you?

• What can I do to truly fulfill that need instead of using you as a substitute?

• What can I do to help change or alter this habit? (Be specific.)

5. Following this dialogue, consider your responses. With your dominant hand, write down one thing you learned that you can do right now. (For example, eat more nutritious food or develop a behavior that would satisfy some of these needs.)

6. Do something specific about the information you received. Some examples are:

• Posting this information in a prominent place where you can see it and act upon it

• Telling your mate or close friend so that they can help you with your goal

• Stocking a healthier alternative in your cupboards and getting rid of the old unhealthy items

• Forming a new cooking or eating habit

Becoming clear about why you are saying no to some of these things will give you *internal* power over your *external* desires. It is important that you take immediate action on this information. Doing that will strengthen your resolve.

Your baby will help you with your nutritional needs throughout pregnancy. Dialogue with him or her, often asking if there are any specific needs you are not meeting. Food will give you the internal fuel to keep you going through pregnancy. You also need nourishment from others.

Nurturing Relationships

One way that we nurture ourselves is through relationships with other people. Learning to create mutually supportive and nurturing relationships feeds the soul. This is especially true in pregnancy.

In this era of fast food and instant gratification, we often forget that relationships take time, attention, and consistency. (That is, if they are satisfying.) It takes time, shared experience, and common ground for trust and respect to grow. This is especially true of intimate relationships, as in a marriage or deep friendship. That's what makes relationships with loved ones such a treasured gift.

Before you became pregnant, you had a *support system* or network that helped you through your day. Your support system may consist of family, friends, members of the community, or your religious group, and so on. In pregnancy, however, the idea of a support system takes on new meaning. The system will be a carefully selected group of people who will be your birth team. They will become the "welcoming committee" when your baby is born. Natalie's story is a good example of how to structure a support team:

> My support team throughout pregnancy consisted of my husband; my best girlfriend, Deirdre; my parents; and my sister. Of course the OB/GYN was part of the team, as was my chiropractor/nutritionist, whom I'd been seeing since before I got pregnant.
>
> A month before the baby was due, Deirdre and I toured the labor-and-delivery wing of the hospital. We reviewed the various options and asked about regulations regarding who could be present at the birth. We chose an alternative-birth room because we could have our support team there as long as each person had an active role.

At the time I went into labor, my core support team took me to the hospital as planned. My sister and my mother joined us a little later. I had specific tasks for each of them. Deirdre guided me in breathing and also acted as my focal point. My husband provided emotional support and physical strength if I needed to be moved, propped up, and so on. My sister was the "gofer" who got me anything I needed, such as water, ice, a chair, and so on. My mother was the official photographer of the entire event, including the birth. My chiropractor came in and did adjustments while I was in labor.

Having all that support made me feel very safe. My support team all knew what I wanted in terms of medication, surgery, and so on. If there were any emergencies, I didn't have to worry about anyone doing anything to me or the baby that I didn't want them to do. I had a lot of confidence in my OB/GYN because I had already talked to him about what I wanted. The birth of our baby was definitely a team effort. Yes, it was painful and it was scary, but it would have been much more so if I had not had my support team there backing me up.

The following exercise will provide useful tools to begin structuring your support team:

Getting Help: *Picturing My Personal Support Team*

Materials: Journal and felt-tip pens
Optional: large paper and art supplies
Purpose: To assess your resources and form your birth-support team
Technique:

1. Ask yourself, *Who are the people I turn to for understanding, support, or assistance?* These people are your personal support system. Picture them in your imagination, and experience your feelings toward each one of them.
2. Using your non-dominant hand, create a picture of you and your support system *in relation to your pregnancy and the approaching birth.* Make a picture or symbol of yourself in the center of the page. Surround the picture of yourself with images or symbols for each person in your support team. Label each person.
3. With your dominant hand, on a separate page write down ways in which you would like each person to support you.
4. Each week do something specific to strengthen and coordinate your support system.

Conclusion

As your pregnancy progresses and your baby's due date draws closer, you will find that your support team becomes an increasingly important part of your birth preparation. Not only will you feel more nurtured by having a strong support system in place but you will also be giving your baby a beautiful gift: a community or welcoming committee that is waiting to greet him or her into the world with open arms.

5

Birth Plans

Now that you have given some thought to the various aspects of childbirth and researched some of your options, it is time to be specific and make your dreams a reality. You have probably gathered facts about various methods of childbirth, heard different opinions, and reflected on your own needs and wishes. Choices need to be made about which method of childbirth you prefer.

As mentioned in Chapter Two, Choosing Your Health Care, when we consider spending a lot of money on an important purchase (house, car, personal computer, or household appliances), we usually shop around. First we get clear about what we want and need. If we're on a budget, such a purchase may involve long-term planning and saving money. We usually gather information, research prices, and consider our options. We think about our decision a lot before making our purchase.

Prenatal care is the most important investment you will ever make. It requires more time and thought than any other purchase. The care you receive during pregnancy, labor, and birth will impact your life and the life of your baby forever. Be an informed consumer.

Most births in the United States today take place in a hospital setting and are attended by obstetricians and nurses. However, increasing numbers of women are choosing alternative methods and locations for their delivery. Some examples of alternative birthing are:

- Underwater births

- Free-standing birth centers

- Home births

- Midwife delivery in hospital

- Doula-supported birth (a definition of a doula and her function appears later in this chapter)

What sets these methods apart from the most widely used hospital care is that they tend to emphasize the emotional and relationship aspects of birth along with the physical.

Regardless of the method used, everyone agrees that the safety and health of mother and child are of the utmost importance. There are different opinions about what a safe birth is and how to attain one. For instance, in the name of safety many hospitals rely heavily on numerous *routine medical interventions*. To name a few:

- I.V.'s (intravenous needles)

- Electronic fetal monitors (both external and internal)

- Administration of pitocin

- Routine use of medication, painkillers, mood-altering drugs, sleeping pills, and so on

- Intrauterine catheter

- Urinary catheters

- Artificial rupture of membranes (breaking the bag of waters)

- Vacuum extractors for delivering the baby

- Use of forceps for delivering the baby

- Cesarean-section surgical delivery

- Episiotomy

- Eyedrops or creams (put in baby's eyes)

- Vitamin K shots (for the baby)

- Clamping and cutting the umbilical cord immediately upon delivery

- Separation of mother and baby after birth (baby taken to hospital nursery for "observation")

For a general overview of methods of birthing available today we recommend:

Your Baby, Your Way, by Sheila Kitzinger

Alternative Birth: The Complete Guide, by Carl Jones

A Wise Birth, by Penny Armstrong and Sheryl Feldman

Midwife Means with Woman, by Elizabeth Hallet and Karen Ehrlich

(See the Bibliography for more titles.)

Doula or Childbirth Assistant

A recent development in the field of childbirth is the doula, or childbirth assistant. The word *doula* comes from the Greek, and, literally translated, means "in service of." A doula is a woman who helps a mother with birth and early postpartum. She stays with the mother continuously during labor and birth, supporting her in whatever way necessary. The doula is familiar with hospital policies and procedures and has extensive training and birth experience.

The doula's presence allows the laboring woman to relax and to feel safe and in control of herself. She is now free to focus on her body and the normal birth process, while the medical personnel monitor the birth with their instruments. The doula blends the best of both worlds.

Many women feel they have prepared for birth. However, when attended by strangers in an unfamiliar hospital setting, they feel unprepared and frightened. For instance, just when a woman is getting to know one set of hospital personnel, the shift changes and she has to adjust all over again.

A woman who is not used to hospital terminology may feel as if she is in a foreign country where she does not understand the language. It can be frustrating and alarming to be ignorant about what is being done to her and why. Even if a woman asks, the response is often obscured by technical jargon. Having a guide is vitally important. This is where the doula comes in. She acts as a guide, translator, and interpreter.

American society prizes "safety first." To most people more technology means "safer." Birth has moved away from a simple, natural home setting, requiring little or no intervention, to the complex, high-tech environment of the hospital. Due to the increase of medical technology some level of intervention has become routine in almost all hospital births.

Women's labor, a natural event, has been forced into a technological system driven by policies, procedures, and profits. All of this is done supposedly in the name of "safety" for mother and child. Unfortunately, following these "safe births" many women feel vaguely unhappy, disempowered, and depressed. And they don't know why. They have a healthy baby and they've been told that everything is fine. They "should" be happy, but they aren't.

Since medical technology is here to stay, and home birth is not an option for every woman, there needs to be a "bridge over the gap." One answer is the use of a professional childbirth assistant (doula) as part of the birth team.

Angela was a trained doula. She was assisting Brita and her husband, Rolf, during labor and birth. Angela was aware of their birth plans and knew how adamantly they wanted to avoid an internal fetal monitor (FSE). When Brita went into premature labor, her physician was out of town. His partner attended the delivery. Angela knew that this particular doctor routinely used the internal fetal monitor.

During an exam the nurse asked the physician if he would like an "FSE." Rolf was confused and alarmed. He whispered to Angela, "What is *that?*" Angela explained that an FSE means "fetal scalp electrode," which is an internal fetal monitor. In this procedure an electrode is inserted under the skin of the baby's scalp. (If you are having a difficult labor with fetal distress, this medical intervention may be very helpful. Talk to your physician or midwife before birth about when the use of a FSE would be appropriate and how often your caregiver finds it necessary to use this device.) Knowing about their Birth Plan, Angela queried, "Is that what you both want?" "No," he replied. Rolf then asked the physician if an internal monitor was *really* necessary and the physician admitted that it wasn't; the external monitor was adequate. Brita's labor progressed smoothly, and they had a healthy girl. Rolf felt included and supportive of Brita during the birth, and she felt loved and protected. The couple felt in charge of their baby's birth.

In the last decade six medical studies showed that with the presence of a doula, women have had fewer episiotomies and babies have had less traumatic births. Length of labor has been reduced by 25 percent, and several medical interventions have also been cut back by the following amounts:

- Cesarean section—50%

- Oxytocin (pitocin)—40%

- Pain medication—30%

- Forceps—40%

- Epidurals—60%

These statistics translate into cost-effectiveness because intervention procedures (often accompanied by extended hospital care) are very expensive. The doula offers experienced, objective assistance. Also, unlike most caregivers, she is available to follow through with care after the birth. This continuity of personal attention for the mother and baby is perhaps one of the doula's greatest contributions.

Many women are waiting until they are older to experience birth. They choose to have only one baby. With only one chance to create a joyful birth experience, it is vital to make that one birth as fulfilling and happy as it can be.

The Birth Plan

One way to become an informed consumer of prenatal care is to create a Birth Plan. *A Birth Plan is a written description of what you want and need for your labor, delivery, and eatly postpartum.* Your Birth Plan is a reflection of you. It grows out of your personal feelings and needs and out of your understanding of labor and birth. A good Birth Plan is a guide both for asking questions and for communicating your wishes to others.

Getting Clear

The first step in preparing a Birth Plan is getting clear about what you want and what you don't want. If you are not clear about how you want your birth to happen, other people, often following routine procedures, will make the decisions that should be yours. In a hospital setting, if you and your caregiver have not decided upon and written a Birth Plan and don't know what you want, your labor and delivery will probably be controlled by health professionals. This is not because they *want* to decide for you or are taking the decisions out of your hands. The fact is that all hospitals have "routine" orders and "standard procedures." They must follow these unless directed otherwise. Therefore it is important to learn about the practices, procedures, and philosophy of birth applied in hospitals, home settings, and birthing centers.

Instead of making a Birth Plan, Cindy thought she should leave everything to her doctor. When she got to the hospital, she had to do whatever the staff wanted. They inserted an intravenous device (heparin lock) into her wrist vein immediately upon arrival in the maternity ward. When Cindy questioned why they were doing this, the staff said, "Just in case you need an I.V. later." They also told her, "Don't worry about it, these are just routine orders." She felt powerless. Her unexpected pain and fear caused her labor to slow down.

When her physician arrived, Cindy was very emotional and couldn't discuss her questions about hospital procedures calmly. Not having voiced her wishes in advance, it was too late now to be making last-minute demands. Understandably her doctor became defensive. This patient, who had previously been docile and unassertive, was now uncooperative and highly volatile. Communication broke down. Cindy soon became reactive and fearful and was not in a good frame of mind for problem solving or birthing. The staff followed hospital routine. Because she was having trouble communicating her desires, Cindy left it up to her husband, Bob, to communicate with the staff for her. This put him in an awkward position. He felt stuck in the middle and unable to help her. The whole experience was dissatisfying for both Bob and Cindy. Although they had a physically healthy baby boy, his birth was not a joyful experience. Most of the negative, panic-inducing experiences could have been avoided if Cindy and Bob had prepared in advance.

Make a Birth Plan. Talk it over with your health care professional. *When it is signed by your doctor or midwife, it becomes doctor's orders and should be followed by the hospital staff.* There is power in decisiveness. It sets up a reaction in the brain, which is transferred to the body. When you make a clear decision, your mind will automatically begin helping you move toward your goal. With this frame of mind you can more effectively communicate and problem-solve.

During your pregnancy decide what you want and exercise your right to have it. *Never forget, you are paying for your prenatal care and you have rights as a consumer.* However, with rights there are responsibilities. As a consumer it is your job to know what you want and to make responsible informed decisions. Health care professionals are not mind readers. If you want something, you have to ask for it.

Inventory: *Raise Your Standards*

Materials: Journal and felt-tip pens
Purpose: To clearly define what you want and don't want for your labor, delivery, and early postpartum
Technique:

1. Divide the paper into two sections. At the top of the first column write, *Things I Don't Want.* Over the second column write, *Things I Do Want.*
2. Using your dominant hand, quickly write a list of things you don't want for labor, delivery, and postpartum. Do not stop and think about what you write. After completing this list, relax for a moment.
3. With your non-dominant hand, in the second column make a list of all the things you *do* want for your labor, delivery, and postpartum. After completing your list, review your responses. Just observe your feelings. You do not need to *DO* anything more.

Ch. 5 pg 7 Raise Your Standards

Don't Want

epideral
Epeesiadomy
Drugs of any sort
Don't want to not have my way.
IV
Don't want them taking the baby away right after Delivery.
Don't want a mean nurse but one that will work w/me.
Sea Section
Complications that could harm me or the baby

Do want

1. Natural Birth in the hospital w/ my husband as my coach.
2. fast Delivery
3. Healthy baby
4. Be able to stay on top of things through transition.
5. spiritual experience.

This exercise is a very good one to repeat throughout your pregnancy to identify specifically what you want. It is good training in developing decisiveness, a trait you will need in the months ahead.

Blueprint for a Healthy Birth: Preparing to Make a Birth Plan

In preparing to write a Birth Plan, you will be using right-brain visual techniques for envisioning exactly what it is you want for labor and delivery.

In Chapter Three you cultivated your mental garden by reinforcing positive thoughts and images of birth. Now you will create a visual manifestation of a healthy, happy birth experience through the ancient art of mandala making.

The word *mandala* means "magic circle" in Sanskrit. In a mandala the design radiates out from a central point. There is always a frame or border, which may be round, square, or any other geometric shape. That border is believed to contain and protect the magic within the mandala.

Mandala motifs have appeared in virtually all cultures throughout history: the rose window of Gothic cathedrals, the sand paintings of native Americans showing the four directions and seasons, clocks, compasses, and the astrological horoscope are all forms of mandalas. Mandalas also appear in nature, for example: daisies, sunflowers, and many other flowers and plants.

Mandala making has been used as a form of healing in psychotherapy and art therapy for many years. This form is especially suited for visual representations of one's inner and outer world.

The purpose of making a *birth mandala* is to help you envision a joyful delivery and lay the foundation for your Birth Plan. The very structure of the mandala, with the design elements radiating out from the center point, puts you at the center of your birth experience.

Birth Mandala: *Unfolding Your Dream*

Materials: Drawing and collage materials

Purpose: To put yourself at the center of your birth experience. To create a visual affirmation of your dreams and desires for a joyful birth.

Technique:

1. Draw a very large circle on your paper. Select and cut out magazine pictures, phrases, and words that speak to your heart about the birth experience you want.

2. Sit quietly for a moment and relax. Focus on the Creator, or whatever you call the source of all creation. In the center of your page place a magazine picture that symbolizes the *Creative Source* (God, Higher Power, Inner Self, Universal Mind, Mother Nature). Some people have used pictures of the sun, the moon, a flower, a tree, the ocean, a religious figure, and so on. Find the image that speaks to you personally.

3. Create a mandala that depicts the birth experience you desire. Radiating out from the center point, lay out your pictures, phrases, and words. Follow your intuition about where to place them on the page. Move them around until you are happy with the design. Then glue all the pictures, phrases, and words in place. You may want to draw some images as well. As you create, keep in mind: your birthing environment, your support persons, your physical positions during labor and birth, your care and the care of your baby. Include any other aspects of delivery and birth that are particularly important to you.

4. Display your birth mandala in a place where you can look at it every day. You may want to expand or add to it as time goes on.

The Birth Map

Whenever you plan a journey, it is helpful to visualize where you're going and how you're going to get there. Perhaps you've traveled to Hawaii. You probably saw television or magazine ads with people sunning themselves on white sandy beaches or surfing in crystal-blue water. That enticed you to make the trip. These visual images motivated you to take all the steps necessary to get there and enjoy yourself.

Maps have been used from time immemorial to chart the course of journeys and adventures. A Birth Map is just such a tool. It helps you take charge of the birth through visual affirmations of your goal and the steps you will take to arrive there.

Mapping The Journey: *Finding My Hidden Treasure*

Materials: Collage materials
Purpose: To create an accurate picture of the kind of birth you want. To clarify on paper how you will reach your goal.
Technique:

1. Relax and visualize your "hidden treasure" (the birth outcome that you want to realize). It usually helps to close your eyes and shut out distractions. Let the images crystalize in your mind's eye.

(*continued on next page*)

2. In the top right-hand corner of the page, create an image or symbol of your "hidden treasure." You can draw or use a magazine picture for this symbol. If you draw it, use your non-dominant hand.

3. With your dominant hand, start in the lower left-hand portion of the page and draw a pathway leading to your "hidden treasure." The path represents things to do or skills and attitudes to develop in order to reach your goal.

4. Now draw yourself along the path, actively doing the steps it takes to attain your goal. Include pictures of helpers along the way (guides, resources, support people, spiritual helpers, etc.).

5. With your dominant hand write affirmations on various places around the map.

6. Display your birth map in a place where you can look at it frequently. Use it as a visual affirmation.

Birth-day Party

In preparing to write your Birth Plan, keep in mind that the big event is your baby's *birth*-day. Why not plan for it as you would a party? A festive attitude will provide a counterbalance to your more serious adult planning. By planning the birth as you would a party, you can anticipate, in advance, the joy of your baby's arrival.

Throughout this book you have been developing an awareness of your unborn child. If you are going to make a birth plan, it is crucial that you take your baby's desires into account. After all, the party is for your baby. This may sound strange, because the baby hasn't been born yet. If you've done the dialogues with your unborn child in earlier chapters, you know by now that your baby can definitely communicate with you. So why not ask what he or she wants?

The following exercise is especially fun to do with your partner and birth team.

Welcoming: *Birth-day Party*

Materials: Journal and felt-tip pens or clay sculpting materials
Purpose: To "lighten up" the planning of your baby's birth. This activity will help you have some *fun!*
Technique:

You and your main support person can do this separately and then combine your drawings, or you can both share the same drawing.

1. First relax and go into your safe place. Imagine your baby and ask her what she wants for her special day: her birth-day.
2. Using your non-dominant hand, draw whatever symbols of group fun you and your baby would enjoy. Create a picture of what your baby wants for her *birth*-day party. Add lots of color to your picture and add statements about her desires. Allow your wording to be simple, fun, and even silly.

Later you may write up your Birth Plan based on the desires your baby has expressed in this picture. Some people have even used this art form to present their Birth Plan to the hospital staff. It has created a lighter, more fun atmosphere. The hospital staff has generally enjoyed it and been responsive.

Note: This exercise lends itself to clay. You may want to do this exercise by sculpting with terra-cotta.

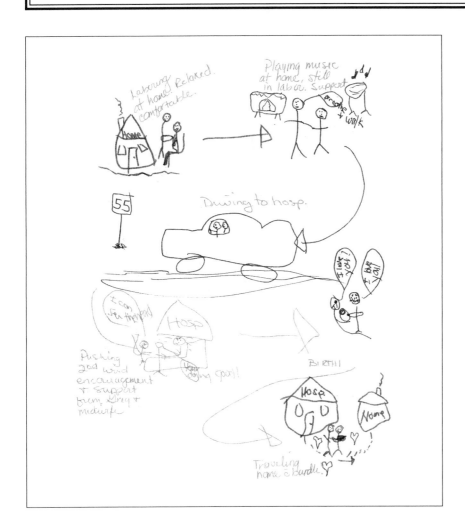

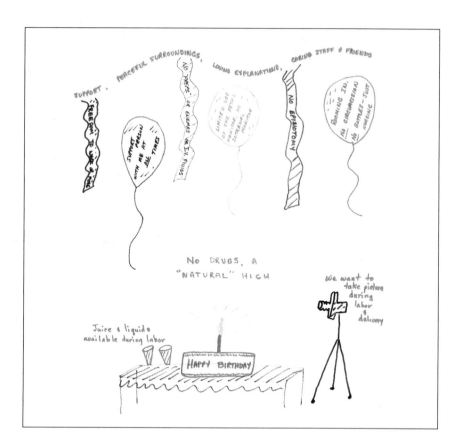

Janice and her support person, Audrey, did this exercise together. First they journaled and had fun drawing symbols of the birth-day party. Then they worked with clay while listening to music. They used audiotapes that Janice had been using during her pregnancy. She intended to use this music during her labor and delivery.

At one point Janice closed her eyes and allowed her hands to shape the clay without planning to make anything in particular. When Janice opened her eyes, she saw that her hands had formed a flower with open petals. It had a fluted center, like a daffodil. She let it dry and put a special candle in the center. This light became the focal point through most of her labor.

Getting What You Want

The following exercise is designed to help you set goals and take action toward the pregnancy, labor, and birth that you want. It can help you begin creating your Birth Plan.

Action Plan: *Walking My Talk*

Materials: Journal and felt-tip pens
Purpose: To help you learn to take actions that support your goal
Technique:

1. Using two facing pages in your journal, on the left-hand page write the heading *Values/Goals.*
2. On the right-hand page write the heading *If . . . Then . . .*
3. Sit quietly for a moment and reflect on what you want for your labor, delivery, and postpartum. With your dominant hand, on the left-hand page write a list of your values and goals. Leave space between each goal.
4. Using your non-dominant hand, on the right-hand page fill in the columns labeled *If . . . Then . . . .*

Example:

If (I want to take charge of the birth), *Then* (I need to tell my doctor what I want, make a Birth Plan, visit the birth place, and communicate what I want with my support team).

The Power of Focus

The mind is powerful but undisciplined. It chases after every thought. In order to harness the power of the mind, you need focus. *Focus* is the ability to concentrate your mind on one image, thought, or goal. Without the power of focus your mind would be continually wandering, directionless. Like a sailboat without a rudder, the unfocused mind is dominated by external circumstances. By contrast a disciplined mind uses focus to achieve strength and arrive at goals.

Directing the Mind

Your brain receives input through your five senses. It stores the images of all your past experiences for future reference. It doesn't decide if information is good or bad, useful or useless, important or unimportant; it simply provides you with data so that you can make decisions and take action.

Although there are several ways to focus, they all depend on the use of questions because your unconscious mind continually asks questions. It is constantly searching for meaning. As you encounter different situations, your unconscious mind asks, "What does this mean?" "How should I respond?" "What should I do?" It scans your memory for similar situations and how they were handled. Based on that information you make a conscious decision.

Your conscious mind is also asking questions, and by asking the right questions you can make effective decisions. By asking the wrong questions you will not arrive at a coherent conclusion.

Bernadette was expecting her second child. Her first child had been delivered by cesarean section. This time she wanted to have a vaginal birth. A few weeks prior to the due date she was overcome with fear that she couldn't do it.

Bernadette's physician referred her to Co-Creations. We introduced her to the concept that how we phrase questions affects our response and our attitude toward the situation. First she observed the questions she asked herself when she felt stressed. "Why am I so afraid?" "Why can't I get myself to practice relaxation?" "Why isn't my partner more interested in our baby?" "What if I can't handle a vaginal birth?" "What if I get too tired to push?" Bernadette noticed that her reactions to these questions were fear and self-doubt.

We pointed out that these types of questions do not help in finding a solution; rather they lead to confusion. They produce a negative physical and emotional state because the brain acts on the command in each question. Even if Bernadette were to find the answer to "why," her problem would still remain. Her goal to change the situation requires that she learn to ask proactive questions, which elicit answers she can act upon.

Once she understood this, Bernadette was able to calm herself down. She wrote out two lists in her journal. She listed the questions she was asking herself. Then she turned them into proactive questions, which could give her solutions.

Ineffective Questions	Proactive Questions
Why am I so afraid?	How can I conquer my fear?
Why can't I get myself to practice relaxation?	What can I do to practice relaxation regularly?

Why isn't my partner more interested in the baby?	How can I get my partner more involved?
What if I can't handle a vaginal birth?	What can I do to prepare for a vaginal birth?
What if I get too tired to push?	How can I prevent myself from getting too tired in labor?

Following the exercise we worked with Bernadette to help her understand the concept of hidden negative commands. The hidden command is usually embedded in the last words of a sentence. Your brain acts on that command. The ways you experience feelings of success, vitality, or frustration are affected by hidden commands in the questions you ask. These commands determine what you focus on and your ultimate outcome. Your power of focus will automatically produce a conscious response. For instance, look at Bernadette's last proactive question in the example above, "How can I prevent myself from getting too tired in labor?" This question contains a hidden negative command, "getting too tired in labor." Bernadette's brain will hear that command and automatically respond, thus defeating her purpose.

We pointed out to Bernadette that all of her other proactive questions were stated in the positive: "conquer my fear," "practice relaxation regularly," "get my partner more involved," and "prepare for a vaginal birth." These thoughts will elicit the response she wants. After learning this principle, Bernadette rephrased her last question to read "How can I create more energy during labor and birth?" Now her brain will respond to the command "create more energy."

While preparing your Birth Plan, pay close attention to the wording you use in the questions you ask yourself.

Questions: *The Power of Focus*

Materials: Journal and felt-tip pens
Purpose: To learn about and change the questions you ask yourself
Technique:

1. Observe yourself for a week. Write down the times when you felt frustrated, stuck, unhappy, sad, lonely, depressed, angry, and so on (any negative emotional feelings). In your journal make note of the questions you were asking yourself.

(continued on next page)

2. Reflect on your questions. How does each one make you feel? Does it motivate you to take action or cause further frustration and indecision?

3. Divide a journal page into two columns. At the top of the column on the left put *Ineffective Questions*. List the questions that caused you frustration and indecision.

4. At the top of the column on the right put *Proactive Questions*. In this column rephrase the question in a way that moves you to action.

5. How does each new question make you feel? Record your feelings in your journal. In the future notice those feelings and what triggers them. Reflect on your questions and self-talk.

Communicating

Communicating what you want is one of the most important things you can do to protect yourself and ensure that your baby's birth is orchestrated as you intend it. Here are a few suggestions:

- Know exactly what you want and why.

- Write what you want in a Birth Plan.

- *Don't* make negative assumptions about another person's motivation. If you disagree with others' behavior, question them.

- Avoid judging others. This destroys communication. When people feel judged, they become uncooperative. Look for another way to communicate.

- Think the best of the people with whom you are communicating, and expect that from them.

- Phrase your questions, statements, and responses to reflect love and safety instead of fear. Notice how you are stating them (even to yourself). When communicating their desires, people are either coming from a place of love and safety or they are defending themselves.

- When you feel conflict in your communication, notice it and reflect upon what is happening. This is a good time to do some journaling if at all possible.

- Master your communications with yourself. (Take charge of your inner family: your Protective Parent, your Nurturing Parent, your Playful and Creative Child.)

- Use short "I" sentences that state your feelings ("I feel, I want, I see, I hear . . .")

- Notice your body language, voice tone, facial expression, body position, timing, and eye contact.

Writing Your Birth Plan

After becoming clear about your wants, you are ready to begin writing your Birth Plan. Make a conscious commitment and put your plan into action. The following is an outline to give you an overview of the steps in preparing a Birth Plan. Once you have begun the process, refer back to this list to see how you are doing.

Birth-Plan Overview

1. Get clear about what you want

   - Notice your internal voice: What are you saying to yourself? What questions are you asking?

   - Define your beliefs and values about any specific aspect of birth that is important to you.

   - Identify your concerns about birth.

   - Identify what makes you happy or excited about the thought of giving birth.

   - Gather information.

   - Share your thoughts with your support person(s).

2. Decide and make a conscious commitment

   - Get clear and focus on your purpose and goals.

   - Use affirmations like "My partner is" or "I am in charge of taking action."

   - Formalize a Birth Plan (write it out).

3. Take action

- Discuss your Birth Plan with your support team.

- Condition your response. Imagine yourself *over and over again* succeeding in carrying out your plan.

- Use others who have succeeded as role models.

- Talk to your doctor or midwife about your Birth Plan. Get their support for your plan and have them sign it.

- Make an extra copy of your Birth Plan to take with you to the birthplace. Be sure this copy is signed by your care provider. Once it is signed, your Birth Plan should be considered to be official orders.

4. Make your goal real

- See yourself having the power to give birth the way you want to.

- Believe in your birthing goal. Image it over and over again.

- Physically practice what it will take to achieve your goal. "Repetition is the mother of skill."

- Reinforce your physical commitment with an immediate reward. (Attach *pleasure* to your effort—reward yourself.)

5. Have patience, be flexible

- Be ready for obstacles to your goal. Make alternative action plans.

- Pay attention to what works and what does not work. Be willing to make minor changes until you reach your goal.

- Don't give up (on your support team, yourself, your body, your baby, or your birth process)!

To begin writing your Birth Plan, go back through your journal entries and gather the ideas you have had for your baby's birth (for instance, the ideas from the exercises entitled "Raise Your Standards," "Birth

Mandala," "Birth Map," and "Birth-day Party"). Having done this, organize your wishes and goals into categories. For example:

- Normal labor

- Normal birth

- Early postpartum care for mom

- What to do about unexpected outcomes (such as C-section, interventions, trauma for the baby)

- Care for your baby (*Note:* Make your baby's care plan on a separate page, because after the birth it will go into the baby's medical chart.)

Before you write your formal Birth Plan, allow yourself some time to think about all of these ideas and your desires.

After a few days begin writing out your wishes. You can do a rough draft (or two) first to be sure that you have included everything that is important to you, your partner, and your baby. The words you use will convey what you want. Be careful; avoid language that will create defensiveness in other people. Words and phrases that reflect a spirit of cooperation and flexibility are better received. Use terms such as *please, I prefer, if possible, will you help us,* and so on.

Avoid making demands or telling others what to do. Instead state what *you* want. Focus on your needs and wishes. Be firm, but also respectful of others' needs. In your requests indicate that you are aware that it may be *medically necessary* to adjust some of your plans. You can state that you are willing to take personal responsibility for any of your birth plans that may be contrary to state or hospital policy.

Your Birth Plan should be a reflection of you: *your* attitudes, values, and beliefs. It should begin with an introductory paragraph that reflects your personal style for approaching the situation.

Writing an Introductory Paragraph

The initial paragraph of your Birth Plan introduces you to the hospital staff. It briefly describes some of your personality traits and includes your values and beliefs. It sets the stage for the rest of your Birth Plan and personalizes it. Write it your own way. You may want to include the following:

- What you normally do to relax.

- How you usually prepare for an event or project (for example extensive planning, procrastination, or hesitancy).

- What your lifestyle is like. Mention your sleep patterns (early or late riser) and your eating habits (vegetarian, meat eater, food allergies).

- What makes you feel safe in new situations.

- How do you respond when you are uncomfortable, stressed, or angry.

Following are two examples of introductory paragraphs to Birth Plans. Notice how they tell something about the woman's personal feelings. This important feature of your Birth Plan lets the hospital staff know how they can best serve you.

Samples of Introductory Paragraphs

Sonia

I first want to thank all those who will be a part of my birth team. I am very excited to welcome my baby in a quiet, loving, and gentle way. I've chosen this hospital and staff to help me do that.

For several years I have been a busy career woman in a large corporation. I'm a general manager and have a large staff working for me. My personal life is a lot like my professional one: I like a lot of organization. I usually carefully plan most events well in advance. For instance, I have done quite a lot of preparation for this birth: reading, childbirth classes, exercise and pain-management classes, additional birth videos, and birth counseling. I'm not comfortable with sudden, unexplained changes in my routine. For relaxation I like to curl up where it's warm and read. When experiencing something new, I feel the best when I can know about each thing before it happens. Throughout birth please be patient with me and explain what is happening often. If you don't do that, I may feel neglected or bossed around and respond by withdrawing and becoming sullen. I am the adult child of an abusive, alcoholic family. My own birth and childhood were unpleasant. I am in group therapy concerning these past fears and upsets.

My husband and I plan to have one child. Therefore I want this birth to be special for both of us. I sincerely seek the advice and guidance of all medical professionals involved with the birth of my child. I wish to experience (as much as possible) a natural-biological birth. In preparation for that I have formulated the following Birth Plan.

Jessica and Michael

I am a housewife, and we have one little boy, Brandt, who is three years old. I love to take walks with him and play outdoors when I'm relaxing. I like to walk or bike ride. If that's not possible, I like to imagine a nature scene from my memories. When I have a project to do, I usually go with the flow of it. I first plan it, but it's okay with me when it goes in another direction.

My husband, Michael, is my closest friend. He makes me feel the safest just by being with me. We do a lot together as a couple, and also as a family. Being together makes experiences really seem great. I don't usually get angry, but when I feel uncomfortable or frustrated, I sometimes cry.

We have a lot of wishes for this birth, but the most important one is to be together as a family. Following is our detailed Birth Plan.

The Body of Your Birth Plan

After your introductory paragraph begin writing your individual plan. It may be easier for your birth team if you prioritize the sections in order of importance to you. However, you can organize them any way you like.

This sample Birth Plan is meant only as a suggestion. Create your own based on what you want and what is available to you. In formulating your own Birth Plan, you may want to include other concerns, such as:

- Use of forceps and/or vacuum extractors

- Artificial rupture of membranes

- Methods used for induction of labor

LABOR

- If able, I prefer to walk to the labor and delivery rooms. I would like to stay in the same room and bed for labor and delivery.

- I would like my husband or support person to stay with me at all times and not be excluded for any reason.

- I request a childbirth assistant (doula) as an additional support person during my labor and delivery.

- I don't want my pubic hair shaved. (Clipping is okay if surgical intervention is required.)

- I do not want an enema (except if it's absolutely necessary for medical reasons).

- I want to use nipple stimulation to strengthen my labor contractions. I do not want labor induced unless my physician, my husband, my doula, and I agree that an induction is medically necessary for my safety or the safety of the baby.

- I want no I.V. fluids unless my physician, my main support person, my doula, and I agree that I am dehydrating (or if absolutely necessary for medical reasons).

- I want the freedom to walk about even after rupture of membranes.

- I desire the freedom to move about or to change positions frequently when confined to bed.

- I would like liquids, such as juices, high-energy drinks, tea, and ice chips for rehydration. If I want them, I'd like soft foods as well.

- I prefer limited use (ten minutes every hour) of the *external* fetal monitor, unless longer use is deemed medically necessary for safety of the baby. I do not want internal fetal monitoring.

- I do not want anesthetics and analgesics administered to me unless I request them.

- I would like the freedom to use the toilet as necessary.

- I request that we use a camera or camcorder in the labor and delivery room.

- I want the use of the shower, bathtub, and/or Jacuzzi. I request that my main support person be allowed to shower with me in order to give me a massage.

BIRTH

- I want to give birth in any position and place that feels comfortable for me. (I do not want to be on my back.)

- I prefer to follow my own natural urge to push and deliver my baby spontaneously. I do not want people directing me about how to push the baby out at the time of delivery.

- I want soft lighting at the delivery. (No bright lights in the room.)

- I would like to hear soft recorded music played at the birth of my baby. We'll bring the player and the tapes.

- My partner or main support person will cut my infant's umbilical cord after it is no longer pulsating. My partner will assist with the delivery in other appropriate ways.

- I want to touch my baby's head as it emerges from my body.

- I do not want an episiotomy. I request that at the time of delivery warm, moist compresses be placed on my perineum. I want to move into a favorable birth position in order to help prevent an episiotomy.

- I would rather have some small tearing than have an episiotomy. If an episiotomy is indicated for medical reasons, I prefer a medial incision, as small as possible.

MEDICAL INTERVENTION

- I request that all non-medical intervention be tried first.

- I request that my main support person not be excluded from any phase of the procedure, including preparation, and so on.

- I prefer using vacuum extractor instead of forceps, if my caregiver believes intervention is medically necessary.

- In the event of a cesarean-section birth, I request the following:

  - Epidural anesthesia
  - My partner or main support person to be with me throughout the surgical delivery of the baby

- To hold and nurse my baby in the recovery room

- My partner or main support person to be able to assist with the baby's care in the nursery

- The screen lowered at the time of delivery so that I can see my baby's birth

- To have my partner sit beside me and hold our baby after birth, if the baby is all right.

- In the event of a stillbirth or premature death, I request:

  - That my baby be washed and wrapped in a blanket and given to me for contact immediately after delivery. I would like my partner or main support person with me. I request privacy at that time.

  - Copies of the birth records of my baby.

  - The fingerprints and footprints of our baby to be put into our birth book.

  - A small piece of the baby's hair (if any) saved for our birth book.

  - Pictures taken of my baby.

POSTPARTUM (immediate)

- I would like the immediate care of my baby to be done on my abdomen (skin to skin if possible).

- I would like the Leboyer bath routine for my baby (warm bath, low lights, soft music).

- I prefer the use of mild eye medication for my baby (erythromycin) as opposed to harsh eye solutions (such as silver nitrate drops). I request that its administration be delayed as long as possible. (*NOTE*: Talk to your physician about the possibility of waiving this requirement.)

- I ask that all newborn care (weight, measurement, bath) be done in my room. I do not want the baby to be away from me. If that is not possible, I request that my partner be allowed to accompany our baby to the nursery for care.

- I request immediate contact of the pediatrician of my choice if there is any sign of infant distress or abnormality. (Provide your pediatrician's name and phone number here.)

- If the baby is male, no circumcision will be done.

- I request rooming-in with my baby.

- Since I intend to breast-feed, I request no drugs be given or procedures be performed on me that will inhibit lactation.

- I request as early a discharge from the hospital as my care-giver deems feasible.

- I request oral vitamin K for my baby instead of injection. (Talk to your physician about possibly waiving this require-ment altogether.)

SPECIAL NURSERY CARE

- If my infant requires special nursery care in the same hospi-tal with me, I request access to him or her at any time.

- If my baby needs to be transferred to another hospital, I re-quest open phone contact with his or her nurse.

- If our baby must be fed by bottle or other means, I would like to pump my breasts and provide my breast milk throughout the hospital stay.

- Please do not give my baby sugar water or additional feeding.

- Please do not give my baby a pacifier. Bring him or her to me or have me come to the nursery to provide the comfort needed.

The preceding Birth Plan is hereby approved and will be followed as closely as possible commensurate with prudent medical practice.

_____   _____
Physician   Date

_____   _____
Mother   Date

For the Partner: Sharing the Birth Experience

Preparation for labor, birth, and early parenting can seem nearly overwhelming for the woman's partner or main support person. The best advice we can offer you is that you take action. It's also best to take action *before* you are in the delivery room. Be an active participant in your partner's Birth Plan so that you can be an active participant at the birth. If you don't get involved during the pregnancy, delivery, and birth, it is easy to feel excluded, left out, and powerless. To be a participant in the birth experience is truly a gift to the baby, to the mother, and to yourself. Witnessing a new life come into the world is an awesome experience.

It is helpful to remember that it is normal to feel inadequate in the face of this unforgettable event. If you are emotionally close to the woman who is giving birth, your important gift is that emotional support. Tenderness is more important than technique in childbirth. You are invaluable! Your presence and offering your love and support will provide the greatest security the new mother needs.

Besides offering general support and love, most partners also want some specific suggestions on how to be helpful. We suggest the following:

- Share the experience of preparation together. Talk about the impending birth; daydream with her.

- Notice your feelings and the questions you ask yourself.

- Practice breathing and relaxation exercises with her. Master them so that she feels confident you will be able to help her during delivery.

- Journal with her and the unborn baby.

- Become involved with her support team.

- Become informed. Read, watch birth films, go to classes and interact with her caregiver.

- Provide her with the support she needs to feel safe such as financial help and a loving, "listening ear."

- Pay attention to her moods.

- Be interested and help her make decisions about creating her Birth Plan.

Birth Plans for Survivors of Sexual Abuse

In Western society one in every three to four women has been or will be sexually abused. Many times survivors of abuse feel confused about what feels safe and what is appropriate behavior toward them. Their abuse experience often impairs their sense of boundaries and their ability to set limits.

During pregnancy, when safety becomes an important concern, abuse survivors need to get clear about what they do and don't want. This may be difficult for them. But because of their past experience it is important that they take steps to ensure that their wishes are met. Some of the exercises presented earlier in this chapter can help tremendously in this regard.

Learning to translate desires into a plan of action helps develop the ability to focus and feel "in control." A Birth Plan is an empowering tool to a woman with a hisory of past abuse (sexual, verbal, physical, or emotional). A carefully-thought-out Birth Plan enables her to *claim the territory*!

Establishing and setting limits by defining her rights is the most important thing an abuse survivor can do for herself. Safety begins within, and is developed through re-parenting the wounded Inner Child. The Protective Parent within can be clear, firm, and assertive and can help us say no to others and yes to ourselves. The Inner Protective Parent puts the best interests of the Inner Child first and will defend its rights.

Esther had been sexually molested in her childhood and teen years by her family physician. Her abuser threatened her with physical violence if she told. As a result of living in fear for so long, Esther found it extremely difficult to tell others about her true feelings. She felt easily intimidated, especially by men in authority.

When she became pregnant, her fear intensified to such a point that she delayed seeking prenatal care. She was referred to Co-Creations. In counseling she finally opened up about her history of sexual abuse and shared her grief and fear. Through the technique of dialoguing with her Inner Protective Parent, Esther learned how to set limits and boundaries to create safety for herself. She became empowered to seek prenatal care and to select as her caregiver someone who felt safe and trustworthy.

Esther created a Birth Plan outlining what she did and did not want for the pregnancy and birth. This helped her to choose a gentle and patient woman doctor who had experience working with abuse survivors. Her sensitive woman physician made all the difference in the world to Esther. She was finally able to relax and trust a health care professional. She also resolved much of her early trauma simply by having a healthy, joyful birth.

Whether or not you are an abuse survivor, if you need to become more assertive about setting limits and boundaries, the following exercise is for you. It will help you tremendously in implementing your Birth Plan, for there are times during labor and delivery when you may have to say no clearly and emphatically.

Inner Dialogue: Finding Protection Within

Materials: Journal and felt-tip pens
        Optional: Large sheet of art paper and drawing materials
Purpose: To find your safety within through strengthening your Inner Protective Parent. To develop assertiveness, clear boundaries, and limits on the intrusive behavior of others.

Technique:

1. Sit quietly for a while and remember a time when you felt protected and safe. Where were you? What was happening around you? Recall what it felt like. What was it that made you feel protected and safe? Picture this protective power in your life. What does it look like?
2. With your non-dominant hand draw a picture of your protective power. What color is it? What shape? Does it look like a person or an animal? Is it an abstract form or something from nature?
3. Write a dialogue with this protective power. Using your non-dominant hand, let your Inner Child ask the protective power to help you in threatening or unsafe situations. Be specific. With the dominant hand let your protective power tell your Inner Child how it will help her in these situations. This protective power is your very own Protective Parent Within. You have it with you at all times. All you have to do is call upon it.

Safe
vibrant
smiles
happy
trusts
self
self-
confidant
grounded
radiant

In preparing a Birth Plan the following are some suggestions for the sexually abused woman to consider:

- Hire a childbirth assistant (a doula), who will be with you during the entire labor and delivery. If this is not possible, ask a trusted friend *who has experience with healthy birthing* to be with you and your partner.

- Write a Birth Plan that really reflects what is important to you. Make it as detailed as you need it to be. Focus on your strengths when you are writing about yourself and your wishes.

- Write an introductory paragraph about yourself so that the hospital staff will know something about you—especially your personality and your likes and dislikes.

Will you keep me safe? Especially when we go to the hospital & they want to do things to me that I don't want? Yes! I'm arranging to have people we love & trust to be a us. Jeremy will be there, talking & holding you/us. Faith is a good midwife & very knowledgeable & she'll be there. We will consult w her before we decide to accept or decide against any intervention. KT will be there too. And we'll stay home till the best time to go to the hospital. Jeremy, Faith & KT will support you/us in having a very positive birth experience

- It is very important for your caregiver and your support team to know about your desires and wishes. Communicate these to them.

- Use the power of focus while writing. Think about the questions you are asking yourself.

In this book we have included many exercises that will help you clarify your goals and plans. However, we have noticed that abused women sometimes have unrealistic expectations. Although they want things to be a certain way, it is difficult for them to take action. The following exercise is particularly useful in helping to design *realistic* Birth Plans.

Before you finish your formal Birth Plan, we suggest that you do this exercise.

Transitions to Responsibility: *And That Means . . .*

Materials: Journal and felt-tip pens

Purpose: To formulate a realistic Birth Plan. To accept responsibility for each decision made.

Technique:

1. With a pen in your dominant hand begin by stating what you want to do. End your statement with "and that means."

   Example:

   I want to avoid an episiotomy, *and that means . . .*

2. Using your non-dominant hand, complete the statement with an action you will take to implement your goal.

   Example:

   I want to avoid an episiotomy, *and that means . . .* doing regular perineal massage, doing squatting and Kegel exercises daily, not pushing too hard when the baby is coming out, writing on my Birth Plan that I want perineal support during delivery to prevent tearing, asking for warm packs on the perineum during delivery.

3. Continue this process with each goal stated in your Birth Plan. Doing the "Transitions to Responsibility" exercise will reveal exactly how prepared you are. It will also reveal any areas that may need more preparation and commitment.
   (See example on Page 160.)

I commit to having a short labor.
And that means practicing, relaxing, exercising, eating right

I commit to having a relaxing/comfortable postpartum.
And that means being with baby & Greg, taking it easy, not overdoing it, allowing family to help with house, chores, allowing time for self, & time. with greg.

Conclusion

Devising a clear and complete Birth Plan is one of the best ways that you can prepare for your baby's birth. The research that goes into devising such a plan will inform you and remove much of the uncertainty connected with childbirth. Of course there may be some unexpected situations that arise; but having a strong support system and a good plan will help you to face surprises. The preparation of a good Birth Plan will also strengthen your relationship with your support team: partner, health professionals, family and friends, and so on. Most importantly a Birth Plan puts you at the center of the labor and delivery process, with others there to support you in realizing your dreams and desires for the birth of a healthy, happy baby.

6

Welcoming Your Baby

From Pain to Pleasure

The waiting has come to an end. The big event you have been anticipating and planning for is here. The most dramatic changes of pregnancy are about to take place: the three phases of labor and birth. We will guide you through these stages by focusing on the *power*, the *passage*, and the *passenger*. By *power we mean the Birth Energy*, the natural ability of your uterus to function during labor and delivery. By *passage* we mean the journey you and your baby embark upon to bring him or her into the world as a separate being. The *passenger* is the baby with his or her needs during the actual delivery.

Power

The Birth Energy is a power from within. It flows through your body, mind, emotions, and spirit. Since your baby's conception the Birth Energy has been bringing about all the changes you have been experiencing. The Birth Energy is enhanced by safe, supportive relationships within your own Inner Family. Then it extends to your baby and support team. As the arrival of your baby draws near, you will experience the movement of the Birth Energy. Besides being a natural physical force the Birth Energy has an emotional and spiritual dimension. It is facilitated by the emotional and spiritual bond between mother and baby.

The Birth Energy is very fragile and sensitive to the environment. During labor there is nothing more empowering for you than feeling supported. This allows you to relax and surrender to the natural unfolding of the Birth Energy. Some women become aware of the Birth Energy in their bodies early on in pregnancy. Others may not feel its rhythm until a few weeks before the baby is due. This rhythm prepares your body for birth (a kind of uterine calisthenics, if you will). You may notice emotions arising along with these contractions.

Having a dialogue with the Birth Energy will increase your awareness of this power in your body. This exercise is based on the work of Rahima Baldwin, a renowned childbirth educator and midwife (see Bibliography).

Dialogue: *Surrender to Life*

Materials: Journal and felt-tip pens
Purpose: To become aware of the Birth Energy. To face the fear of the unknown by discovering the power of the Birth Energy.
Technique:

1. Find a safe, quiet place. Allow yourself twenty to thirty uninterrupted minutes to do this exercise. Sit calmly and relax your body.
2. In your mind go to your "special place." Focus on your baby and the Birth Energy. Get a sense of the strength of this natural power that you have in your body.
3. Using your non-dominant hand, draw a picture of the Birth Energy. Put words around the picture that describe what the Birth Energy means to you.
4. Do a dialogue between yourself and the Birth Energy. Your dominant hand speaks for you, and your non-dominant hand speaks for the Birth Energy. Ask the Birth Energy any questions you may have.
(See example on page 163.)

Who Are you?
   I am your helper
What are you?
   I am the incredible energy + power
that comes meraciously to bring
the baby into the external world
when will you come?
   I will come at precisely the
right time. I want to have the
timing right for the baby + you. I
want your body to be
I b's to do it + want to be
to be ready.

light, energy, love, safety

Following is an example of the power of a joyful birth that resulted from good preparation and strong support.

Karen and Paul were ecstatic about being pregnant. They involved themselves wholeheartedly in the childbirth preparations. Seventeen days before her due date Karen awoke in the middle of the night thinking she had wet the bed. The water continued to leak slowly throughout the night. She had experienced this once before during pregnancy when she had a bladder infection. Somewhat concerned, she called her nurse-midwife to ask what she should do.

The nurse-midwife told Karen to go to the hospital to learn whether the fluid was urine or amniotic fluid. Karen learned that her water had broken and that she was in the early stages of labor. Paul and Karen were advised to return home, relax, and wait.

Paul stayed home from work to support Karen. She ate a light breakfast, and they went for a walk in the park. After lunch they snuggled up and took a nap together. It was a day of self-nurturing for both of them. That evening they watched a videotape of their favorite movie, *Big*. During an especially funny scene Karen's belly laughs coincided with the onset of heavy labor. Turning the movie off, they focused more completely on the labor. When the contractions felt quite strong and were coming every three to four minutes, Karen knew intuitively that it was time to go to the hospital.

Upon arrival a hospital staff member offered Karen a wheelchair, but she chose to walk to the birth center. Karen and Paul were greeted warmly and shown to the room they had chosen for labor and delivery. The birth center was familiar to them because they had taken tours in early pregnancy.

In the room Paul helped Karen settle in with her favorite pillow and stuffed animal from home. She changed into her own nightie rather than wear a hospital gown. Paul played Karen's favorite music on their tape player. The room had a rocking chair, where Karen sat for the admission procedures (blood pressure, temperature, and pulse reading). Karen stayed in the chair for the ten-minute fetal monitor reading. The nurse examined Karen to determine the *dilation* and *effacement* of the cervix, as well as the baby's position. The nurse found Karen had dilated six centimeters, the baby was engaged in the pelvis, and Karen was in active labor.

Following her exam Karen chose to use the Jacuzzi. Paul sat beside the tub massaging her back. They brought their tape player into the bathroom and played soothing music. Karen relaxed, staying in the tub for a little over an hour. During that time their nurse came in to check the baby's heartbeat.

While in the tub Karen remembered to drink often and to change positions frequently. During each contraction Karen focused on her breathing and on her "special place" from her "Birth Cave" imagery. Paul whispered loving words to her and praised her often. When the nurse came in again, she found that Karen was almost fully dilated. The baby was nearly ready to be born.

Karen tried various positions. Squatting, with Paul supporting her, felt the best. In his arms Karen found it easy to tune in to their baby and to the Birth Energy. She could feel her baby descending through the birth canal. When she felt pressure in her bottom and a burning sensation, she lay down on her side with Paul supporting her upper leg. With each contraction Karen felt the urge to push.

Paul was in awe at the sight of the baby's head emerging from Karen's body. He exclaimed, "Oh, honey, our baby's almost here!" Karen reached down and touched the baby's head. After another push or two their little girl was born. The baby was placed on Karen's chest. She and Paul wept tears of joy. For the next hour the three of them spent time alone just being together.

Breathing

Breath is life. If breathing stops for several minutes, life ends. It has been proven that deep breathing enhances well-being. When people are frightened or stressed, they tend either to hold their breath or to hyperventilate. Due to stress and fear, shallow breathing has become a habit with most of us. Breathing too fast (hyperventilation) increases anxiety. Holding one's breath cuts off oxygen to the brain and body. Your baby is seriously affected by both.

If a laboring woman holds her breath, she decreases the oxygen supply to her own body and to her baby. This can slow and sometimes even stop labor. If the woman hyperventilates, she can become terrified and may even become out of control. One would think that hyperventilation (breathing fast) must be getting more oxygen to the baby. Actually the opposite is true. Due to the body's chemical balance, the blood carries less oxygen and has a difficult time releasing it.

During labor the uterus is the strongest muscle in the body. Maintaining its strength requires an abundance of oxygen. Deep breathing provides the fuel that keeps the Birth Energy flowing and the uterus functioning optimally.

It isn't necessary to follow any particular method of breathing during labor, as long as it is *deep and rhythmic.* Your body will guide you to use the breathing patterns you specifically need. The wisdom of the body is innate—trust it. After all, women have been giving birth since the beginning of time.

Sound in Labor

Making specific sounds can help alleviate various discomforts. Specific sounds resonate in particular parts of the body and activate the nerves that transmit messages to the brain. As we have previously stated, once these messages reach the brain, they access information about painful or pleasurable memories.

Different sounds elicit different feelings. Many women who are survivors of abuse are afraid to allow themselves to make sounds. Complying with the abuse meant being silent. Therefore expressing deep body feelings during labor can be threatening. However, there comes a point during birth when the energy is so primal that women naturally express their physical responses to it by making sound. The woman who has survived abuse can be terrified or horrified by this reaction. In order to circumvent the possibility of this reaction, we recommend practicing making sounds daily throughout the pregnancy.

You can tell you're doing well with practicing if making the sound produces energy for you and your feelings of fear or disgust are lessened. As with affirmation exercises you will want to repeat specific sounds daily, allowing your feelings to surface. Use your journal to record those feelings.

Making sounds is also a very good breathing exercise, because you must breathe deeply in order to make sound. Practice making the following sounds. Notice where they resonate in your body, and journal with that particular part.

- Vowel sounds (A, E, I, O, U)

- HUMMMM—resonates in lungs and sinuses

- NNNNNN—resonates in lungs and sinuses

- MMMMMM or MA MA MA—resonates in sinuses

- YA YOU YAY—moves the jaw

- HA HA HA (like laughter)—is good for indigestion or heartburn

After practicing and journaling about each of these sounds, try putting them into a chant or mantra. One of the side benefits of practicing the same sound repeatedly is that your baby becomes familiar with it. When you make your sound in labor, it will produce feelings of safety and calm for the baby if you have *cleared a space* around that sound.

Believe in Yourself

Trust your ability and your body's ability to do the right thing. Having a baby is a totally natural occurrence, very much like learning to walk. A child takes steps, falters, stumbles and falls, but keeps trying until she succeeds. The *pleasure* of learning to walk far outweighs the *pain*. The child *never* sees her efforts as "failure." She just picks herself up and persists until she is walking.

However when it comes to the *natural* event of birth, many women question their ability. They focus only on the *pain* of this *pleasurable* event and fear failure. Mistrustful of her body, the laboring woman often loses confidence and asks or allows others to intervene.

Numerous women have told us that their beliefs about labor come from two primary sources: the media and other people's horror stories. Films and television depict labor and delivery as a traumatic and excruciatingly painful experience. In one study of 296 television births, only one was portrayed as happy and true to life. All of the others were sensationalized, dramatized, and guaranteed to stir up conflicting emotions in the viewers.

We have discovered an interesting phenomenon among women who seem to enjoy telling others about their horror stories. Those who go on and on about their difficult birth experiences are usually carrying around unresolved grief. Telling their story over and over again is an unconscious attempt to heal the pain. Unfortunately it doesn't work. Repeating the painful details only reinforces a negative attitude about birth. It also instills fear in those who listen.

During birth we suggest you remember the simple analogy of the baby learning to walk. Focus on the *pleasure*, not the *pain*. Keep going! Focus on the solution. Focus on your goal and believe in yourself. Use the tools you have learned in this book, such as the Power of Silence, and the Power of Focus. Don't put an earthly limit on a heavenly matter.

Birth is highly charged with emotion. Media portrayals and horror stories about labor have created and perpetuated frightening images of birth in many people's minds. Associating fear with labor is detrimental. Not only does fear cause stress, but expectant mothers who are fearful of labor often *react* emotionally to information about birth rather than *responding* productively. It is possible, however, to strengthen yourself through what we call stress inoculation. This is done by exposing oneself to the very thing you are afraid of and clearing any negative feelings. For example, watching an actual video of a birth may bring up fear at first, especially if all your mental images of birth are frightening. Repeated viewing of a birth video can neutralize your emotions.

Remember, fear is created by the beliefs you have about a particular image. If fear is a big issue for you, we suggest that you repeat "The Power of Focus" exercises found in Chapter Five concerning questions, beliefs, and values. The exercises in Chapter Three, "Verbal Affirmations: Clearing a Space" and "Visual Affirmations: Picture Perfect," can also be helpful.

Other forms of stress inoculation have been introduced to you in this book, such as visual and verbal affirmations. If you have had stress inoculation, by the time labor begins, much of your anxiety will have been cleared.

Mandala: *Stress Inoculation*

Materials: One large sheet of white art paper plus a pad of colored construction paper (variety of colors), felt-tip pens, scissors, glue

Purpose: To help you inventory the skills you've developed for managing pain in labor

Technique:

1. Draw a large circle in the center of your art paper. Inside the circle print the word *PAIN* in large letters.
2. Sit quietly for a moment. Review the skills you have learned for dealing with pain and discomfort, such as birth information, support team, Power of Focus, imagery, breathing, Power of Silence.
3. Locate the center of your circle. Using different colors of construction paper to represent each skill you have learned, cut pie-shaped wedges to fit into your large circle. The size of each piece will be determined by how well you

have developed that particular pain-management skill. For instance, *Information* may be a large piece, while *Breathing* may be a smaller one. Label each slice of your pie.

4. Arrange and glue the pieces into your pie. The goal is to cover the *Pain* circle with colored pie pieces. Display your mandala where you see it frequently and acknowledge yourself for having developed these pain-management skills.

5. As you continue doing pain-management exercises in this book and develop more skills, you can make another circle and expand the pieces of the pie until the circle is filled with labeled wedges.

Passage

Passage encompasses the events of labor. Labor is the process of the baby moving down through the pelvis and birth canal. The woman's body must adjust to accommodate for this movement. The Birth Energy makes itself known at this time through an increasingly powerful chain of events: the latent, active, and transition phases of labor. For more detailed information about the phases of labor, we recommend the following:

Pregnancy, Childbirth and the Newborn, by Penny Simkin, Janet Whalley, and Anne Keppler

A Good Birth, A Safe Birth, by Diana Korte and Roberta Scaer

What to Expect When You're Expecting, by Arlene Eisenberg et al.

When labor is graphed, it is measured according to time and centimeters of cervical dilation. This is called a Friedman curve (see page 170). According to this chart, women are supposed to dilate 1.5 centimeters every hour. This purely physical standard is based on statistical norms. Physicians and nurses tend to become alarmed if labor deviates from the Friedman curve. However, if a woman doesn't follow the norm, it isn't always indicative of a problem.

When a woman is in labor, she is not thinking about centimeters and Friedman Curves. Rather, she is experiencing a broad range of emotions that accompany each phase of labor. You need to know about the emotional hurdles along with the physical signs of progress during labor. While in labor a woman can become discouraged and depressed if she focuses only on physical signs. Penny Simkin has pointed out that these emotional hurdles during labor parallel the Friedman Curve. Just as there is an increase in physical activity, there is an increase in emotional tension with each phase of labor. The following graph shows these emotional hurdles:

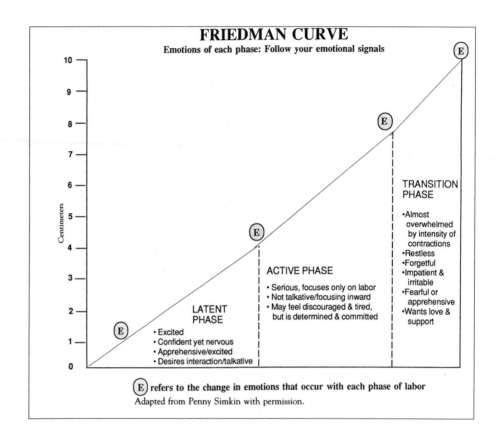

FRIEDMAN CURVE

Emotions of each phase: Follow your emotional signals

TRANSITION PHASE
- Almost overwhelmed by intensity of contractions
- Restless
- Forgetful
- Impatient & irritable
- Fearful or apprehensive
- Wants love & support

ACTIVE PHASE
- Serious, focuses only on labor
- Not talkative/focusing inward
- May feel discouraged & tired, but is determined & committed

LATENT PHASE
- Excited
- Confident yet nervous
- Apprehensive/excited
- Desires interaction/talkative

(E) refers to the change in emotions that occur with each phase of labor
Adapted from Penny Simkin with permission.

Pain in Labor

The uterus is a hollow muscle. As your baby grows, the uterus stretches to accommodate its increasing size. Then, during labor and delivery, the different fibers of the uterine muscle work in harmony to birth your baby. In addition to this principal muscle, two other sets of muscles, the abdominal and perineal, function like supporting actors in this drama of life.

As any athlete knows, if muscles are stretched without gradual preparation and sufficient oxygen, pain will result. Without oxygen lactic acid in the bloodstream increases, resulting in painful muscle spasms.

Hence the most important conditioning for the abdominal and perineal muscles is gentle stretching accompanied by deep, rhythmic breathing. Doing these exercises during pregnancy will help decrease labor pain.

Deep, rhythmic breathing and gentle stretching also release endorphins into your bloodstream. The word *endorphin* comes from the word *endogenous*, meaning "coming from within," and morphine, the strongest painkiller available. Endorphins are your body's own natural way of producing morphine.

Endorphins are very potent, but their life span is short. Since they are best released through movement and breathing, it is important to do both during labor. If one form of movement or breathing doesn't make you feel comfortable, try another. For instance, walking may not work, but yoga stretches might. The following are books that contain specific exercises for uterine, abdominal, and perineal muscles:

Positive Pregnancy Fitness, by Sylvia Klein Olkin

Prenatal Yoga and Natural Birth, by Jeannine Parvati Baker

Guide to Moving Through Pregnancy, by Elisabeth D. Bing

Working with the abdominal and perineal muscles also tends to release emotions. These areas of the body often hold unacknowledged feelings. In addition to doing the physical exercises, do the Cluster Writing activity subtitled "A Quick Look at Feelings" in Chapter Three. Use some of the following words: *abdomen, pelvis, vagina, birth canal, pushing,* and *squatting*.

Early Labor

The first stage of labor is called the *latent* phase (1 to 4 centimeters' dilation). During this stage you will face the big question "How will I know if I am really in labor?" Relying only on the due date to let you know when labor will begin may make you feel indecisive, unsure of yourself, and frustrated. Your uncertainty may be accompanied by fear. However, during the last month of pregnancy you will begin to feel signs that your body is preparing for birth. Penny Simkin developed a graph to help couples identify these changes (see *Pregnancy, Childbirth and the Newborn* by Simkin, Whalley, and Keppler). With her permission we have adapted it on page 172 for your use.

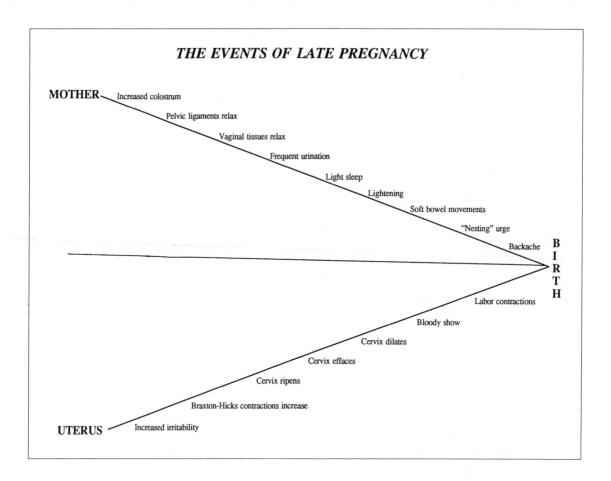

THE EVENTS OF LATE PREGNANCY

MOTHER — Increased colostrum

Pelvic ligaments relax

Vaginal tissues relax

Frequent urination

Light sleep

Lightening

Soft bowel movements

"Nesting" urge

Backache

B I R T H

Labor contractions

Bloody show

Cervix dilates

Cervix effaces

Cervix ripens

Braxton-Hicks contractions increase

UTERUS — Increased irritability

Inventory: *Tuning In*

Materials: A large piece of art paper and felt-tip pens
Purpose: To observe the changes occurring in your body and detect with greater accuracy whether or not labor is about to begin
Technique:

1. Place your paper so that the shortest dimension is running from top to bottom.
2. Using your dominant hand and drawing from left to right on the page, make a large arrow-shaped graph like the one above. Label it as shown: *Mother* and *Uterus* on the left side of the graph, and *Birth* at the point of the arrow.
3. Over the days leading up to your due date, observe your body and note the different changes that are occurring (e.g., light sleep, frequent urination, backache, soft bowel movements, nesting urge). Record them under the heading of *Mother* on your chart.

4. Under *Uterus* write down your experiences of the changes in your uterus, such as increased Braxton-Hicks contractions and bloody discharge. Include any observations made by your caregiver regarding changes in your uterus or cervix.
5. With your non-dominant hand, in the center of the graph write any feelings and reactions to your physical changes (e.g., serious, tense, restless, becoming discouraged).
6. Post your graph where you can see it frequently and add to it. (If you have a special room for your baby, it is a good place to display your artwork.)

Active Labor

In the next stage of labor dilation extends from 4 to 8 centimeters. At the beginning of this phase the birth energy is still very fragile. Most animals inhibit labor unless they are in a private place where they feel safe; humans have the same reactions. Unusual changes can cause a woman's labor pattern to slow down or stop as a protection device. For instance, if a woman is not having a home birth, the onset of active labor is usually the time when she thinks she should go to the hospital or birth center. When she arrives, it is not uncommon for labor to stop completely. The frightened Inner Child is likely to be activated by unfamiliar surroundings and clinical procedures performed by strangers. She perceives the hospital as a strange and therefore unsafe place. Because the Inner Child lives in the body, it may shut labor down as a form of protection.

Tawana's labor stopped when she arrived at the hospital.

Labor started in the night. For about an hour my contractions were coming every five minutes. My sister was with me, and although we weren't sure I was in labor, we decided to go to the hospital. We remembered to bring some familiar things. I was glad we had, because soon after arrival my labor pains completely stopped. I felt really weird because I couldn't get them started again.

We asked the nursing staff to leave us alone for a while. We put pillowcases from home on the pillows and put out my own colored washcloth and face towel to use. I decided to wear my own nightgown because it made me feel more normal and comfortable. I even set my cosmetics out where I could see them on the shelf. I remembered what I had learned in class about "claiming the territory."

We got through setting up the room and went for a walk in the corridors so that I could scope it out. It really worked! After an hour and a half my labor started up again. The rest of my labor went really fast. The nurses were great. They allowed me to do what I wanted, and I delivered my healthy baby daughter soon afterward. I believe that "claiming the territory" is really important.

You are in active labor when contractions are coming three to four minutes apart (or closer together) and are demanding your full concentration. (When a contraction occurs, you must stop whatever you are doing and focus on it completely.) When your labor pattern is well established, it will be less likely to stop. (It may slow down, but generally it won't stop completely.)

As Tawana discovered, utilizing her five senses really helped reestablish her labor pattern. The following section will give you ideas as to how to do this.

Being SENSE-able

The senses are sharpened or enhanced during labor. Impulses from your five senses (sight, hearing, taste, smell, touch) travel faster to your brain than pain sensations. When activated in a positive manner, your senses can decrease or slow up the ability of your brain to recognize pain. Your conscious mind can only hold one thought at a time, and your body will automatically act on that thought. If information from your five senses gets to the brain first, you will be better able to control the pain sensations surrounding your labor and birth experience. Following is a review of information that will help you use all five senses during labor.

SIGHT
- Visits to your chosen birthplace before labor begins.

- During pregnancy visualizing yourself in labor in the birthplace—"claiming the territory."

- A focal point—move the focal point closer to you as your labor progresses.

- Things of interest in the room or outside.

- Your partner's face—focusing on eyes is sometimes too intense; use another part of the face.

- Pictures in your inner mind that you have created, such as your "special place."

- Pictures or artwork from home that make you feel comfortable and safe.

HEARING

- Making frequent visits to your chosen birthplace and becoming used to the sounds there—part of "claiming the territory."

- Your partner's voice.

- A recording of comfortable, familiar, safe sounds from your own daily environment.

- Taped music you enjoy that has a pronounced rhythm or beat.

- Imagining the sound of your baby's hello or having a conversation with your baby.

- Enjoying the rhythmical sound of the baby's heartbeat on the fetal monitor. (Link up the sounds of your baby to your "special place.")

- Hearing the comforting sounds you have chosen to make during birth (we call them birth songs). Remember, keep your jaw loose and your mouth partially open when making your birth sounds.

TASTE

- Kissing your partner frequently during labor.

- Drinking cool or warm beverages (such as ice chips or tea).

- Using mouthwash or breath freshener.

- Sucking on your favorite lollipop (lemon flavor or sweet-sour tastes seem to be the favorites). *Never* use small hard candies; you might choke on them.

- Sucking on your favorite flavored Popsicle.

- Drinking power beverages. (This tastes good in labor, gives you energy, and balances fluid and electrolytes in your system.)

- In long labor, eating soft or liquid foods, such as soup or pudding.

- Eating easily digestible high-energy snacks.

SMELL

- Visits to your birthing place to become accustomed to the different smells.

- Your partner close to you. (Note to partners: Don't wear clothes that have strong odors such as cologne, body odor, or toxic chemical smells, such as gasoline or paint.)

- Familiar smells, such as your or your partner's pillow.

- A blend of odors you have created that smell good to you. (Remember to avoid strong odors.)

TOUCH

- Your partner holding you.

- Any pressure on your skin such as someone holding your hand, rubbing your back, or massaging your tummy.

- Moving your joints, walking, rocking, rotating your hips as in dancing. (Remember to change positions frequently in labor.)

- Moving your face, smiling, laughing, yawning.

- Pressing your feet firmly on the floor (also foot rubs and cold or hot applications to your feet).

- Warm things, cold things, wet things, such as warm, moist compresses on your bottom, back, or lower abdomen.

- Pressure on your perineum (sitting on a hard surface, such as a rocking chair, or putting a pillow between your legs so that it presses on the perineum).

- Vibration, especially on the mid and lower back.

- Stroking your hair or having it brushed. (Remember to brush in the direction that your hair grows.)

- Breathing deeply and rhythmically.

- Laboring in water.

Stress

Paying attention to your body movements and the emotions they create is great preparation for birth. Notice what you do when you have strong emotions such as anger, stress, worry, or fear. Also notice what brings you out of these emotional states. Is it a hug, kiss, or smile? Is it a positive thought, a change in the questions you're asking yourself?

Get to know your body's response. *Claim the territory!* You can do a lot of this by yourself, but it helps to have other people's input. Get your partner or main support person to begin noticing your movements and your emotions. Notice what creates stress and what reduces or relieves it. Whatever way you react to stress is the same way you will react during the stress of labor.

Sometimes couples instinctively know what their partner likes and dislikes, but often the opposite is true. You can't communicate what you want until you are aware of it yourself. Sharing the following exercise with your main support person will help you do that. It builds a stronger support team.

Communication: *Stressing Out*

Materials: Journal and felt-tip pens
Optional: Large paper, crayons, markers
Note: Do this activity with your primary support person
Purpose: To observe and better understand how you communicate under stress.
To develop a stronger support team for birth.
Technique:

1. Become quiet. Think of a time when you were under stress. Using your dominant hand, respond to the following questions:

   • How did you react to the stressful situation you thought of? For example, did you cry, sleep, get angry, hit things?

   • What did you say under stress? Did you swear, yell, or were you silent?

   • How did you move your face? Did you bite your lip, clench your jaw, or furrow your brow?

   • How did you clear your stress? Did you laugh, change the scene or activity, or say or do a particular thing?

(continued on next page)

2. Ask your birth partner or main support person to do this next part of this exercise. Think of a time when your partner was under stress. Write your observations about her during that time. Answer the following questions:

- How did she react to the stressful situation you thought of? Did she cry, sleep, get angry, or hit things?

- What did she say under stress? Did she swear, yell, or was she silent?

- How did she move her face? Did she bite her lip, clench her jaw, or furrow her brow?

- Were you involved in clearing her stress? If so, how did you do it? Did you get her to laugh, change the scene or activity, or do something in particular?

3. Take turns sharing your journal responses with each other.
4. Using this information, decide *specifically* what your partner can do to help you when you are under stress. Can she squeeze your hand, sit quietly beside you, crack a joke, hold you, or massage your feet and shoulders?
5. Write this list in your journal and share your ideas with your partner.

Now that your partner knows how you react to stress, it will be easier for him or her to support you during labor. As listed in the "Being SENSE-able" section, there are several ways you can help yourself during labor. The most commonly overlooked way is through the use of music. Unfortunately most hospitals have not figured this out, because they do not have the equipment available for taped music. Therefore *do not* forget this important part of your birth equipment. Make sure to bring a portable (battery-operated) tape player, extra batteries, and music tapes of your choice.

Music

As you listen to various styles of music, you may notice that the rhythms, pitch, and tempo have different effects on your body. High-pitched, faster, more vibrant music creates a playful and happy mood. Low-pitched, quiet, and slower rhythms create a feeling of calm. Music activates the flow of memories stored in the right hemisphere of the brain. During labor if you play music that is associated with pleasant memories, your body will *automatically* respond favorably.

Your baby is also highly responsive to music. By the fifth month she hears sounds clearly and can distinguish between your voice and other people's. She can also express her likes and dislikes about music. Therefore she will respond with less stress if you are playing her favorite music during labor.

Heidi found that when she listened to "hard rock," her baby moved in a very vigorous manner. She felt like he was really "rocking out," either "having a ball or getting upset." She wasn't sure which. Heidi experimented with other upbeat but more mellow music. The baby's movements were active, but not as agitated. Heidi sensed that he did not like the "hard rock" music. Her journal dialogue with the baby confirmed her feelings.

Pay attention to your baby's response to various types of music. Note the movements she makes. See if you can tell which kinds of music she likes and doesn't like.

Child Chat: *Listening In*

Materials: Recorded music of your choice, journal, felt-tip pens
Purpose: To help you learn more about your baby's response to sound by noticing his likes and dislikes
Technique:

1. Listen to different styles of music. How do you feel about the music? Write down your feelings.
2. Make a note of any movements your baby makes while listening to the music.
3. Ask your baby how he feels about that particular piece of music. Use your non-dominant hand for his response.

• You may want to try listening to some of the following music:

Dolphin Dreams, by Jonathan Goldman
Rain Dance, by Philip Elcano
Music to Be Born By, by Mickey Hart
Transitions, by Placenta Music
Relax with the Classics, by the Lind Institute
Canon in D Minor: With Nature's Ocean Sounds, by Pachelbel
Love Chords: Music for the Pregnant Mother and her Unborn Child, compiled by Thomas Verny

(continued on next page)

Soothing "popular" music
Your favorite religious music

Note: Sources for these recordings are listed in the Resource Guide.

- Your baby may really enjoy relaxing to baroque and baroquelike music. Because of the slow and consistent rhythm it most resembles your resting heartbeat. Try listening to music of composers such as Mozart, Handel, Haydn, Boccherini, Vivaldi, and J. S. Bach.

Transition Phase of Labor

The third and most challenging stage of labor is called *transition.* The forces of the labor contractions are so intense that it is easy to feel overwhelmed by them. By this time fatigue may have set in, and emotions may be pretty raw. Commonly it is during transition that the woman says, "I don't know if I can go on with this." She knows she can't turn back, but she wishes it were over with. Does she have the energy? Does she have the courage?

Transition is also the most challenging time for those in attendance, particularly for the woman's partner or main support person. The intense physical sensations accompanied by strong emotions produce an energy that is sometimes overwhelming for everyone in the room. If you saw your partner looking flushed and glassy-eyed one minute and cold and shaking involuntarily the next, followed by sounds of desperation, what would you think? Most people think that normal expressions of this phase of labor are signs that something is seriously wrong, that the woman is ill. However, all of these behaviors are normal and appropriate. Rather than indicating that something is wrong, they show that birth is imminent.

People attending the birth should learn about the emotional as well as the physical signs of each phase of labor. Inform your support persons about how to recognize this phase of labor so that they can reassure themselves and you that everything is normal and fine.

The good news is that though this is the most intense stage of labor, it is also the *shortest.* Another advantage is that your body responds most easily to new stimuli at this time. If you are feeling overwhelmed by powerful emotions, a fast way to shift them is to alter your breathing and your movement. Here are some guidelines:

1. Breathing and vocalization during contractions

   - Emphasize the "out" breath

   - Keep your vocalization low-pitched (no screaming)

   - Do rhythmic breathing and vocalization simultaneously with your coach

2. Movement

   - Listen to your body and change positions often

   - Move your face, smile, laugh, relax your jaw, open your mouth, yawn

   - Squat to open the pelvic outlet so that your baby can turn more easily

In Chapter Four you began creating your "special place" through imagery. To help you prepare for the final stage of labor, we will introduce the Birth Cave imagery. The goal of Birth Cave imagery is to experience a womblike environment and help you focus on your baby's birth. Some women actually experience memories and feelings of being in their own mother's womb. This is a natural reaction to Birth Cave imagery. If you need to clear unresolved feelings about your own birth, do some of the journaling exercises from Chapter Three, such as: "Drawing the Inside Out," "Full of Feelings," or "Cluster Writing."

Imagery: *The Birth Cave*

Section A

First, do this part alone and record your feelings in your journal. Later you can share this with your main support person.

As with the earlier exercise, you may want to record the following narration. The wording and phraseology are just like the exercise done previously in Chapter Four. The dots following each phrase indicate places to pause as you read the text.

1. Cross the hallway into your "special place." . . . Once there, take a walk . . . On the walk you come across a cave. Stand for a moment at the entrance to the cave and contemplate going in. . . . How do you feel? Is the cave inviting or scary? . . . Notice if you are willing to enter the

(continued on next page)

cave. . . . When you feel ready to do so, go into the cave. . . . (It may take more than one imagery session before you feel comfortable entering the cave. That's okay. Just keep doing the exercise until you can enter it.)

Inside the cave there is a warm glow. You are surrounded by a soft light and a peaceful atmosphere. . . . Stand inside the cave and notice your feelings (allow at least one minute here). . . .

2. Come out of the cave into the light of your "special place" and walk back across the hallway in your mind. Slowly and gently become aware of your physical surroundings and your body.

3. In your journal write your feelings about having been in the cave.

Continue going back into the Birth Cave daily. If questions or strong feelings present themselves, seek out the answers or reasons for those feelings. You may want to talk to a family member or close friend of your family who knew you when you were a child and can answer your questions. When you are able to claim the Birth Cave as your present baby's space, continue with the next phase of this exercise.

Imagery: *Birth Cave (continued)*

Section B

This section is to be done with your partner. Read the instructions together first and then begin the imagery exercise.

1. Go to your "special place" together. . . . Describe your Birth Cave to your partner. . . . Invite your partner to enter the Birth Cave with you. . . . Once inside, allow an image of your baby to emerge. . . . Talk to your baby. . . . After both of you experience the baby and your feelings about the cave, come back to your "special place." Cross the hallway in your mind and return back to an awareness of your physical surroundings and your body.

2. Sit and share with each other what you felt and experienced. With your non-dominant hand, each of you draw the image of how you saw your baby. Write down what he or she said.

Note: Some partners find it quite difficult at first to imagine their baby, let alone talk to it. If this is true for you, don't worry about it. Just keep going to the Birth Cave together and focusing on your baby. Your partner will eventually become comfortable with the experience and feel included in your preparation. If this does not happen, be sure to do this exercise alone. It will be an important image for you during labor and birth.

The following section of the Birth Cave imagery works well in combination with perineal massage, described on the next page. This is generally done during the last six weeks of pregnancy.

Imagery: *Birth Cave (continued)*

Section C

1. In your mind's eye continue going into the Birth Cave daily. Examine and notice the walls. Repair and strengthen any places that seem weak. (Don't question whether this works, just do it together. The power of the mind is very great.)
2. As you examine the cave walls, you find a tunnel. . . . (Before continuing, in your imagination put the baby in a safe place and tell it *not to follow you*. Tell the baby that when the time is right, you will come and help it through the tunnel. Once the baby is in a safe place, you and your partner may begin to explore the tunnel.)
3. You notice some interesting things about this tunnel. It is moist and the walls are soft. They give to your touch. . . . As you continue exploring you see that the tunnel opens out into your "special place," though in a different part. . . . You recognize that by passing through this tunnel, your baby can one day join you in your "special place."
4. Continue imagining going back into the tunnel, checking it out, and preparing it for your baby to come through. . . . Is it too narrow? . . . Are there rocks or barriers in the way? . . . Are there any other obstructions? . . . (The obstructions may appear in the form of images. When the image appears, dialogue with it, asking questions similar to those in the dialogue exercises you did with your body in Chapter Two.)

Note: Do this daily if possible. When the birth is imminent, the tunnel will be clear and the baby's passage will be opened. At that time you will be physically and mentally ready to open up for your baby's birth. Remember, doing this exercise is a very important way to *claim the territory* and establish feelings of partnership in preparation for your baby's birth.

Perineal Massage

During delivery the pressure of the baby's head moving down through the birth canal opens the folds of the vagina *naturally*. This is the same *natural* way the petals of a rose unfold to the warmth of the sun. In order for this to occur, the muscles of the perineum and vagina must be relaxed, soft, and elastic. Gentle stretching is the best way to prepare these muscles for this natural expansion and opening.

In many cultures this preparation for childbirth is happening inadvertently throughout a woman's life. Squatting naturally conditions the perineal muscles. Women squat for their normal everyday activities, such as sitting, urinating, defecating, resting, and working. These routine daily activities relax the perineal muscles. Therefore at the time of birth the perineal muscles are ready for the work they will do.

Industrialized nations leave women at a disadvantage in this regard. Our habitual patterns of movement neglect the pelvic-floor muscles, which are so important in childbearing. Physically we are not prepared in the course of daily life for childbirth. Seldom do we do any activities that naturally exercise these muscles. We have to take classes and read books in order to learn how to do something that should come naturally. Because of this lack of preparation the likelihood of having an episiotomy or seriously tearing these muscles during delivery is quite high.

If you want to avoid an episiotomy, we suggest that the following exercise be done *daily* (or as often as possible) for six weeks prior to your due date. By massaging and stretching the perineal muscles the pelvic floor is strengthened. By stretching them these muscles become conditioned for the work they are about to do. This exercise relaxes the walls of the vagina and teaches you to focus on it as your baby's "birth tunnel." It complements the part of the Birth Cave imagery you just learned and is most successful when done in conjunction with it.

Before you begin, breathe deeply and rhythmically. Tune in to your baby and visualize your Birth Cave.

Perineal Massage: *Opening to Your Baby*

Materials: A bowl of warm water, washcloth or similar compress, wheat germ oil or K-Y jelly, pillows, mirror. Be sure your hands are clean and your fingernails short. If your hands are rough, it's good to wear lightweight rubber (surgical) gloves. (Don't use mineral oil or petroleum jelly; these substances clog pores, do not properly absorb into the body, and do not help the tissues relax.)

Purpose: To strengthen and relax the perineal musculature. To help you prepare emotionally and physically for birth.

Technique:

1. First do this exercise alone so that you can get to know this part of your body and begin to address emotions that come up during the exercise.
2. It helps to put a mirror in front of you so that you can see the perineum. You should be seated with your legs open, knees bent (squatting but leaning back into pillows that support your body so that you can relax).
3. Dip the washcloth into the bowl of warm water and wring it out. Press the warm compress to your perineum. Hold it there for about half a minute. This warmth relaxes the muscles in preparation for the massage. Repeat this while focusing on your Birth Cave imagery and the birth tunnel.
4. Lubricate your thumbs with oil or a water-soluble jelly. Rub enough of the oil or jelly into the whole perineal area so that your fingers and hands move smoothly over it.
5. Insert your thumbs into your vagina up to the second knuckle. Once your thumb is well inside your vagina, press down toward your anus until you feel a stretching and burning sensation. Once you feel that pressure, stop and hold it. Breathe into the burning sensation. Relax while imaging clearing a space in the birth tunnel. Pay attention to your feelings.
6. Slowly move your thumbs in an outward and upward direction, sliding in a **U** shape up the walls of your vagina. Notice your feelings; what are you saying to yourself while doing this?
7. After massaging this area, remove your thumbs from your vagina. Again lubricate your thumb and forefinger. With your thumb inside your vagina and your pointer finger on the outside, gently pinch the muscle that runs between your vagina and anal opening. Gently massage that sling of muscular tissue in a back-and-forth movement. (This is the major muscle that will sustain the pressure of the baby's head as it emerges. It needs to be made more flexible by exercise and massage.)

(continued on next page)

> *Note:* Stop anytime you feel like you need or want to stop. For instance, you may want to stop just after putting your thumbs inside your vagina, or partway through the exercise. That is perfectly okay. Stop and process whatever feelings are coming up. Remember, the goal is to *clear the space* and *claim the territory*.

We encourage you to do this exercise. Let go of your doubts and fears. If you find you are unable to do this exercise because strong emotions such as fear, repugnance, and revulsion get in the way, talk to a professional counselor or to your caregiver. You need to know how to get past your upset feelings, because your baby is going to pass through this area of your body. It is best to face and challenge any uncomfortable feelings now. Your goal is to think of this part of your body comfortably, even joyfully.

Women who have suffered sexual abuse that involved violation and penetration in this area very often have strong emotional feelings come to the surface when they attempt this exercise. Should this happen at any time, stop and acknowledge your feelings. Allow yourself to cry or experience these strong emotions. Do not proceed until you have cleared your negative feelings by journaling about them. (Repeat the exercises found earlier in this book, such as those found in Chapter Three concerning the Inner Child.)

It may take some women many days or weeks to come to a place of feeling comfortable about this phase of the exercise. That's all right. Stay with your feelings. Don't turn this exercise into a "have to" or a "should." When you feel ready, invite your partner to do this exercise with you. (If you do not feel love and safety with your partner, do not have him do this exercise with you.)

Your partner does the same preparation of your perineum, but lubricates his forefingers, instead of his thumbs. Inserting the forefinger of each hand, up to the second knuckle, he presses down *slowly* toward your anus. Direct him as to how much pressure you can handle. He then *slowly* slides his fingers up the sides of your vagina, exerting gentle pressure and stretching the vagina open as he does so.

Next your partner removes his forefingers and inserts his thumb into your vagina. With his forefinger on the outside and thumb in your vagina he gently but firmly grasps the sling of muscle between your vagina and anal opening. He massages that sling of muscle in a back-and-forth movement. Again, if emotions come up, process them together. You must let any negative or fear feelings out.

(*Note to partners:* This is one of the most beneficial exercises you can do to help with birth preparation. Do not be afraid to exert gentle but firm pressure against the perineal muscles. This will produce a burning feeling and sensations of stretching, but so will the baby's head. Your goal is to help prepare this area by gently stretching the vaginal opening prior to birth. Follow the woman's lead and do as she requests. Stop immediately and do not push if she does not want to. Help her share any difficult feelings that may come up. Pay attention to your own emotions. Journal your difficult feelings as well as loving feelings about the experience. You may want to share these feelings with your partner. Repeat this exercise daily or as often as possible. After doing this exercise for a couple of weeks, you should see a noticeable difference in the elasticity of the perineal muscles. Eventually you should be able to do the exercise using two forefingers—on each hand.)

During this exercise pay attention to your feelings as they arise. As you and your partner release any fears or blocks you may have stored in this part of your body, acknowledge your feelings and discuss them together. To reinforce your good feelings, write about them in your journal. This is a very good opportunity to strengthen your relationship with your partner and with your baby as you prepare the birth tunnel for her.

During late pregnancy Paulette combined Birth Cave imagery and perineal massage. Several times throughout labor she focused on the Birth Cave and tunnel as her son, Geoffrey, pushed his head through the birth canal. As the perineum stretched to accommodate her baby's head, Paulette was able to relax into the experience instead of feeling fear. Geoffrey's birth was fulfilling and enjoyable.

Passenger
Welcoming Your Baby: From Pain to Pleasure

Until the last decade medical experts still believed that the brain of newborns and infants was not completely formed and that therefore babies had no feelings. Physicians believed that a newborn couldn't feel and react as an older baby would. The idea that birth would have any lasting emotional impact on the baby was considered impossible. We now know that this is *not* true. (Unfortunately there are some medical professionals who still hold this belief.)

Over the last three decades medical research has discovered many fascinating facts about the unborn baby's ability to learn and remember. Following are some of the facts about the innate capabilities of your unborn baby:

Seven Weeks:

- Sensitive and aware
- Makes facial expressions (squints, scowls, sneers)
- Makes combative movements
- Cries audibly
- Expresses pain
- Shows perplexity, disdain, and fear

Fourteen Weeks:

- Discriminates between sweet and bitter tastes
- Listens throughout the skin
- Reaches and grasps the umbilical cord
- Finds her toes and sucks on them
- Stretches, scratches, rubs hands and feet together, and yawns
- Is aware of light

Twenty-eight Weeks:

- Hears and recognizes speech patterns

At Birth:

- Has heightened sense of smell
- Distinguishes odor of mother (e.g., breast odors and perfume)
- Has adequate vision for intimate distances of 12 to 16 inches (distance from mother's face to her breast)

- Recognizes songs and stories that he was exposed to in the womb

Your baby remembers birth quite clearly. Reactions to any trauma are stored in your infant's body and memory. These memories of trauma can be accessed months or years later. This has been documented by psychologist David Chamberlain in his book *Babies Remember Birth*, and by psychiatrist Thomas Verny in *The Secret Life of the Unborn Child*. Our own personal life and clinical experience brought us to the same conclusion. *Babies have feelings and consciousness in utero and at birth. The birth experience has an impact on one's entire life.* This conviction has shaped our approach to labor, delivery, and early parenting.

Because your baby is so sensitive and aware at birth, it is vitally important that you begin protecting and nurturing her from the start. This is especially crucial during labor and delivery. Question any pain-producing procedures that are suggested. If you think a procedure will hurt you, it will definitely affect your baby. Many physicians and nurses are still unaware of this fact. They still tell parents that newborns don't feel pain the way an adult does. This is simply not true.

Birth Positions

During labor your baby moves down through your pelvis and on through your vagina. To descend your baby must make several small but very important turns. These are called "cardinal movements" and have been clearly described in childbirth preparation books such as *Pregnancy, Childbirth and the Newborn*, by Simkin, Whalley, and Keppler, and *Special Delivery*, by Rahima Baldwin and Terra Palmerini Richardson.

Throughout the stages of labor various birth positions enhance the baby's movements. For centuries women from other cultures have instinctively birthed in the squatting position. They have squatted to labor and deliver because they found that the baby births more easily in this position. In this culture we are starting to rediscover why this is true.

Attached to the pelvic bones and running down to the knees are two very strong ligaments. When you squat, these ligaments pull on the pelvic bones and widen the birth cavity. In late labor (7 centimeters' dilation) squatting is most beneficial because it provides additional room for the baby to get into a favorable birth position. In addition gravity assists with the downward descent. When you squat, visualize your baby turning and descending through the birth canal.

To combine squatting and visualization, you can prepare a "storyboard" of the descent of your baby. A storyboard is like a comic strip with pictures showing the desired sequence of events.

Birth Storyboard: *Moving into Place*

Materials: Large sheet of art paper, colored felt-tip markers, book or pamphlet with pictures and explanations of the baby's six cardinal movements during birth: engagement, flexion, internal rotation, extension, external rotation, and birth

Purpose: To visualize the five cardinal movements the baby makes during delivery. To combine imagery with practice in squatting for birth.

Technique:

1. Place your paper horizontally so that the shortest dimension is running from top to bottom. Draw a comic strip of six boxes from left to right. Begin in the box on the extreme left side. Using your non-dominant hand, draw your baby making the first cardinal movement.
2. Proceed across the page, drawing each of the six cardinal movements. The sixth box shows your baby being born.
3. Display your storyboard where you can see it while you are practicing your squatting exercise.
4. In a squatting position look at your Birth Storyboard. Imagine your baby making these movements as you mentally see yourself giving birth.

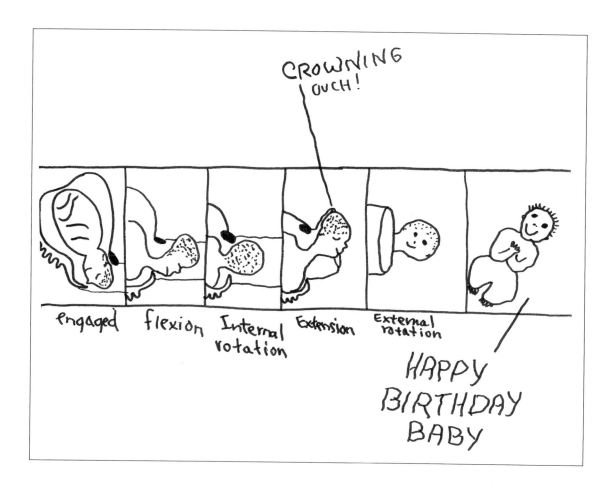

Your and the Baby's Comfort During Delivery

When most people think of sound and labor, they hear women scream-ing, out of control. When we speak of sound during delivery, that is *not* what we are talking about. On the contrary, purposeful sound produced consciously and with preparation is an important part of a joyful birth. We call sounds of birth "birth songs." Appropriate sound produces vibrations that calm and soothe the baby. If you have been practicing chanting throughout pregnancy, the sound you will be making during delivery will be familiar and reassuring to your baby, like a lullaby. Vocalizing or making chanting sounds requires deep breathing, which energizes and relaxes you and your baby. Chanting has been used by almost all cultures throughout the world for healing purposes. This tradition continues today in the practices of Native American shamans, African medicine men, Australian aborigines, and Indian yogis.

Here are some specific recommendations about "birth songs" in labor:

- On the out breath make the sound of one of the vowel tones you have been practicing. Stay with the open vowels, such as *ah-aaaaaaaaaaaaa* or *oh-oooooooooooo*. Imagine you are singing a lullaby to your baby. These vowel tones relax the jaw.

- *Avoid* tones like *AYE-IIIIIIIIIIII* or *EEEEEEEEEEE*. These tones cause your jaw muscles to tighten, which produces tension in your body and pelvis. This muscle tension closes down the relaxation of the uterine muscle and inhibits the dilation of the cervix. These sounds also frighten your baby.

- Keep your vocalizations low pitched. (Do low moaning versus high-pitched screams. The latter tightens muscles and breeds tension.)

- Make sounds that follow a rhythm or pattern (such as chanting a mantra or repetitive syllables). These work quickly and maintain relaxation.

- Practice the sounds you will make in labor so that your unborn baby gets used to them.

Breath and Pushing

Breath during the pushing stages of labor is an area of controversy in the Western medical establishment. During delivery most doctors and nurses instruct the woman to hold her breath for a specific count (usually 10) and bear down forcibly to expel the baby. Studies show that holding the breath while forcefully pushing during delivery is actually detrimental. It blocks the oxygen supply to your baby at a time when she needs an abundant supply. When you hold your breath, the uterine muscle is deprived of oxygen and cannot perform optimally. It has been our experience that holding the breath during delivery also makes the amount of time in the pushing phase longer. When the uterine muscle is deprived of oxygen, it tires more easily and functions less efficiently. Delivery becomes longer and more difficult.

Instead of holding your breath, breathe naturally during pushing contractions. Only bear down when you feel your body needs to bear down. (This is like the type of pushing done when starting to have a bowel movement. Your body tells you what to do naturally.) Be patient and *push only when your body tells you to do so*. As long as you and your baby are both doing well, there really is no need to rush this part of birth. (Of course if there is an emergency for your baby, you will be directed to hold your breath and to push forcefully.) If you have been breathing naturally, as suggested, your body won't be overly tired. You will have the strength to push as directed: hard and fast. Between pushing contractions reach down and touch your baby's head. Doing that can bring a feeling of connectedness and renewed energy.

Birth

Perhaps the most joyful and emotion-filled experience of your life occurs at the moment of your baby's birth. The first sight of your newborn is an image that will stay with you for the rest of your life. The moments and first hours that follow this event are profoundly meaningful for you, the baby, and your partner. For this reason we have included a detailed discussion of the postpartum period in Chapter Eight, "Growing into Parenthood."

Placenta

Birth is not complete until the delivery of the placenta. This usually occurs fifteen to twenty minutes after your baby is born. At this point it's very important that you focus your attention on your uterus. The placenta has two large arteries and one vein. After the birth the uterine muscle continues to contract while working to expel the placenta and close down the blood vessels.

When the placenta detaches from the wall of the uterus, major bleeding may occur. To stop the bleeding, the blood vessels must close down. One way to control the bleeding is by massaging the abdomen. When profuse bleeding continues despite abdominal massage, drugs such as pitocin may be used to stimulate the uterus to contract.

As an alternative, we suggest that you use the power of your mind and the Birth Energy to stop the bleeding. Many times women have done this when abdominal massage did not work, thus avoiding medical intervention. They have prepared for this moment with the following exercise:

Imagery: *Think Sponge*

Materials: Sponge or washcloth

Purpose: To create an image of a contraction as preparation for delivery of the placenta

Technique:

1. Observe what you normally do after you have finished using a sponge. You squeeze it until it's no longer dripping.
2. Imagine that following the birth of your baby your uterine muscle is squeezing, just the way you would squeeze a sponge.
3. During pregnancy every time you squeeze a sponge out, tell your body, "Following the birth of the baby, this is what my uterus is going to do."
4. Be sure to share the word *sponge* with your main support person so that he or she can remind you to "think sponge" after the delivery of your baby. The moment that you "think sponge," your body will automatically respond to the conditioning you have given it.

7

Unexpected Outcomes

Birth is a mystery. We cannot control it, nor can we fully understand it with our rational minds. As any woman who has been pregnant or had a baby knows, we do not "make babies." They simply pass through us, as Kahlil Gibran tells us in his book, *The Prophet:*

> *Your children are not your children.*
> *They are the sons and daughters of Life's longing for itself.*
> *They come through you but not from you,*
> *And though they are with you yet they belong not to you.*

We can surrender to birth by honoring and supporting it. We can respect and care for ourselves and the new life with which we have been entrusted. However, we must remember that each human being has a life of his or her own. We are only witnesses to that life. There is a greater, higher power that is in charge of life and death. The name that each person gives to this Higher Power is very personal: God, the Creator, the Spirit, Universal Mind, Yahweh, and so on. When we receive custodianship for a child (which is what we do when we accept a pregnancy), we are surrendering to this mysterious co-creative power.

Without the Creator, birth would not be possible. Without parents this particular child would have no way of incarnating, of embodying its spirit. Whether a child comes to full term, is born, and remains with us (for whatever period of time) is ultimately out of our hands. The moment of birth and the time of passing beyond this life are between the individual and the Creator.

We can do everything in our power to prepare ourselves to welcome the newborn. However, there are things that are out of our control. The Serenity Prayer is relevant: "God, grant me the serenity to accept the things I cannot change, the courage to change the things I can, and the wisdom to know the difference."

Up to this point we have offered tools for cultivating "the courage to change the things we can." Now we turn to another skill: acceptance of the things we cannot change. Birth, like the rest of life, is full of surprises. Sometimes there are unexpected outcomes and surprises that we could not have foreseen and certainly haven't planned for. Some of them are joyful and others may be full of sorrow. It's the chance we take when we accept our part in welcoming a baby into the world. Uncertainty is part of the human condition.

At this time we want to address some of the unexpected outcomes that some parents face. We do this not to frighten you but to be honest about some of the risks. It is better to talk about these risks openly than to carry the fears and anxieties around without expressing them. This is another form of "stress inoculation."

In pregnancy the unexpected can appear in many forms and at different times. Some problems surface during pregnancy, such as toxemia, threatened miscarriage, gestational diabetes, and anemia. Other conditions may appear during labor and birth, such as abruptio placentae, premature birth, or malpresentation of your baby. It is difficult to predict if a labor will be particularly long or painful. Stillbirths and early infant death are unexpected, as is the birth of a handicapped child. Yet these do occasionally occur.

Even if unexpected outcomes cannot be predicted in advance, we can prepare ourselves by learning to accept what life gives us and by allowing and expressing our true feelings about it. It doesn't matter how serious or seemingly unimportant the unexpected outcome is; it is still a blow. The degree of disappointment can vary. Perhaps we were counting on a "natural" childbirth, but an emergency requires medical intervention. Or maybe the surprise element is that the baby arrives much earlier than expected and must be put on life-support systems. Yes, the baby may survive, but parents and family probably feel frightened, sad, angry, or guilty.

In the face of the unexpected outcome, it is crucial to acknowledge your feelings. To glibly pretend everything is okay when it is not simply drives the feelings inward. Sooner or later we need to face them, feel them, and heal them. Our growth is on the other side of our grief.

Like all natural processes, grief unfolds in cycles, as follows:

PAIN	PLEASURE
GRIEVING	**GROWTH**
Steps in the grieving process	Steps in the growth process
1. Shock - denial	1. Shock - becoming aware of: a. What you don't know b. What you can't do c. What you don't have
2. Anger	2. Frustration - Anger
3. Bartering	3. Negotiating Bartering, dealing
4. Sadness	4. Feeling of hopelessness a. Dejection b. Fully aware of the situation c. Sadness
5. Acceptance	5. Getting on with the issue breakthrough - "DO IT"

In this chapter we share with you the experience, strength, and hope of others who have been faced with the unexpected. They have graciously agreed to tell their stories so that those in similar circumstances can be inspired to go on. You might even have friends or family members who have encountered such situations. Their willingness to talk openly about unexpected outcomes can be extremely valuable to them as well as to you.

When There Are Complications During Pregnancy

Difficulties that arise during pregnancy can require additional tests and careful observation by your doctor. Special medication or other precautions may be necessary. This naturally causes fear and concern in a pregnant woman and in her family. It is valuable to journal with your condition and with your unborn child in such circumstances. Ask specific questions about your individual condition.

Lara, a young mother of two healthy babies, faced an unexpected complication in both of her pregnancies. She described it as preterm labor: contractions of the uterus that occur long before the baby is full term. Lara's contractions began at thirty-two weeks with her first pregnancy and at twenty-four weeks with her second pregnancy.

"I had some fear when I found out about the condition," she told us. "I was pregnant for the first time and was concerned." She dealt with the fear by informing herself: reading, asking questions, getting more information, finding out all she could about her condition. She read *The Premature Baby Book*, by Helen Harrison, and found it very helpful. In her reading, Lara found that the chances of a healthy outcome were very good if the baby was born after thirty-two weeks. Lara was given a special medication by her health care practitioner and put on bed rest for the last six weeks of each pregnancy.

Lara's most difficult challenge was staying in bed. To counteract restlessness and boredom, she filled up the time reading and crocheting. "Eight afghans!" she laughed. Adding to her restlessness was the fact that the medication for slowing down the contractions seemed to *activate* her nervous system, making immobility more difficult to handle. Lara got through her first pregnancy successfully and had a happy, natural delivery after a seven-and-a-half-hour labor. Her son, Scottie, was born in an underwater birth at the Upland Birthing Center in

California. Lara spoke in glowing terms of the experience, of her physician, and of her birthing environment.

When Lara became pregnant again three years later, she had to deal with the same condition. This time the uterine contractions began much earlier: twenty-four weeks. "I was a lot more afraid when it happened in the second pregnancy," Lara remembered, "because it was so early." As with her first pregnancy Lara's physician prescribed the same medication and bed rest.

This time Lara faced twelve weeks in bed. As she put it, "This time I knew enough to get myself organized for the long stretch ahead." Her husband set up a mattress in their home office where Lara could use the computer. With the Prodigy program and a modem she joined a national computerized support system, hooking up with others who were dealing with the same condition. Lara used the Parenting Bulletin Board on Prodigy, and found the support network for people on bed rest very useful. She received and shared information and experiences. Through the Prodigy network Lara encountered a twenty-year-old man who had been born around the twenty-fifth week of pregnancy. He was now a healthy adult and an honor student. His survival had been considered a miracle, and now he was sharing it with others who needed strength and hope. Lara was encouraged by his story.

Lara also discovered Sidelines, an organization with national outreach, for women who had been put on bed rest. Lara's second pregnancy ended happily with the full-term birth of another healthy son after a three-and-a-half-hour labor. Like his brother, Timmie was delivered underwater at the Upland Center in a truly joyful birth.

If your pregnancy is challenging and fraught with difficulties, the course of labor may be subject to a lot of medical management. A cesarean delivery may be involved. It is very important for a woman who must have a cesarean that she not see it as a failure on her part. It is not a sign of her inadequacy or an indication that she wasn't giving birth "the right way." If a cesarean becomes unavoidable and is done for the baby's or mother's health or survival, the woman needs support to accept it. The principles we have presented in this book apply to preparation for prevention of or acceptance of cesarean birth. For more insight into cesarean births, see Jane English, *Different Doorway*, in the Grief and Unexpected Outcomes section of the bibliography.

High-Risk Birth

Any high-risk birth need not frighten you if you can retreat to your Birth Cave imagery and enter your "special place." Sharon's story is a perfect example of a high-risk birth:

Following a series of miscarriages, Sharon was in her early forties when she conceived again. Early on in her pregnancy her body threatened another miscarriage with heavy bleeding. Due to the bleeding and her advanced age, an amniocentesis was strongly recommended.

The procedure seemed to go well, and it was determined that indeed she had miscarried. However, another fetus was lying peacefully and safely beside the sac of her miscarried baby. She had been carrying twins. The baby that remained in utero was a healthy boy. Sharon and her husband, Hal, were elated! However, within hours following the test Sharon began having contractions and losing fluid vaginally. The test had ruptured the amniotic sac, and it appeared that she might miscarry the second baby. Over the following days the fluid loss continued, and the situation was critical. She was given only a 10 percent chance of bringing the pregnancy to term. It was even suggested that Sharon and Hal might want to terminate the pregnancy and "try again." Instead Sharon was determined to do everything she could to save this pregnancy. She stayed focused on her goal throughout this challenging pregnancy, labor, and birth.

Sharon was placed on bed rest and given Terbutaline in an attempt to stop the uterine contractions. Despite these medical interventions she continued to experience contractions and fluid loss. She felt afraid and out of control because she had to rely on drugs to get her body to "work right."

Forced to safeguard the baby by remaining quiet and taking medication, Sharon explored her mind's power of control. She was aware of the body-mind connection because of her background in psychology. Her inner guidance found alternatives to the drugs. Her two sisters, who had experienced successful home births, suggested that Sharon try homeopathic remedies, so she sought professional advice from a naturopathic physician. She found that homeopathic remedies work effectively and would not endanger her health or the baby's. She decided to try the remedies suggested. The natural remedies worked, and her condition improved. She was able to discontinue the Terbutaline and bed rest. Sharon was very cautious as her pregnancy progressed.

Her naturopath referred her to Co-Creations. We introduced Sharon and her husband to the Creative Birth Journal techniques. The couple were excited about the concepts they learned. Feelings of joy and expectation began to reawaken. We also introduced the idea of having a doula. One of Sharon's dreams had been to have a home birth, but her high-risk pregnancy made it necessary to deliver in the hospital. However, choosing a doula helped her and Hal imagine a more personal birth in the hospital setting.

At thirty-five weeks Sharon began having contractions again. These contractions were different from the others, and she knew that their son was on his way. Sharon and Hal called their doula. With the doula present she and Hal felt calm enough to stay home for a while. Her sisters were also there supporting them. Together, feeling safe, Hal and Sharon enjoyed the intimacy of early labor at home.

When active labor was well established, they all went to the hospital. Sharon maintained an inner sense of power in spite of potential problems with the interim physician assigned to her case. (Her own physician was out of town.) She and Hal remained in control of the situation and had the kind of labor and birth they wanted. Their baby son was delivered without interventions.

As Sharon held their beautiful son, she reflected on her difficult pregnancy and her present feelings. The patience and fortitude needed during those months contrasted sharply with the joy and satisfaction she felt now.

Fear and Pain

The two primary areas of stress that women identify with labor and birth are fear and pain. Doctors use external medical interventions to relieve pain. Using the medical model, the birthing woman becomes a "patient" and allows the doctor to define pain as being unnatural, an indication that something is wrong. In the hospital setting the woman seldom receives clear and continuous assurance that the way her body is coping with labor is natural. Often she assumes that the pain associated with her birth experience is not normal.

As medical management of her labor increases, she subsequently loses the feeling of being in control. Her fear escalates, her body tenses, and an increased need for intervention follows. A laboring woman often allows external means (such as epidural anesthesia) to alleviate her pain and fear.

During a stressful time such as difficult labor and birth, the mother-to-be needs lots of physical and verbal support. She needs to maintain her confidence and sense of security. Having a doula present before the fear/pain cycle seems insurmountable can help her center herself and gain control.

There are steps you can take to deal with the panic that may occur during a difficult labor:

- Get clear and decide on your plan of action *before* panic hits.

- Learn to communicate feelings of stress and panic to your partner or support person.

- Know your coping strategies. How will you handle an emergency?

- Focus on your support person and follow his or her lead.

Under stress you may find it very difficult to control your own emotions and behavior. If your support person is prepared for an unexpected outcome, you will be able to cope more easily.

For the Support Person

When you are the main labor coach and you must make a difficult decision, try to decide, act on the decision, and then forget it and move on. Sometimes this is easier said than done. The following suggestions can help:

- Catch the conflict by preparing for it and coping with the feelings early.

- Relax: take two or three deep breaths and release your muscles.

- Realize what is happening. Think to yourself, *I am getting upset and need to stay calm.*

- Get your mind off the "problem" and focus on the alternatives.

- Avoid focusing on only one solution.

- Explore. Weigh the benefits against the risks.

- Make the best decision you can based on the information you have and then move on.

If the laboring mother begins to panic or lose control, hold her firmly. Use eye contact and breathe with her. Guide her through the contractions. Never ask her a question *during* a contraction. She needs to concentrate on what is happening in her body. Questions and unnecessary talking distract her. Except for soothing words of love, encouragement, and support speak to her only between contractions. At all times give her lots of love and support.

Emotional Crisis

Sometimes the big surprise during pregnancy or before birth is an external event. A loved one dies, a catastrophic event occurs, or marital problems arise. This happened to Reana. She faced a crisis in her marriage just before her due date.

When Reana became pregnant at age thirty-nine, she felt her prayers had been answered. However, in the last month of pregnancy her husband, Josh, announced that he was in love with another woman. Reana was crushed. How could such a thing happen, especially at this particular time? Her dreams and hopes all seemed to be dissolving before her eyes. How could she go through with labor and birth feeling hurt, rage, and grief? This was not the way she had envisioned having her baby.

At the height of her despair over the situation, Lucia happened to visit Reana's home with a mutual friend. Lucia sat with the sobbing woman, giving her quiet support. Encouraged to honor her feelings without embarrassment, Reana released them without holding back. She later accepted this crisis as an opportunity to take charge of her own pregnancy.

After a while Reana was able to talk about the situation and to engage in dialogue with her Inner Child. When asked, Reana's Inner Child said she wanted Josh to move out. It was not emotionally safe for her to have him there. She did not feel supported or treated fairly and honestly. Lucia then worked with Reana on identifying her support system. Whom could she trust? Who was there for her? Whom did she want at the birth?

The more Reana talked about what *she* wanted and *how* she wanted the birth to go, the stronger and more self-confident she became. Transformed from a victim of circumstance into a powerful woman, she took charge of her child's birth. Lucia reinforced Reana's ability to have the birth exactly the way she wanted it. She built up Reana's sense of her totally lovable and capable self.

Five days later Reana gave birth to a beautiful baby girl. She had a vaginal birth even though a C-section had been strongly recommended because she stalled at 6 centimeters' dilation for six hours. Josh did attend the birth after all, with Reana's permission. Her support system (a childbirth coach and another friend with whom she talked on the phone) were really there for her, she reported. Although Reana's labor was long and painful, birthing her daughter was a joyful experience.

Sexual Abuse: How the Past Impacts Birth

During labor a woman who has a history of sexual abuse often faces unexpected challenges. She may experience the birthing baby as an invader in this traumatized area of her body. Even though the "attack" is not coming from outside (as it did in the past), it still feels like an invasion. This shuts down the Birth Energy. When this happens, the woman's fear and tension increase dramatically. This complicates the birth, endangering both mother and child. Frequently this leads to interventions such as vacuum extraction, forceps delivery, or even a C-section.

Sexually abused women who have done Inner Child dialogues throughout pregnancy have been able to have healthier, less painful births. In most cases they have avoided medical intervention, such as C-sections and episiotomies. Lisa's birth story is a good example:

> My first baby was delivered by C-section. With my second pregnancy I wanted to experience a vaginal birth. Creative Birth Journaling helped

me get in touch with the things I wasn't aware of. Journaling was very helpful, not only for me but for my partner and my other support people. If my support people don't know what I want, how can they be supportive? My support group got to know my moods and what I need to feel safe. When labor began, I felt ready.

I remember that during the last part of the pushing there was some part of me holding back. I didn't seem to have the energy I needed to make progress. It felt like there was something psychological holding me back. My doula suggested that I do a dialogue between my adult self and my Inner Child. I asked my Inner Child what was going on. She needed to know that no one was going to order her around this time. I then shared the dialogue with my physician and birth team, and they helped me to relax and not feel pressured to hurry up.

It seems there was a deeper significance to the timing of Lisa's baby's birth. Her baby was born a few minutes past midnight on Lisa's own father's birthday. (He had been her abuser in childhood.) The baby came to bring joy. Never again would this day hold unpleasant memories for Lisa. It was a beautiful labor, birth, and healing. As a result of this profound birth experience Lisa felt empowered. As she put it, "If I can do that, I can do *anything*."

Labor for Survivors of Sexual Abuse

As labor becomes more intense, strong emotions may arise. Sometimes this can be frightening. There is no more vulnerable time in a woman's life than when she is giving birth. Being able truly to "let go" and trust the safety of her environment is very important. Trusting and "letting go" must happen first from within herself. For the woman who has been physically or sexually abused, this is often quite difficult because she associates being vulnerable and open with her past abuse. One of her coping mechanisms was to dissociate from her body, to just not "be there." This survival tactic, which served her during the abuse, is not helpful during labor and birth. Her tendency to leave her body, to escape it and deaden her physical sensations, may interfere with the birth process. The labor will generally slow down or even stop. In labor the goal is to remain *present* and *aware* in the body.

Women who have been abused also feel more fear and vulnerability when they are sick. They are afraid of being a "patient." Being a patient in the hospital often connotes *helplessness,* another painful memory from the past. The sexual-abuse survivor needs to keep in mind that pregnancy is not an illness.

For the abuse survivor the best preparation for labor and birth will be establishing her boundaries and creating a strong support team. That may include her partner, a close friend, or a family member. A professional childbirth assistant (doula) can also be an invaluable addition to her birth team.

Some of the following problems may arise as "unexpected outcomes" for sexual-abuse survivors.

- Fear of I.V.'s, vaginal examinations, or any other medical probing that feels invasive

- Feelings of violation and mutilation evoked by an episiotomy

- Difficulty breast-feeding

- Postpartum depression

When a Baby Is Ill or Handicapped

One of the most difficult challenges for a parent is giving birth to a baby who is ill or handicapped. Not only are such parents filled with grief, but they also feel powerless. Grief and powerlessness can lead to obsessive worry. Some people turn inward and become inactive and indecisive. They can't sleep or eat; they get depressed and isolate themselves. Others may try to escape their fear by turning outward. They distract themselves with drinking, compulsive talking, watching television, or keeping busy every minute.

One way to deal with these feelings is to acknowledge them. Parents of babies who are ill or handicapped have feelings they have never experienced before. Physically exhausted and emotionally drained, these parents feel extremely vulnerable. The two most important survival tools are a strong support system and patience (with oneself, one's partner, and the baby).

One couple who faced the heartbreak of having a handicapped baby were Maggie and Jim.

Jim and I were so excited that I was pregnant. I had been very ill, and we weren't sure I could conceive, so it was quite a thrill for us. I took very good care of myself throughout the pregnancy. We found a wonderful midwife to help us have our baby at home.

My labor progressed rapidly and was fairly easy. When my baby was born, we were told that Zachary had a cleft lip and palate. At first we weren't sure what that meant exactly other than that his little face looked different.

The difficulties started to surface in the first twenty-four hours. Breast-feeding was extremely difficult. I tried everything. He was not able to suckle or swallow the milk and was losing weight. I was terribly disappointed because I had wanted so much to breast-feed. When it was determined that we had to turn to bottle-feeding, I was devastated. My childbirth educator suggested that I focus on *emotional nourishment* for both me and my baby. My husband echoed her words. He urged me to be kind to myself, accept the reality, and love and care for Zachary the way he was. This helped bring my situation into clearer perspective.

Dialogue: *What Can We Do to Help You?*

Materials: Journal and felt-tip pens
Purpose: To get in touch with the spirit of the baby who is ill. To bond with your baby.
Technique:

1. With your non-dominant hand draw a picture of the baby.
2. Using two different-colored pens, write out a dialogue with the baby. Your dominant hand writes for you (the parent or support person), and your non-dominant hand writes for the baby. Ask the baby the following questions:

   Dear Baby, what do you want me to call you?
   How do you feel (physically and emotionally)?
   What caused you to feel this way?
   What can I do to help you?

3. With your non-dominant hand draw a picture of the baby *after* it has received the help it asked for.
4. Write a love letter to your baby.

When a Baby Dies: Grieving and Growth

There are many major transitions in life that call for us to mourn the death of our hopes and dreams: divorce or separation, physical death, leaving or losing a home or a job. Even in our everyday lives when our expectations are not met, when our fondly held wishes are not fulfilled, we experience an "inner death." We may blame ourselves or harbor regrets or resentments. We may feel guilty or ashamed, supposing it must be our fault. Or perhaps we explode with rage and shake a fist at heaven, demanding, *Why? This is unfair. I did everything I could. How could this happen?* The stages and styles of grief have been well documented. But when we are faced with our own personal grieving, firsthand experience is all we really have to guide us through the grieving process.

Two weeks into the writing of this book Lucia's father died. Around the same time her younger daughter happily announced that she was pregnant. Here are Lucia's reflections on the grieving process and how she dealt with it:

When I began work on this book, I read Jessica Mitford's *The American Way of Birth,* a hard-hitting study of birth practices in the United States today. In off hours I was also devouring a compelling book about death, *Grace and Grit,* Ken Wilbur's story about his and his wife, Treya's, struggle with her cancer for the last five years of her life.

Both books had a strong emotional impact on me. Mitford's book fired me up and strengthened my resolve to work toward changing how we give birth in this country. The Wilburs' book broke my heart open. I wept during the entire last section of *Grace and Grit,* in which Treya's death process is described in her own words and in her husband's. Because she was so spiritually conscious and had embraced her humanity, her life, and her death so completely, it felt more like reading about the birth process. The parallels between birth and death had never been so clear to me before. I didn't know then that within the week I would be dealing with birth and death in my own family. The next week my father died.

Although he was aged and had been ill for a while, my father's passing came as a surprise. I wonder if we're ever really ready for the death of a loved one. There was also a sense of irony about it. Here I was, two weeks into writing a book about pregnancy and birth, and I was confronted with both birth and death in my own family: my father's death and my daughter's pregnancy.

While grieving my father's death I was keenly aware of my feelings and thoughts. They jumped to the surface and could not be buried beneath busywork, socializing, and all the other things that often distract me from my internal life. At one level I felt as if I were experiencing an abortion. I had begun work on the new book and had been sailing ahead, the words flowing, the creative juices gushing out in torrents. Then I hit a big stop sign: death. That had not been in my plans. Hadn't one of the doctors said that my father's death was *not* imminent? After all, he had survived surgery and thirty radiation treatments two and a half years before at age seventy-nine. His physician used to commend him for being "tougher than cancer" and for defying the odds. He wasn't supposed to die *now*, or so I thought. But the inevitable had happened. And I had to deal with it.

All my other plans and schedules had to be put aside. I had to surrender to feelings, to memories, to grieving, and to the burial. As his only child I was responsible for the funeral arrangements. I had to carry on with adult decisions and plans, when my Inner Child was feeling dev-astated that her daddy was gone. But as in past crises, I found that the support system I had consciously built up over the years was well in place, like a net under a trapeze artist. I knew I could trust them to be there for me when I needed them, and my gratitude knew no bounds. My family members and friends all came forward now and offered what-ever help they could give. And I thanked God for all the inner work I had done over the years. It all prepared me to keep my heart open to the gifts of love and time and empathy that were being offered now. In dealing with the pain of loss, once again I learned about the power of a support system. The trust and deep affection that brought all of us together in our shared grief was profoundly beautiful.

At this time I also reconnected with my beloved journal in a much deeper way: A letter written to my father brought a feeling of acceptance of his death; expressions of gratitude for all the support I was receiving brought home to me how loved and cared for I was. But most important, simply writing about the little daily occurrences and memories that triggered overwhelming emotions throughout the day provided great solace.

My father died just before Christmas. After he was gone, it was very difficult getting through the holidays, which we had planned to spend together. Christmas Eve, Christmas Day, and New Year's. Glancing at his gifts (wrapped before I received the news of his death) prompted a depth of emotion that I hadn't expected. The smallest incident: a glance at a family photo, hearing "Have Yourself a Merry Little Christmas" on the radio (a song from a movie he had edited years ago), all brought grief crashing down in waves.

Surrendering to the sadness and letting it be okay was most helpful. This often meant reaching out to be with people who understood and were supportive of tears as a natural part of life and a necessary part of healing. At other times it meant embracing solitude, not to isolate myself but to treasure time alone in order to feel, accept, and honor my feelings. Sometimes I journaled and wrote out dialogues with his spirit. At other times I looked at old photos of my father as a child and young man. I felt much closer to him at these times than I ever had when he was alive. His spirit seemed very near. This blessed solitude also provided me with time to meditate, pray, and be with the Great Spirit.

We share Lucia's story with you because some of the ways she dealt with her grief may help those who are facing the death of a baby. Of course there is an added element of poignancy when a baby dies. As the saying goes, "When your parent dies, you've lost your past; when your child dies, you've lost your future."

The birth of a child is accompanied by high hopes. Babies symbolize new beginnings, a fresh start, life and exuberant energy. Expectation burns so brightly. We refer to a pregnant woman as "expecting" or we speak of "expectant" parents. But if something *unexpected* happens, the grief can be overwhelming.

Feelings of guilt and remorse may be mixed with rage and emptiness. These powerful emotions can cause a sense of shame, alarm, and restlessness. All of these reactions to death are normal. It is important to embrace the whole range of emotions.

There are many ways to deal with the death of a baby:

Hold, bathe, dress, and talk to your baby.

Name your baby.

Sit together, hold the baby, and allow yourself to cry.

Acknowledge your grief.

Invite family and friends to be with you and your baby.

Honor the baby's spirit through some kind of ceremony or ritual, such as creating your own funeral or arranging a conventional one.

Pay attention to your primary relationship. Be patient and respectful of each other's different ways of grieving and coping.

Write a letter, telling the baby how you feel about your loss.

Ask God or your Higher Power for comfort and guidance.

Collect keepsakes: I.D. bracelet, set of hand and foot prints, birth certificate, lock of hair, picture of your baby, receiving blanket your baby was first wrapped in, the umbilical cord.

Be patient with yourself. Don't make any major decisions right away.

Later on, join a grief support group.

Letter: *Dear Baby*

Materials: Journal and felt-tip pens

Purpose: To communicate your feelings directly to a lost baby. To express your grief. To accept compassion and love from your Higher Power.

Technique:

1. With your dominant hand write a letter to your baby. Share your feelings about your loss. Be totally spontaneous. This may be very difficult to do. If the feelings become overwhelming, you may need to stop and cry or seek comfort from a member of your support team.

2. With your dominant hand ask your Higher Power (or whatever you call your Inner Self) to speak with you. Ask it for specific guidance, consolation, and help. Now, with your non-dominant hand, allow your Higher Power to speak to you.

3. With your non-dominant hand draw a picture of someone who embodies the spirit of compassion. It could be someone you have known, or perhaps a spiritual figure such as Christ, the Blessed Mother, Quan Yin, the Buddha, an angel, White Buffalo Woman, or Mother Earth. In your picture show this figure of compassion holding your baby or in some way caring for its spirit.

Bill wrote his memories and feelings about the stillbirth of their daughter, Caitlin.

It's Sunday morning and Moe and I are at the hospital. Moe hasn't felt the baby move in the last twelve hours or more. A staff doctor put a fetal monitor on Moe's belly but couldn't see any heartbeat. Our baby girl was dead! I really thought I could wake myself up and find out that it was all just a bad dream.

The doctor started some I.V. medicine. We have to wait for the uterus to dilate, then hopefully Moe will go into labor. We waited all night. We talked about how we'll look at Caitlin when she comes out and wish her good-bye and tell her we love her. The doctor says we can try again after two months and one period. How can we think of that? We're both so sad right now. During the night Moe cried and cried and cried. Then in the morning I cried when I told my best friend, Mark, what had happened.

Moe and I talked about our feelings a lot. I was very scared about the delivery. The thought of going through the whole birthing process all for a dead baby was just about unbearable. Finally we slept.

Then in the early morning Moe complained of a lot of pain, which could only mean she was ready to deliver. I became extremely nervous and prayed over and over for strength and understanding for Moe and me. Moe had to work really hard to push our baby out. It was an absolutely beautiful experience, working together to deliver our baby.

When she was born, she was a beautiful baby. Brown hair, long legs, big feet. We both held her, talked to her, and told her we loved her. We gave her her name: Caitlin. At that moment she gave us both so much joy and happiness. We both cried a lot, and I thought I could cry forever.

When we came home, it was very sad. Everything in the house reminded us of Caitlin. I've been staying very close to Moe. She really needs a lot of support right now. My business will just have to take care of itself for the time being.

All of our friends have been very supportive. The house was filled with bouquets of flowers for weeks after. Together we joined a support group for grieving parents. I really benefited from sharing my feelings with other couples. Hearing how other men dealt with their grief was very comforting. Moe and I developed a close friendship with two other couples in the group. Since then, like ourselves, one of the other couples has had a live birth.

Jane wanted very much to share her story in the hopes that her baby, Crystal's, birth/death would help others who are dealing with the loss of an infant:

My pregnancy was perfect. The baby and I were really healthy. I was happy to be pregnant. My husband, Ernie, was pleased too. At eight months we had the baby shower. During the shower I felt the baby make a pretty big movement. It was as if she had turned. I immediately felt that something happened. The next day I couldn't feel the baby moving anymore. I was crying because I knew something was wrong. I told Ernie and a couple of other people, but everyone just told me "that happens toward the end of the pregnancy." Despite my gut-level feelings I chose to believe them. But I *really had known it* right away, *from the moment that big movement happened at the shower.* I knew that I was going to the doctor's in a couple of days, so I tried not to worry.

I went into the doctor's office by myself. When the doctor listened for the heartbeat, there wasn't one. He called Ernie and told him. Then he called the hospital and arranged for some sonograms. I met Ernie later that day at the hospital. We still didn't know anything. Nobody came in and actually acknowledged that our baby had died. We were kind of sitting there waiting and waiting. Finally a woman came in and started sort of counseling me. And Ernie said, "What happened? Would someone please tell us what happened?" She said that our baby had died. The placenta separated from the wall of the uterus and she bled to death. Essentially her blood just went into my blood. That was a really big shock.

My first thought was to have a cesarean. I kept thinking, "Just do it, get it over with." The doctor and the hospital nurses explained to me that they don't do that. They felt that it was better physically and psychologically for my body to birth on its own. Later that day they started the pitocin to induce labor, but it just didn't work. Our baby was not ready, and frankly neither was I. My body just held on and wouldn't let go. We decided to go home and wait.

I had two weeks to prepare for our baby's birth. A lot of people had problems with that—I mean a lot! They felt that the doctor should perform a C-section. Some people just could not see me. They didn't know what to say or how to react. I didn't take it personally, because I had a strong support system and I could understand that they felt uncomfortable.

Waiting was really good. A network of people was there for me all of the time. They totally cared for me. Those two weeks were a blessing. Instead of just rushing in and "getting it over with," I had a chance to think about what I wanted to do and how we wanted to celebrate the baby's life and death. I had a chance to really think and to communicate with the baby.

I had a bookstore. I read a lot about death and I did a lot of journaling. I got my feelings out so they wouldn't be totally internalized. The journaling also gave me something to look at, which put things in perspective. I'd get insights and feelings from journaling. Somehow it was really healing, like honoring the fact that our daugher had lived.

Finally they called me from the hospital. I was told that I needed to come back, because they were worried. I could get sick and toxic. So

I packed, and we went in. The hospital and my doctor were so supportive. They were really there for me! Whatever I wanted was okay with them. They started the pitocin, but nothing happened. I spent the night in the hospital.

Early in the morning I awoke suddenly with a chill. I thought it was nervousness. But then I felt this real calming presence that was very reassuring. I just lay there feeling that warmth and trying to go back to sleep. A few minutes later a nurse walked in and saw I was awake. She checked me and told me that I was fully dilated and ready to have the baby. I was shocked because I hadn't had any pains. I didn't even know. The doctor and Ernie raced to get there in time. They made it about twenty minutes before the birth. The doctor was wonderful. They were very, very compassionate. After about three pushes our baby was born. The doctor told us that we had a little girl, which we had intuitively known during the pregnancy. After they wrapped her up, he gave her to me.

Everything about her was perfect. Even her placenta was heart-shaped. The doctor stayed with us for a little while after her birth and talked about her. He unwrapped her and showed us every little part of her body. Her beautiful little hands and feet. She was so delicate. It was really nice that he did that because I probably wouldn't have thought of it.

While I was still pregnant, we had named her Crystal. I had my altar set up in my hospital room. The nurses were really respectful of that. We took pictures, got a lock of Crystal's hair, and put blessing oil on her. We kept her with us for quite a while and had our own private time. I needed to hold her.

We left the hospital in the late afternoon. A friend of mine from the childbirth classes had delivered her baby just four days before Crystal's birth, so we went to visit them. That was kind of hard, but somehow I just felt the need to do that. Then two days later we went back to the hospital to get Crystal's body. We wrapped her in a beautiful blanket that a friend of ours had made for her. I carried her out of the hospital in my arms and held her all the way to the mortuary.

Another friend of ours had made a little casket for her. When we got to the mortuary, we put her into it and placed crystals and potpourri around her little body. I remember that it was real hard for me to let her go again. We left while she was being cremated. While we were waiting until it was time to go back for her ashes, we took our little son to the toy store, had lunch, and went to the mall. That waiting was hard too.

We had decided to take Crystal's ashes to the Atlantic Ocean and scatter them over the water. From the minute she died until her burial, there had been ravens everywhere I went. The raven is a very special and symbolic bird to me personally. When we got to the ocean, we were trying to decide exactly where to go. Looking around, we saw two ravens sitting on a rocky point. Ernie looked at me and said, "Well, I guess that's the place."

We went out onto the point. Crystal's burial was beautiful. I sang a couple of lullabies I had sung all during pregnancy. Then I spread her ashes. They were beautiful. They glittered and sparkled, I guess because of the crystal dust mixed in with them.

Jane wrote the following poem to Crystal shortly after the ceremony at the sea:

> Crystal, my vision of loveliness, clarity
> enchanting of the star nation
> Crystal, ethereal,
> her spirit never to have boundaries,
> never tied, freedom.
> Crystal, embodiment of love itself,
> raven, our connection.
> Magic surrounds us.
> We are one.

Jane continued doing journal work, expressing her feelings of grief.

One-week anniversary of your birthday.

Oh, my little angel. My arms ache for you. You reminded me this morning that your mission was to heal and that you could reach more people and do it better in the space you're in now rather than this physical world. "After all, isn't that what all this is about?" you asked.

Three books that Jane found to be very helpful were:

Risk to Be Healed: The Heart of Personal and Relationship Growth, by Barry Vissell, M.D., and Joyce Vissell, R.N., M.S.

Empty Arms: Coping after Miscarriage, Stillbirth and Infant Death, by Sherokee Ilse and Linda Burns

Empty Cradle, Broken Heart, by Deborah L. Davis, Ph.D.

We also recommend:

When Hello Means Good-bye, by Pat Schwiebert, R.N., and Paul Kirk, M.D.

8

Growing into Parenthood: Birth to Two Months

You have just gone through a profound change. Giving birth was probably the most dramatic experience of your life. Make time to record your impressions and feelings about your labor, your birth experience, and your baby. You can do this in your journal or make an audio or video tape of your memories and feelings. Invite your partner to do the same. A record of your birth story will be a wonderful keepsake for you and your baby in years to come. Include the following:

- Memories and feelings about my labor and birth experience

- Impressions about the care I received

- The first sight of my newborn (what I noticed, how I felt)

- Observations of my baby today

Prenatal education focuses on you and your partner with birth as the "goal." Usually very little information is given about the baby and infant care *after* the birth. If any guidance is offered, it normally pertains to immediate postpartum care of the newborn. Although parents may feel prepared for birth, they are often at a loss about what to do with the actual baby.

You may find that society does very little to help. Some assistance is offered, but it is often difficult to access. In this section and in the Bibliography and Resource Guide that follow, we provide you with support and guidance on how to care for your baby.

What Is Good Parenting?

Every expectant parent wonders, *Am I capable of being a good parent? Will I do a good job? Can I nurture and protect my child?* These are normal questions, and it is perfectly natural to have these concerns, especially if you are a first-time parent.

The truth is that there is no single "right" way to parent your child. You will be defining your own style of parenting. There really are no ready-made formulas, no matter what anyone tells you. The key is awareness (of yourself and your baby), willingness to do the best you can, and patience with yourself and your baby. Listen to yourself and to your innate maternal instincts. Listen to your baby and his emotional as well as physical needs.

It is also valuable to get information and guidance to help you solve problems that arise in the everyday care of your baby. Rather than rely exclusively on your pediatrician, who is probably very busy, there are other excellent resources. One thing you can do is draw upon the ideas and experiences of seasoned parents and parent educators. We recommend the following books on parenting:

The Baby Book: Everything You Need to Know About Your Baby—From Birth to Age Two, by William Sears, M.D., and Martha Sears, R.N.

The First Six Months, by Penelope Leach

Pregnancy, Childbirth and the Newborn, by Penny Simkin, Janet Whalley, and Anne Keppler (Chapters Eleven and Twelve)

There are also some highly informative videos on infant care, such as:

Diapers and Delirium, by Jeanne Driscoll

Baby Basics, by T. Berry Brazelton, M.D.

Following is some information about the changes that your baby will experience so you can react positively to your new baby and to the role of parent.

Your Newborn

Your baby needs to be treated with great tenderness, love, and compassion following birth. In order for you to give thoughtful care to your baby, it is important to know what happens to babies in most births.

The baby has just left a "home" in which the temperature averaged 98.6 degrees Fahrenheit. He enters a room at least 15 to 20 degrees cooler.

Previous to birth the baby's oxygen supply came through the umbilical cord. Within minutes of birth the baby's body must adjust to breathing on its own. Often the umbilical cord is clamped before it has stopped pulsating. In effect this "chokes" the baby because his oxygen supply is cut off before his lungs are fully functioning and breathing.

He has spent the last forty weeks immersed in water and covered with a thick layer of vernix caseosa (natural protective coating). When born, he enters a dry atmosphere. His extremely sensitive skin is immediately exposed to rough, sterile towels.

From the dark, cocoonlike environment of the womb, his sensitive eyes are subjected to bright lights. Accustomed to sounds muffled by water, his ears are now bombarded by loud, harsh noise. His body, which lay tightly curled up and cradled in a weightless state, is now subject to gravity's pull. After spending months rocking rhythmically in a safe, protected space, the baby is often moved about rapidly in a hectic, stressful manner.

Understanding the difficult transition a baby makes at birth can help you treat your baby with the utmost sensitivity and gentle concern.

The following considerations should be taken into account when you make your Birth Plan:

- *The temperature of the delivery room:* You may want it heated to at least 75 to 80 degrees Fahrenheit.

- *Cutting of the cord:* You may request that the cord not be cut immediately after birth; cut it after it has stopped pulsating.

- *Placement of the baby after birth:* You can ask for your

baby to be placed on your abdomen or chest, skin to skin, with a warm towel or blanket covering her.

- *Bonding with your baby:* You may want your baby with you for at least an hour immediately following delivery. Ask that during that time minimal care procedures be done, such as monitoring his respiration, heart rate, and so on. This is a time when you may want to be alone with your baby and family.

- *Physical contact with the baby:* Consider gently holding and breast-feeding your baby during the hour immediately after birth.

- *Atmosphere during and immediately following birth:* Some possibilities are low lights, soft music, lowered voices, and slower movements.

- *Father's participation in birth and postpartum care of baby:* Consider his helping with the delivery, placing the baby on your abdomen, cutting the cord, and giving the Leboyer tub bath with low lights, soft music, and warm water at your bedside.

- *Suctioning at time of birth:* At birth your baby usually has fluids removed from nose and mouth through a procedure called suctioning. You can ask that it be done gently and only when necessary. Ask that after the initial suctioning your baby be allowed to cough or sneeze out the mucus rather than undergo repeated suctioning.

- *Rooming-in:* You can ask that your baby stay in your room rather than being taken away to the nursery. This is referred to as rooming-in. You can also request that all care and examinations of your baby be done in your room.

- *Sleeping patterns for the baby:* You can have your baby in bed with you, either beside you or lying on your chest.

Finding a Pediatrician

It's a good idea to look for a pediatrician before your baby's birth. If you haven't selected one in advance and there is an emergency, the hospital will assign you a pediatrician.

Lucille had given no thought to choosing a doctor for her baby. When her daughter, Deborah, was born after a breech delivery, it was discovered that her foot was twisted. The staff pediatrician was called in and diagnosed it as a clubfoot. The information was delivered through a nurse, who offered no explanation or comfort. Lucille was in shock at the news that her baby girl was handicapped. She spent an agonizing night alone in her room (there was no rooming-in at the hospital, and the baby was in the nursery).

The next day her OB/GYN brought in another pediatrician to examine the baby. This doctor visited Lucille and told her that the first diagnosis had been incorrect. Due to malposition of the baby, her foot had been twisted, a temporary condition that could be easily treated. By putting a cast on the baby's foot for a couple of weeks, her foot could be straightened out. The impersonal treatment Lucille received from the staff pediatrician might have been avoided if she had already established rapport with a pediatrician of her choice.

In finding a pediatrician, use the same approach you did in selecting health care for yourself. Decide what you want and then research your options. In making a "shopping list," consider some of the following questions:

- What are the doctor's credentials?

- Does he or she have privileges at the place you are planning to give birth?

- Does he or she come to the hospital to examine newborns?

- What does the infant examination include?

- Does the pediatrician's feeling about circumcision correspond with your own? How does he or she deal with feeding? Sleeping and eating "schedules"? Baby-wearing and baby-carrying devices? Immunization? Common ailments such as colds, flu, ear infections, diaper rash, and allergies?

- What are his or her fees? Hours? Single or group practice? What do they do in an emergency? Who takes the calls?

- What books does he or she recommend?

If you have chosen to birth at home with a lay midwife, you may want to find a pediatrician or family-practice doctor who is sympathetic to home births. Look for someone with a philosophy that is compatible with yours.

As you research pediatricians, visit the offices of the ones you are considering. Notice if the office is pleasant for children. How are they treated? Is there a place for them to play? Are the sick babies separated from those who are well? How does the doctor treat babies and children? How does the staff relate to babies and children? Is there usually a long wait? Talk to other parents who are waiting with their children and find out how they like the doctor.

Changing Feelings: The First Six Weeks

Childbirth classes present you with a preview of what to expect during labor and delivery. Emotional changes that occur *after* the baby arrives are rarely addressed in depth. There is no way to know exactly what feelings will come up after the birth of your baby. You can be sure that they will be profound and intense, but the specific emotions are impossible to predict. Every parent is different, every baby is different, and every situation is different.

Even if you cannot predict what lies ahead emotionally, you can *prepare* for it by learning to deal with your feelings. Of course you have already been doing that throughout this book. By honoring feelings during pregnancy you have been getting ready for the powerful emotions that arise when you finally have a real live baby in your arms.

As any new mother will testify, the strong emotions surrounding birth stay with her for days after the birth experience. Feelings of awe, joy, and gratitude frequently well up in her heart. She has been deeply touched, and the early days of motherhood are a wonderful period of spiritual opening. In many cultures the postpartum period is honored as a special time. Birth is seen as a spiritual awakening requiring a time to "gather the soul." In some Latin countries the mother and newborn are separated from society and allowed private time together for forty-one days. They are watched over and protected carefully. The mother is relieved of any work-related tasks so that she can be attentive to the inner work of re-collection.

Birthing mothers today are faced with a real dilemma. We do not have the extended family (common in other cultures) to help mothers and allow them to take time with their newborns. In the nuclear family a mother is expected to take care of the baby and the household. She feels required to be up and functioning "normally" within a very short time (often a week or less) after giving birth. In our fast-paced society we no longer make "sacred time" following birth. We are not talking about maternity leave but about quality time in which to concentrate on nurturing the self and the baby: physically, emotionally, and spiritually.

The high spiritual energy of birth, together with the intense physical output, is a perfect setup for breakdown. Usually this is referred to as postpartum depression, or the "baby blues." Lack of sleep, limited time and energy for self, poor eating habits, and trying to do too many things (laundry, meals, housework, etc.) often lead to behavior that appears to be depression.

Studies show that postpartum depression occurs most frequently and with greatest intensity among women who have birthed in a hospital. Depression also seems associated with cesarean sections, heavy medication, and other unplanned interventions. This is understandable when you consider that people recovering from *any other major surgery* would never be expected to take care of a baby immediately afterward. But that is not the case for new mothers.

Many who have been depressed after giving birth say they have felt irritable, teary, confused, vulnerable, sad, exhausted, unsettled, and somewhat disoriented. These feelings are usually accompanied by a sense of guilt and apprehension about being an adequate mother.

Katrina was a young mother who had to face this dilemma. She shared her story with us:

> Before getting married I had a successful business as an interior decorator. My husband, Miklos, and I decided that I wouldn't work outside the home for the first two or three years after the baby was born. I really wanted to concentrate on taking care of the baby and learning how to be a good parent. I'm not sure what I expected, but in looking back, I think my head was full of images from television and magazine ads showing happy babies with their doting parents. It all looked very sweet.
>
> What I was hit with, first of all, was a real feeling of isolation. I had never been home alone all day every day in my life. I had either been a student in school or been running my business. Both ways there were always a lot of people around. To make matters worse, we moved to a totally different area where I knew no one and I didn't have time to make friends because we were so involved in painting and decorating our house before the arrival of our daughter, Nadya.

The birth had been very difficult, and I was very tired for a long time afterward. It took me several weeks to really recover. Meanwhile I had to adjust to all of the things it takes to take care of a baby: erratic sleep patterns, lots of laundry (especially because we had chosen to use cotton diapers), simply adjusting to an entirely new lifestyle. I also suffered from postpartum depression for the first month after Nadya was born.

It was very difficult because I felt guilty for not feeling joyously happy to have such a beautiful baby. I was ashamed to tell anybody that I was depressed and miserable a lot of the time. I only talked to other people about the happy moments, but the negative feelings just got swept under the rug.

I couldn't even talk to my husband about it very much because he was starting a new job and was very preoccupied with that. It was my lifestyle that had changed the most, and it was difficult for him to understand what I was going through. He thought I should be blissfully happy too. After all, we had what we had wanted: a healthy baby girl. This reinforced my feelings of guilt and my fear that I wouldn't be a good mother. It wasn't until some years later when I went into therapy that I was able to acknowledge all of those feelings and to realize that they are common for someone in my situation.

Experiencing some depression after the birth of your baby does not mean that there is anything wrong with you. Changing feelings are typical of the postpartum period. If you sometimes feel low, sad, or "blue," see it as an opportunity to go inside and talk to your Inner Child as you did during pregnancy. Return to the practice of being in touch with your feelings and taking good care of yourself. Also, create a support system of people you can be yourself with. It is crucial to have people in your life who can allow you to have your feelings, whatever they are. Remember, it is not bad to feel sad.

In rare cases depression can be severe. If the depression becomes so severe that you are unable to care for yourself and the baby, seek professional help. Warning signs of severe depression are:

- Difficulty getting out of bed

- Inability to respond to the baby's cries

- Loss of appetite

- Insomnia (can't sleep)

- Feelings of helplessness and hopelessness

It is not uncommon to experience some of these symptoms during the postpartum period. However if they become severe seek professional help. Don't put it off.

It is also important to acknowledge the grieving stage associated with the ending of your pregnancy. Paradoxically birth is a beginning but also an ending to a phase in your life. Grieving and growth are synonymous.

Letting Go: *Saying Hello, Saying Good-bye*

Materials: Journal and felt-tip pens
Purpose: To express your feelings about letting go of your pregnancy and birth experience. To focus on saying hello to the things you want.
Technique:

1. Sit quietly and reflect on your baby's birth. Think about things you've *had* to let go of (your pregnancy, freedom, peace and quiet, sleep, money, time, organization, friends, etc.).
   Think about the things you *want* to let go (pain, anger, aches, fear, feeling overwhelmed, disappointment).
2. Use two pages side by side. On the left-hand page write *Good-bye.* On the right-hand page put *Hello.*
3. Using your non-dominant hand, under *Good-bye* draw a hand holding a bunch of balloons on strings. Label each balloon with the things that you have had to let go of and those you want to let go of.
4. After labeling the balloons, sit and imagine them floating away.
5. Using your non-dominant hand, under *Hello* write at least three words that express things you want to say hello to.

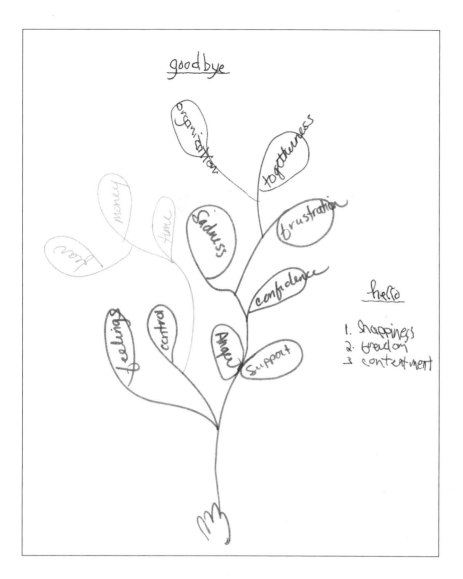

goodbye

organization
togetherness
money
time
sadness
frustration
action
confidence
feelings
control
Anger
support

hello

1. happiness
2. freedom
3. contentment

You can also repeat earlier exercises for dealing with your changing feelings. One of them that is especially appropriate at this time is the following:

Drawing the Inside Out: Full of Feelings

Go back to Chapter Three, page 71, and repeat the exercise "Drawing the Inside Out." Do this exercise from the new perspective of life as a parent.

Your journal is a wonderful place to acknowledge any postpartum depression you may feel. However, avoid allowing yourself to stay stuck in grief or depression for too long.

In addition to exploring emotions, take care of yourself physically. Get plenty of rest, eat good food, and do some gentle exercise. Go out in the fresh air if possible. Avoid isolating yourself. Get help for household chores such as cooking, laundry, and cleaning. Hire a helper or get assistance from family or friends. This is an important time to call upon your support system. If physical problems arise, check with your health care professional to determine if your discomfort is normal in recovery from birth. We recommend the following books:

> *After the Baby's Birth: A Woman's Way to Wellness*, by Robin Lim

> *Positive Parenting Fitness*, by Sylvia Klein Olkin

If your baby shows symptoms of abnormal discomfort, you can journal with him or her just as you did when you were pregnant. Kathy did this and got great results.

Kathy had been told by her midwife to continue her prenatal vitamins for several weeks following the delivery. When she ran out, she didn't bother to replenish her supply. Her life as the mother of baby Jubilee and her two-year-old son, Kent, kept her very busy, and Kathy soon became exhausted and depressed. Her newborn also grew fussy, restless, and demanded more and more of her attention.

Finally Kathy remembered the dialogue work she had done during pregnancy in which she asked questions with her dominant hand and received answers from the baby with her non-dominant hand. In a written conversation with Jubilee, Kathy learned that the baby wasn't getting adequate nourishment from her mother's milk. After doing the journal dialogue, Kathy was motivated to read more about nutrition and how to improve the quality of her breast milk. While reading about nutrition for lactating mothers, she discovered that her midwife had been right. Kathy needed exactly the same vitamins she had been taking before Jubilee was born. Shortly after resuming the vitamins Kathy got her energy back and Jubilee became contented.

Siblings and Your Newborn

If you are already a parent, the other children in your family will need help in preparing for the newborn. Naturally this should be done during pregnancy and unfold as a series of ongoing discussions about the expected baby and what it will be like to have a new member of the family. Include them as much as possible and help them to make it *their* baby too. It is also important to teach siblings your new needs as a pregnant woman. If they are old enough, this is an excellent time for them to help you around the house by taking on new responsibilities that are appropriate for their age and stage of development. A book that includes valuable information about preparing siblings for the arrival of a new baby is:

Pregnancy, Childbirth, and the Newborn, by Penny Simkin, Janet Whalley, and Anne Keppler

Postpartum Survival

It is inevitable that a variety of difficulties will arise shortly afer your baby's birth, but they don't have to become a problem. Here is a list of some effective ways of dealing with this major adjustment in your life:

- Accept all the help you can get! Forget about being "supermom."

- Set priorities. Decide what's most important to accomplish and don't worry about the rest. Remember, relaxing is *more important* than vacuuming. As one mother of four put it, "Cleanliness is next to impossible!"

- Think ahead about easy-to-prepare meals and snacks. You might suggest to friends that an appropriate welcoming-baby gift would be a meal. And don't forget the paper plates.

- Put your own needs first. Be honest: If you're tired, let people know.

- Take the phone off the hook.

- Keep visits short.

- Sleep when the baby takes naps. Don't use the baby's nap time to get caught up.

- If possible, hire a local teenager or an elderly person to help you. If you can't afford to pay, arrange for trades (e.g., meals, baby-sitting).

- Don't be too hard on yourself: infancy is short and sweet. Enjoy it!

The following exercise should be done while you are pregnant. After the birth go back and read what you wrote. Hopefully your journal will remind you of things that were important to you.

For Myself, for My Baby

Materials: Journal and felt-tip pens
Purpose: To help you focus on nurturing things you can do for yourself, your partner, and your baby
Technique:

With your dominant hand respond to the following:

1. • Three things I will do for myself after the baby is born.
   • Three things I will do for my marriage or partnership after the baby is born.

2. • Names and phone numbers of family members I can call on for support.
   • Names and phone numbers of friends I can call on for support.
   • Names and phone numbers of health care professionals.

As you learned during pregnancy, self-nurturing must begin with the Inner Child. You've probably experienced the vulnerability and sensitivity of this special part of yourself. Immediately following your delivery you may find that your Inner Child wants to speak with you.

Inner Child Chat: *How Do You Feel?*

Now is the time to go back to Chapter Three, page 76 and repeat the exercise "Inner Child Chat: *How Do You Feel?*" In your dialogue focus on how your Inner Child feels about your baby. Is she feeling competitive with your baby? Or does she feel that her needs are being met? If they are not, find out what you can do for her.

Postpartum Weight

Now that you're no longer pregnant, you may feel pressure to lose weight quickly. Some women think they "should" or "have to" look a certain way within a short time after the baby is born. If your baby weighed nine pounds and you only lost five pounds (by the scale), you feel discouraged. We recommend the book *Positive Parenting Fitness* by Sylvia Klein Olkin. It is a very helpful book with many useful ideas and suggestions for getting back in shape. Use the "Power of Focus" skills you learned in Chapter Five. Remember, letting the media or fashion magazines dictate how you "should" look will break down your self-esteem.

Breast-feeding

For many years breast-feeding fell out of favor. For that reason today's generation of mothers may have difficulty finding guidance from women experienced in breast-feeding. Fortunately La Leche League was formed by a group of women dedicated to the natural art of nursing. They provided support and instruction through their book *The Womanly Art of Breast Feeding*, a classic in the field. We highly recommend it. La Leche League continues to be a major support network and source of information concerning any breast-feeding question. Contact your local chapter by calling the number listed in your area phone directory or contacting your local childbirth-education resource center for more specific information.

Two other books on nursing are:

The Nursing Mother's Companion, by Kathleen Huggins

Bestfeeding: Getting Breastfeeding Right for You, by Mary Renfrew, Chloe Fisher, and Suzanne Arms

Following is a list of some of the reasons breast-feeding is very beneficial for you and your baby:

- Breast milk provides all the nutrition your baby needs for the first four to six months.

- Breast milk contains antibodies that strengthen your baby's immune system. Breast-fed babies are healthier.

- Breast-fed babies have higher I.Q.'s.

- Breast-fed babies have better tooth and mouth development.

- Breast-fed babies don't have as many allergies or digestive problems.

- Nursing comforts your baby emotionally.

- Nursing is convenient and economical.

- Breast-feeding strengthens bonding with your infant.

- Women who have breast-fed have a lower incidence of breast cancer.

- Breast-feeding tones the muscles of the uterus and helps the woman's body recover and recondition itself more rapidly.

If for any reason you cannot breast-feed, don't feel badly. What counts is your intention to nourish your baby emotionally as well as physically. Don't lay a guilt trip on yourself. The important thing to keep in mind is to hold your baby while feeding him. Avoid feeding your baby by letting him lie down with the bottle propped beside him. Doing this communicates that eating is an impersonal physical action. Being fed this way is devoid of human contact and emotional nourishment. Rotate the baby from the right side to the left side, just as if you were breast-feeding. During feedings make eye contact and talk with your baby. Again, the important aspect of feeding your baby is developing your bond with her.

If you want to clear negative feelings about breast-feeding, we suggest doing the journal exercise entitled "Cluster Writing: A Quick Look at Feelings."

Cluster Writing: *A Quick Look at Feelings*

Go back to Chapter Three, page 72, and do the exercise again. This time use one of the following as your focus word: *breast, breast-feeding, nursing.*

Turning to Your Support System

Your support system is extremely important after your baby's birth. Developing good teamwork during your pregnancy prepares you for the emotional ups and downs that occur after the baby comes. Your support system can help you avoid going into isolation and feeling burdened or overwhelmed by parenting. Your support system can bring relief, resources, companionship, and encouragement.

Remember, the nuclear family (two parents and a child or children living in isolation) is a recent development. Three generations ago it didn't exist. Parents, children, grandparents, and/or uncles and aunts all lived together or in close proximity. The extended family was the norm. There is an old African expression: "It takes a whole tribe to raise a child." Your support system is your "tribe" and may or may not include blood relatives. Turn to your support team for as much help as you need. This is not a time to go it alone. It's good for you and your baby to have others for companionship, for support, and for celebrating this new life.

Shandrice did not consciously create a support team to help her after her baby was born. She ended up with one by default, but it was not the team she would have chosen. Here's how she described her experience:

> I had a very difficult time giving birth to our first child. It was a long labor, and the baby almost died during the delivery. I was completely exhausted and in a lot of pain afterward. Since my husband and I lived in a semirural area, my mother offered to let us stay at her home and bring in a nurse to help care for me and the baby. It turned into a disaster.
>
> The nurse was a very domineering woman who discouraged me from breast-feeding (a battle that I ultimately won). She insisted on monopolizing the baby. She kept insinuating that I was in no condition to take care of the baby. She hinted that I didn't know how to anyway, so the baby would be better off in her care. Her intimidation was very subtle, but I felt it. The problem was that I didn't have the energy to fight with her most of the time.
>
> The baby and I had to share a room with the nurse, who snored all night so that I couldn't get any sleep. After a few days I complained bitterly to my husband, who came to the rescue. He fired the nurse and took me home. In looking back, I realize my mother had good intentions, but I had given her too much control of the situation. I let her choose the nurse and allowed both of them to "manage" my recovery period and the care of my baby. I let them decide what was best for me and how I should feel. Once I was home with my husband, I had the opportunity to really get to know the baby and care for her in my own

way. I learned an important lesson and did not make the same mistake with my second child.

By contrast Jacquelyn and Bertrand took a different approach. Bertrand reflected back on the birth and postpartum period with joy and satisfaction:

> We had wanted to have a natural childbirth and we did. It was great! We took childbirth classes together and spent a lot of time doing research together and talking about what we wanted. We had a doula with us at the hospital and found that to be extremely valuable. She even made herself available to Jacquelyn after the baby was born, both in the hospital and at home. Having someone to talk to who was both technically knowledgeable and aware of what we wanted was really helpful. After Jacquelyn came home from the hospital, I felt reassured that she had someone to turn to during the daytime when I couldn't be there.

Jacquelyn also had family members and friends helping her. She recollected:

> My sister was available to help with some of the household chores so that I could spend more time with the baby. In the beginning the baby had some trouble catching on to breast-feeding. My doula had breast-fed all of her children. She told me about her experiences and also put me in touch with the La Leche League, who were very helpful. I felt like we were surrounded by people who really cared and were there for me and my family in this time of need. I don't know what I would have done without their help. It made adjusting to parenthood much easier and much more enjoyable.

One of the things that many mothers of infants complain about is a feeling of isolation. In our work we have found that this sense of being isolated contributes greatly to postpartum depression. Certainly there are physical factors having to do with hormonal changes, fatigue, and the transition from pregnancy to motherhood. However, isolation can exacerbate all of these other factors. A support team can go a long way toward preventing the feeling of aloneness that may set in after mother and child are home. This sense of isolation can be extremely difficult if the woman is used to being with other adults all day, such as in an office or other group situations. This abrupt change of lifestyle can prove a real challenge for some women.

Getting Help: *Picturing My Personal Support Team*

Go back to Chapter Four, page 126, and do the exercise again with the focus on your new needs now that the baby is here.

Babies Are People

The cutting of the umbilical cord has been celebrated as a very symbolic event in many cultures. It signals the completely new beginning of life. Despite being fragile and quite vulnerable, your newborn comes equipped to begin life. Though still developing, his five senses function quite well. A few of the skills your baby is born with are the following:

- *Sight:* Your newborn can see quite well at close range, and when you hold him in your arms, he can see your face clearly. He can distinguish dim or bright lights and colors. He prefers patterns over solids, and moving objects over still ones. He loves looking at faces.

- *Hearing:* Your baby has been hearing quite well since she was *in utero.* She knows your voice quickly and is alert to other familiar sounds.

- *Smell:* Smell is perhaps your baby's most valuable skill at birth. He detects your body odor and imprints to it immediately. This is why we believe it is so important that your baby be delivered directly onto your skin. (This same skin-to-skin contact should also occur between the father and child shortly following birth.)

- *Taste:* Studies have shown that babies have acutely functioning taste buds *in utero.* Your newborn distinguishes different tastes and demonstrates this the way adults do.

- *Touch:* Touch was the first sense to develop in the womb. You baby's skin is highly sensitive and actually receives information necessary for growth. Your baby senses and listens with her skin and responds to the quality of physical interaction.

Growing into
Parenthood: Birth
to Two Months

233

Your baby is completely his own separate being and he needs to be treated as such. The next exercise is designed for you to begin observing your baby.

Observations: *Getting to Know You*

Materials: Journal, felt-tip pens, and sheet of blank white paper (8½ by 11 inches or larger)

Purpose: To observe your child and record your observations in order to learn more about his or her personality, needs, and patterns. To bond with and communicate with your baby.

Technique:

1. Write down some of your observations about your baby's way of communicating. What have you learned about how your baby makes his or her needs known? What personality traits seem to be emerging? (Be sure to include the age of your baby in relation to these observations. How many weeks or months old is your baby?)

2. On a separate sheet of paper or in your journal draw a time line. Along this line write in the days or months of your child's age, and vertically above and below the line write in a phrase for behaviors and skills that your baby is demonstrating.

Note: You can do this exercise first while your baby is still in the womb. Focus on how your baby is communicating with you *in utero* through movements, hiccups, changes in position.

It is important that you consider your expectations for your baby. If unrealistic expectations and ideals are imposed on the baby, parents may set a dangerous course of trying to make their baby into something he or she is not. In our work of parent education we have seen this as a guarantee for family disaster. Nothing damages parent-child relations more than a parent's inability to see and accept a child for exactly who he or she is.

Expectations: *What I Want for My Baby*

Materials: Journal and felt-tip pens
Purpose: To become aware of your hopes, wishes, and expectations of your baby
Technique:

1. Using your dominant hand, complete the following sentence in your journal. Complete each sentence as many times as is appropriate.

   - I want my baby to . . .

   - I hope my baby will . . .

   - I expect my baby to . . .

   - I will be disappointed if my baby doesn't . . .

I want my baby to . . .
- Be happy & healthy

I hope my baby will . . .
- Be happy & healthy
- trust itself
- Love itself
- follow its passion & fascination in life

I ~~expect~~ want my baby to . . .
- Learn what it wants in life & to pursue its dreams

I expect my baby to . . .
- Listen & talk to me
- listen to itself & follow its heart & dreams

I will be disappointed if my baby doesn't . . .
- Love itself
- Love Jeremy & I
- Have good health

Growing into
Parenthood: Birth
to Two Months

235

One of the biggest problems new parents face (especially first-time parents) is that reality does not match their fantasies. As a result they conclude they are inadequate and are doing something wrong. These attitudes lower parents' self-esteem and rob them of the enjoyment of parenting. It is important to be realistic about the necessary adjustments that must be made with a newborn in the family. Many people think that having a baby is simply a matter of addition. They assume they will add the baby to their already existing lifestyle. Soon parents realize that having a baby demands the creation of a *new* lifestyle.

Life with a newborn may seem chaotic compared with your old life, especially if you prized order and careful planning. If this was the case, you may be in for some *big* surprises. The fact is it is very difficult to maintain typical adult order (business as usual) with babies around. You can do it, but you have to deny the nature of a baby's needs and impose rigid standards and expectations.

Flexibility and acceptance of change are among the most important skills new parents can have. You will soon find that babies go through many phases, and you will need to adapt to them as they come and go. Nothing is forever. Your baby may be "colicky" from six to eight each night for a while. It may seem as if this nightly pattern of two hours of misery will go on indefinitely. Don't panic! Before you know it, your baby will move on to another phase. As the ancient Chinese philosophy puts it, "Nothing is so permanent as never to change."

Social Adjustments

While adjusting to your new lifestyle, keep in mind that people who have not had children may not understand your new priorities. They'll expect you to remain the "old you": a person who could make a lot of plans, show up on time, and follow through on commitments. We are by no means suggesting that parenthood will make you become irresponsible or flaky, but your values and priorities will probably change dramatically. Your friends who do not have children may be upset by this. They are not used to adapting to your new lifestyle. For this reason you may feel more comfortable with friends who also have a baby or young children. Develop and foster these kinds of relationships before your baby is born. You can also maintain your relationships with your other friends. As with everything, communication can help you to iron out any rough spots.

The bottom line is *babies are unpredictable.* They are individual human beings with their own needs and expressions. Your job as a new parent is to learn to understand your infant and to respond appropriately. This often takes time. Meeting your baby's needs may require you to change plans you have made with other adults. Here are some common situations that may interfere with your plans:

- The baby develops a bad diaper rash and is in a lot of discomfort. You feel he needs you to be with him.

- You can't afford a baby-sitter.

- It suddenly starts raining and you don't want to take your baby out because she's recovering from a cold.

- You don't have a baby-sitter and the place you have been invited to is not appropriate for children.

Adult time schedules are just not the same as those of a baby. *Relax.* Enjoy this new relationship. Let your baby, partner, family, and close friends be your main social outlet for a while.

Baby Talk: Learning to Listen

Babies speak through sound, gesture, and movement. Furthermore each baby has its own unique way of communicating, as any parent of more than one child will tell you. One of your tasks as the parent of a newborn is to decode your infant's messages and to respond appropriately. This is not always easy.

Carlos observed that each of their two children had entirely different personalities from the very start. Here's how Carlos described his observations of his boys:

> I noticed right after each of our kids was born how different they were. The sound of their crying was different. Julio, our first baby, had sort of a high-pitched cry when he was upset. It was a little like a smoke-detector sound. If he was hungry, it was louder. When he was tired, it was a different cry, sort of a whimper. My wife and I learned to tell the difference by watching and listening. Sometimes I felt like an investigator, but it was fun, especially when you guessed right.

> Our second child, Jorge, used to talk to us with his body. After a while we could tell what he wanted by the way he was moving. When he was hungry, he didn't cry as much as Julio had, but he moved his head around a lot and would make loud sucking sounds with his mouth.

Paying attention to the way your baby communicates is very important. It can save you a lot of headaches. If you can learn to understand your baby's own way of "talking to you," you will be well on your way to growing into parenthood. Listening, watching, and taking the time to tune in to your baby is what early parenting is all about. Let your baby be your teacher. Let your natural instincts develop as you attend to your baby's needs.

Remember, your baby is extremely vulnerable and totally dependent upon you. If you do not listen to him or her, who will? As we have seen, listening is an art and can be developed. By learning to listen to yourself, your own feelings, and your needs, and responding appropriately, you have been preparing to do the same for your baby. By honoring your own Inner Child, you have trained yourself to honor your baby's needs. The box below outlines some of the ways your baby "talks":

How Your Baby Talks

- Body movement
- Facial expressions
- Sounds and crying
- Physical symptoms, such as rash, throwing up, diarrhea, and colic
- Waking and sleep states

Learning to understand your baby can be like going on a treasure hunt. Follow the clues. Some good books with valuable guidance in communicating with your infant are:

300 Questions New Parents Ask, by William Sears, M.D., and Martha Sears, R.N.

Families: Crisis and Caring, by T. Berry Brazelton

Crying

One of the most noticeable ways your child communicates is through crying. Deciphering cries is a challenge. It is somewhat easier if you follow a pattern. We suggest looking for causes from the outside to the inside. Start by observing your baby's physical condition. Does he have wet diapers? Is she hungry? Is her clothing pinching? Is the blanket too tight? Is he cold?

Next, move inward and consider his emotional state. Is he acting restless and fussy? Perhaps he needs a change of sights and sounds. Is he expressing a need for comfort or contact? Does he behave as though he wants to be held and cuddled?

Finally, think of the spiritual needs he may be expressing. Perhaps he is fussing because he is "missing the womb." He may just need to be with you and feel safe enough to cry. He may need to express anger and frustration that carried over from a complicated or difficult birth. Closing out light, holding him close, and rocking him can help tremendously. Just hold your baby close to you and let him cry. Don't try to *do* anything more. Sometimes simply *being* there is enough. The gentle rocking, fetal position, and darkness resemble the environment he just left. It soothes his spirit as it reunites him to the rhythm of his life before birth.

The following journal exercise will guide you in your observations of "Baby Talk":

Observations: *Baby Talk*

Materials: Journal, felt-tip pens, and sheet of blank white paper (8½ by 11 inches or larger)

Purpose: To learn to decode your baby's cry for help when he or she is ill, upset, or in need of attention

Technique:

1. Think of a fussy time your baby has that you are trying to understand.
2. With your non-dominant hand draw a picture of your crying baby. Around your picture list the various ways you normally try to comfort your baby and solve her problem.

(continued on next page)

3. On a separate page write a dialogue between you and your baby. Ask the baby how she feels when she's crying, why she feels that way, and what you can do to help her. Ask the questions with your dominant hand, and let the baby answer with your non-dominant hand.

Suffering and Pain

One of the biggest challenges in parenting your baby, as in any relationship, is how to deal with illness or irritability. Babies express themselves in a host of ways: smiles, giggles, and baby talk. They also cry, spit up, fuss, fidget, and are sometimes sleepless, restless, and hyperactive.

Part of being human is the experience of physical discomfort and emotional upset, such as fear and frustration, as well as comfort and pleasure. Naturally we want our baby to be safe and content as much as possible. Any parent will tell you how difficult it is to see his or her baby in pain.

However, sometimes there is no way to avoid pain. It is part of the human condition. In fact discomfort is a survival mechanism. When your baby is hungry, she is experiencing pain and discomfort. She expresses this through crying. When we hear her express pain, it is normal to want to do something about it. Crying gets the attention of caregivers and gets the baby fed. Without this sensitivity to pain the baby wouldn't thrive. Sometimes pain is a useful part of life.

If you think you can prevent your baby from experiencing human suffering, you are setting yourself up for great disappointment. Yes, you can love and protect her, but you cannot control everything that happens to your child. Any attempt to do so robs her of learning, growing, and making her own way in the world. Allowing your child to be a separate person starts when she is a baby.

There are several effective ways to comfort your crying baby. We suggest that you explore and find your own solutions within the following six areas:

- *Position:* Notice which physical position calms your baby: cradled, tummy to tummy, skin to skin, lying over your forearm, held high over your shoulder, or seated.

- *Rhythmic motion:* Combine motion with physical position. Try walking, rocking, swaying, sitting, or using a mechanical device that produces motion, such as an infant swing.

- *Touch and massage:* Touch is one of your baby's most developed senses. Try using firm strokes on the back, gently patting in a rhythm, rubbing your baby's feet, learning and using specific massage strokes.

- *Warmth:* Your baby's sense of temperature control takes time to develop completely. Sometimes being cold causes your baby much discomfort. Try swaddling, cuddling, a warm bath, warm-water bottle.

- *Sucking:* Your baby has been sucking for months before birth. If you are breast-feeding, allow your baby to breast-feed frequently. You can also encourage your baby to suck on his own thumb or fingers. We suggest a pacifier as a last resort. If you choose to use one, find a pacifier that is orthodontically correct.

- *Sounds:* Sound was one of your baby's earliest developed senses. Try soothing sounds (such as speaking reassuring words in a soft voice), humming or singing songs (preferably ones you sang before the baby's birth), or "white noise" (such as an electric fan, dishwasher, washing machine, or clothes drier). Try one of the tapes or crib devices that play intrauterine sounds, or play music you listened to before the baby's birth. Avoid heavy-metal music, as it can make babies irritable.

9

Creative Parenting:

The First Two Years

"Bonding" builds an emotional tie between parent and infant. Like any relationship, parent-child bonding does not happen all at once. It occurs over time and with experience. If conditions permit, trust and safety are developed and a feeling of love is established long before birth.

In Chapter Seven we described the bonding between parent and infant that occurs at birth. This is a deeply personal connection between mother and child and between father and child. There is another form of bonding that should take place: between family and infant. *Family* can be defined as "the extended family of blood relatives and friends."

Family-bonding rituals exist in cultures throughout the world. We already mentioned the Latin custom of allowing mother and child to be honored for forty-one days following birth. In some countries the baby's placenta is buried in the ground and a tree is planted over it. As the child grows, so does the tree. In our culture we have Christian infant baptisms and the Jewish *bris* as bonding rituals. Others have chosen to create their own bonding ceremonies.

Prior to the birth of their son, Rhonda and her husband, Mike, had decided to plant a rosebush in honor of the baby. Looking through catalogs, they had found the rosebush they wanted. On their Birth Plan they requested that the placenta and cord be saved. Returning home after the birth, Mike buried the placenta in their garden and planted the rosebush over it. A couple of weeks later, when Rhonda and the baby were ready for guests, the proud young couple invited their close family and friends over for a "celebration." Each guest was asked to write something special to the baby, Jason, and read it in a little ritual they performed around his rosebush. Each year, on both Mother's Day and Father's Day, the bush yielded beautiful blossoms.

How do you continue building the *emotional* tie between you and your child? How do you embrace your new role as a parent and the changing relationship with your partner? In the first two years of your baby's life, you will see immense changes. Unfortunately there is very little assistance for the parents of young children in our society. This chapter is designed to help you find your resources, within and without. You will learn effective parenting tools to help you and your baby get off to a good start. Let's start by talking about how infants communicate through body language.

Body Language

Over 70 percent of your daily communication is done without words. Your facial expressions, body movements, and posture all communicate who you are. If this is true for you as an adult, it is even more true for a newborn. With the exception of crying and other vocal sounds, a baby relies heavily on body language.

Although medical technology has done much to intervene and save lives, it has also increased the degree of stress and trauma for both the mother and the baby. The emotions of birth are stored in your baby's body. Many body workers, such as masseuses and movement therapists, readily agree. Therapists such as Dr. William Emerson have conducted extensive research on the baby's need for physical touch. Emerson has shown that gentle touch can help the baby release traumatic "body memories" of birth. Many cultures do this naturally through infant massage. In India, Sweden, Haiti, Africa, and New Zealand (to name only a few), infant massage is a regular part of newborn care.

Infant Massage

Touching releases growth hormones throughout the body. Fascinating research done at the University of Miami showed that premature infants grew more rapidly as a result of being touched. In the control group the babies were not touched except for normal routine daily care. By contrast the babies in the experimental group were stroked three times a day for ten minutes. (The research did not call this *love,* but we would.) Both groups received the same basic care and feeding. At the end of the study the results showed that the babies in the experimental group gained an average of 49 percent more weight *per day on the same amount of food.* It was concluded that touch made the difference. It influenced the level of growth hormones in the bodies of these babies.

Massaging your infant helps you to:

- Get in touch with your baby's body signals
- Learn your baby's special needs
- Interact with your baby
- Foster relaxation and contentment in your baby
- Improve your baby's sleep pattern
- Build the baby's self-esteem and feeling of being loved
- Stimulate the release of growth hormones
- Promote brain growth in your baby
- Relieve your baby's stomach and bowel discomfort
- Teach your baby about safety and boundaries

Infant massage also helps parents develop healthy feelings of fathering and mothering. This is especially good for the working mom who has to be away from her baby. Massage is a way to express tenderness and foster feelings of love for your baby. As you massage your baby, you can learn to relax and enjoy this gentle form of interaction.

Massage your baby on a regular basis, such as after a bath. The familiarity of this routine will be reassuring and relaxing for you both. Start learning the various strokes of infant massage when your baby is a newborn. Then when your baby becomes a wiggly infant, you will already know the movements and can be more flexible with your approach. Infant massage should be continued throughout the first two years of life. We recommend the following books:

Infant Massage: A Handbook for Loving Parents, by Vimala Schneider McClure

Baby Massage, by Tina Heinl

Mother Massage, by Elaine Stillerman

Settling In

Coming home with your newborn is often a worrisome event. Assuming full responsibility for your baby's care may seem overwhelming.
The normal behavior of your newborn may cause you to have feelings
of alarm. Coughing, occasional sneezing, erratic breathing patterns,
gagging, and choking sounds are typical. Your baby is getting rid of
extra fluid in her lungs, throat, and nasal passage. Simple measures,
such as laying the baby on her side or on your chest and carrying her
in a sling or in your arms, can be comforting.

At first you will probably be consumed by caring for your baby. As the
weeks pass, you may feel that your life is still out of control. It seems
as if you live only to respond to your baby's needs. This causes some
women to feel "at a loss." They can't see any structure in their life
anymore. If this feeling occurs, it may be useful to create a chart for
yourself. By diagraming your baby's physical and emotional growth, you
will begin to see a pattern. You may observe that you and your baby indeed follow a fairly consistent routine. Sometimes just knowing these aspects of your baby's behavior helps you feel in control of your life again.

Activity Chart: *Peek-a-boo, I See You*

Materials: Two pieces of art paper (18 by 24 inches) or two large pieces of graph
paper, colored markers

Purpose: To help you observe and chart your baby's growth and personality
traits. To help you acknowledge new structure in your life.

Technique:

1. Place your piece of art paper or graph paper like a rectangle in a horizontal
position. Along the top of the paper mark off one-inch squares across the
page. Mark each square with the hours of the day and night. Down the left
side of the margin mark off one-inch squares. Label them with the dates.
When you have finished, you should have a graph of one-inch squares. (If
you are working with graph paper, just highlight the one-inch lines.)

(continued on next page)

2. Each day record your baby's activitites for a twenty-four-hour period of time. Using your colored markers, color in the squares according to the activity. *Sleep* is blue, *awake and crying or fussy* is red, *awake and content* is yellow, *feeding* is green, *parent-baby interaction* is purple, *diaper change* is brown. (Write the specific activity such as bath, car ride, play, etc.)

3. Post this chart in an obvious place (a wall above your baby's changing table or the kitchen where you both frequently go). Add to the chart for one week or longer. Throughout the day mark your poster with the baby's various activities.

Baby Care

The first thing you may have noticed is that everywhere you go with your baby, someone has advice for you. Take heart—remember when people did that to you about your pregnancy? How did you handle it then? Do the same thing now. Weigh the information, balance it against your own lifestyle and needs, and then decide what *you* will do.

Sleeping and Night Care

Of primary concern to most parents of a newborn is the disruption of their sleep pattern. If your baby does not sleep through the night, many feelings of anxiety may arise. Questions might start running through your mind: "Am I a good mother? How come my baby isn't sleeping? My friends' babies all slept through the night at this age. What am I doing wrong?"

Consider having your baby sleep beside you. We realize that many "experts" have advised against this, claiming it is unsafe, unsanitary, and unhealthy. We disagree. Mothers have been sleeping in the same bed as their infants for centuries. Why was it safe and healthy then and not now? Why do we isolate newborns in their own separate rooms? We think this practice is questionable, and so do many other authorities in the field, such as Dr. William Sears, Martha Sears, Dr. William Emerson, and Dr. Gayle Peterson (to name a few).

Sharing your bed with your baby has many benefits:

- The baby sleeps better, and so do you.

- The baby learns sleep and breathing patterns by being near you throughout the night.

- It's easier to get the baby to go to sleep if you lie down together.

- Breast-feeding in the middle of the night is much easier if the baby is in bed with you. It's less disruptive of your sleep.

- It's less upsetting for the baby who is hungry in the middle of the night. He doesn't have to cry as loud or as long to wake you up and get your attention.

- Breast-feeding mothers often find they can anticipate when the baby is hungry and feed him before he is fully awake and distressed.

- Premature babies or others who were not separated from their mother in the hospital bond more easily when they sleep with their mothers. Research shows that they thrive.

How long a baby should share your bed is an individual decision. Eventually your baby will be able to go to sleep and stay asleep without your help. He will usually indicate when he wants a bed or room of his own. Some parents make this transition in stages: a crib beside their bed followed by a move into a room of the baby's own or with siblings.

There are long-range benefits when the baby feels nurtured, protected, and safe. Self-esteem and a sense of security grow stronger. He is more willing to reach out and explore the world if he feels safe in the core of his being. Some believe that babies grow stronger by being isolated and sleeping in a bed alone; our observation is just the opposite. Children who are isolated exhibit fear, anxiety, and restlessness. They tend to be more timid and unwilling to take risks.

Carrying Your Baby

Baby wearing, the practice of carrying the baby in a sling close to the parent's body, is a practice in many cultures. Only in industrialized nations have we abandoned this age-old custom. Babies benefit, both emotionally and physically, from being carried by their mother during her waking hours. Babies carried in this way appear to be much more adaptable and flexible. They seem to be far more contented and appear to interact socially with greater ease.

Baby wearing is a wonderful way for a father to bond with his child. Using a sling, he can still go about his work around the house while cuddling the baby. Several books on infant care discuss baby wearing. Our favorite is:

The Baby Book, by William Sears, M.D., and Martha Sears, R.N.

Baby-proofing Your Home

As your baby grows and begins exploring the environment (crawling, climbing, learning to walk), you need to be aware of the safety of your home and surroundings. One way to see things from your toddler's perspective is to get down on your hands and knees and crawl around the house for a while. Survey the territory. What can you see and touch and grab from this level? Look for some of the following as you inventory your house. Make a checklist of potential hazards:

- Stairways

- Ovens and other electrical appliances

- Computers

- Electrical outlets, wiring, cords

- Open or unsecured cupboards storing toxic detergents, cleansers, or other chemicals

- Bathroom medicine chests with dangerous drugs, nail polish, and polish removers

- Throw rugs that slip easily

- Knick-knacks and other items that are easily breakable

- Small items that a baby can choke on, such as hardware (nuts and bolts, screws, nails, etc.)

- Plants (some may be poisonous or have toxic chemicals on them)

Ages and Stages

During the first two years of life a baby goes through many stages of development and rapid change. During the first few months the baby is simply *being* herself and learning about who she is. She learns that by experiencing how she is treated by others. If she is treated with respect and care, she will feel valued. This period is the foundation for a child's self-esteem or lack of it. (In the case of abuse or neglect the baby draws the conclusion that she is not lovable or capable.)

Probably the biggest challenge for you as a parent during this period of time is to love and care for your child willingly, even when she is colicky, wakeful, demanding, or ill. This period of your child's development of self-esteem triggers unresolved self-esteem issues in the parent. It becomes essential to nurture yourself and strengthen your own self-esteem. If you do this for yourself, you can do it for your infant.

Any time that a behavior or a pattern of your baby's is particularly stressful for you, see it as a mirror reflecting some unresolved feelings within yourself *about* yourself. We recommend that you return to some of the self-nurturing suggestions and exercises in Chapter Four. Review "107 Ways to Take Care of Yourself," page 104, and repeat the exercises below:

Self-Nurturing Lists: *Taking Care of Me*

See Chapter Four, page 105.

More Inner Child Chats: *What Do You Need?*

Chapter Four, page 101.

Two books by Jean Illsley-Clarke that we highly recommend are:

Self-Esteem: A Family Affair

Growing Up Again

The next exercise is adapted from Clarke's work. It is a technique for creating verbal affirmations directed either toward your own Inner Child or toward your baby.

Affirmations: *I'm Glad You're Alive*

Materials: Journal and felt-tip pens
Purpose: To develop self-esteem in you and your baby through positive parenting self-talk
Technique:

1. Sit quietly for a while and imagine that you are in your "special place."
2. Look over the list of affirmations shown below:

   - I'm glad you are alive.

   - You belong here.

   - Your needs are important to me.

   - I'm glad you are you.

   - You can grow at your own pace.

   - You can feel all of your feelings.

   - I love you and I care for you willingly.

3. Choose one of the affirmations. Using your dominant hand, write it in your journal.
4. With your non-dominant hand, write your feelings about the statement you just wrote.
5. Continue writing the affirmation with your dominant hand and responding (with reactions) using your non-dominant hand until your feelings are positive or neutral.
6. At another time continue doing this exercise using other affirmations on the list. Do them one at a time.

As your child continues to develop, she begins to experiment and explore. From about the middle of the baby's first year until approximately a year and a half the child is busy *doing*. During this period she is using all of her senses and initiating, learning, and growing. She is crawling and learning to walk and talk. Everything interests her. She is reaching out to experience her world. Her feelings of being capable begin at this time.

Perhaps the most important parenting skill during this stage is patience. This period can be particularly challenging for a parent if he or she was blocked from exploring and initiating at this age. Using the same format as the exercise above, use the following affirmations and clear the space for healthy parenting.

Affirmations: *You Can Be Interested in Everything*

- You can explore and experiment; I will support and protect you.
- You can use all your senses when you explore.
- You can do things as many times as you need to.
- You can know what you know.
- You can be interested in everything.
- I like to watch you initiate, grow, and learn.
- I love you when you are active and when you are quiet.

From about eighteen months to three years of age, your baby is beginning to express independence. In expressing himself he may throw temper tantrums, test limits, and say no. This stage has been called the terrible twos and coincides with potty training. It is a period when the child is learning coordination and control. She is becoming her own person. By asserting herself, your toddler discovers if you still love and support her as an individual.

During this phase repeat the exercise above with the following affirmations:

Affirmations: *I'm Glad You're Starting to Think for Yourself*

- I'm glad you are starting to think for yourself.
- It's okay for you to be angry, and I won't let you hurt yourself or others.
- You can say no and push and test limits as much as you need to.
- You can learn to think for yourself, and I will think for myself.
- I know you can think and feel at the same time.

(continued on next page)

- You can know what you need and ask for help.

- You can become separate from me, and I will still love you.

Parents as Partners:
Keeping Your Relationship Alive

There is a common belief that having children strengthens a marriage. This is not necessarily true. Having and raising a child is a monumental undertaking and is not something to be taken lightly. After the baby arrives, the couple's relationship changes forever. Caring for an infant requires adjustments in the relationship that can hardly be imagined before the baby actually arrives.

For first-time parents the changes in schedule, lifestyle, and responsibility can often feel overwhelming. For instance, trying to figure out why a baby continues crying in the middle of the night (even after a feeding) can lead to loss of sleep, frayed nerves, and feelings of frustration. If these emotions are held in and not discussed openly, they can seep out indirectly in sarcastic remarks, demands, and arguments between the parents. When fatigue sets in, fuses get short.

Lori and Charles had been looking forward to having a family. They loved each other very much and felt that being parents together would enrich their marriage. After they returned home from the hospital with their baby girl, Tina, they faced many changes. Lori had a difficult delivery, and her recovery was slow and painful. She felt tired and depressed for the first three months after the baby was born. Thinking this was normal, Lori didn't ask for help or counseling but tried to go it alone. It was all she could do to feed and bathe the baby every day. Although she'd always loved cooking, preparing meals seemed like an enormous job. As for companionship with Charles, she simply had no energy left at the end of the day to interact much with him. Also, it seemed that the baby was the fussiest during the hours he was at home.

As for Charles, he had just started a new administrative job. Preoccupied with the adjustment to a different company, schedule, and level of responsibility, it was difficult for him to be supportive of Lori. He felt powerless to deal with her postpartum depression, which seemed to be dragging on. Charles missed having intimate time alone with his wife and wondered when he would have the old Lori back.

Fights began erupting. This was not typical of their relationship. Finally, when Tina was nearly a year old, Charles and Lori came into counseling. They shared how baffled they were at what was happening to them. As Charles put it, "One day we were happy and loving, and almost overnight we started getting crabby and irritable with each other or not talking at all. It all started after the baby was born. Is that what happens when you have kids?" Lori echoed his words and added, "I thought having a baby was going to be so wonderful. Don't get me wrong. Tina is adorable, and we both love her so much. But our marriage is going to pot."

What Charles and Lori were experiencing was a phenomenon that is all too common. Instead of strengthening the marriage, the stress of adjusting to parental responsibility can actually weaken it. At a time when the baby most needs a loving environment, parents start to drift apart. Instead of sharing their feelings and reactions to parenting and supporting each other through the challenge, each of the partners retreats. When this happens, communication breaks down and the relationship is headed for trouble.

As Lori put it, "Our marriage is becoming a business partnership. When we do talk, all we discuss are doctor bills that need to be paid, household repairs, and a lot of nitty-gritty stuff that has no real heart in it. We used to have so much fun together, going places, sharing ideas." Charles agreed, but said he felt powerless to "fix it." He shared that the marriage was "drying up."

In counseling they first learned to nurture themselves as individuals. They discovered their Inner Children and expressed their vulnerability with each other. Over time they realized that although they were parents, they still had their own childlike feelings. Charles admitted feeling jealous of Lori's focus on the baby. Lori was able to express her feelings of guilt about being depressed for so long and neglecting him. Later Charles and Lori did the collage exercise "Visual Affirmations: Picture Perfect" (found in Chapter Three). Doing this activity reminded them of their identity as a couple and also of their individual needs.

Lori and Charles learned to nourish their relationship. Lori developed her own support system consisting of family members and friends. She received individual counseling for her depression. Charles began bringing little gifts home for Lori: flowers or a book he knew she'd enjoy. She left loving messages on his private voice mail at work and asked her parents to baby-sit so that she and Charles could spend one night a week alone. They also joined a support group for re-parenting themselves. When Tina was a little older, they occasionally went away for weekends alone.

By being willing to tell the truth about how they felt and what they wanted, Charles and Lori were able to resurrect their relationship. Learning to take better care of themselves and their relationship had another big benefit. There was a better, more loving atmosphere in the home, resulting in better parenting for Tina.

For more guidance on keeping your relationship alive and healthy, we strongly suggest the following books:

> *Embracing Each Other*, by Hal Stone, Ph.D., and Sidra Winkelman, Ph.D.
>
> *Getting the Love You Want*, by Harville Hendricks, Ph.D.
>
> *The Shared Heart*, by Barry Vissell, M.D., and Joyce Vissell, R. N., M.S.

The following exercise can help you sort out your expectations and values regarding parenting. It is useful to do this exercise with your partner before and after the birth of your baby. Do your journal work separately and then share what you have done.

Family Portrait: *Expectations*

Materials: Felt-tip pens, art paper, collage materials, magazine photos
Purpose: To articulate your expectations, hopes, and dreams about parenthood
Technique:

1. While you are still pregnant, make a photo collage of your ideal family.
2. Using your dominant hand, write a description of the family you want to have. How do the family members relate to one another? How do you feel about being a part of this family?
3. If you did this exercise while you were still pregnant and did it again after the baby was born, compare your collages. Are there any differences between the two pictures? Have your attitudes changed? Explore this with your partner.
4. Do a collage of your expectations, hopes, and dreams about your relationship with your partner now that your child is in your life.

An invitation to **loving couples**

Dates again

Savor the romance.

dinner out

walks

talks

Rediscovering

A MOMENT
A MEMORY

SECURITY
WITHOUT CHANGE

"FAMILY PORTRAITS"

As you reflected on your ideal family, perhaps you asked yourself the question, What is a good parent? Every culture, group, and family has its own definition of what good parenting is. In our society parenting education is not considered a necessary preparation for adulthood. It rarely appears in the school curriculum. It is understandable that new parents often feel totally unprepared once the baby is born. One young mother compared it to being thrown into the ocean with no swimming lessons. "Completely overwhelming," she said. "It was nothing like I expected. In looking back, I don't know what I expected. We were really flying in the dark."

In view of this lack of education for family life, it is easy to see why new parents look around and measure themselves against others. New parents often imitate what they see others doing. Unfortunately they look to those who haven't a clue about healthy parenting themselves. To add to the confusion, there are scores of books out by experts and academics that often present conflicting points of view.

Parenting Styles

One way of finding out about parenting is to talk with some parents. Ask them what it's like. What do they enjoy about parenting? What are some of the challenges? The next activity is a tool for gathering information about parenting. Do it before the baby arrives.

Interview: *Exploring Parenting Styles*

Materials: Journal and felt-tip pens
Purpose: To observe other parents and dialogue with them about the realities of parenting. To identify your own likes and dislikes about parenting styles.

Technique:

1. Find some parents you would like to interview about what it's like to be a parent. Ask them if you can get together for some uninterrupted time (perhaps one-half to one hour) to gather some information and hear about their parenting experiences.

2. Here are some suggested questions for your parent interview. If their children are older, ask about parenting their children during infancy and early childhood.

   - What do you like most about being a parent?

   - What do you like least about being a parent?

   - What kind of support system do you have to help you as a parent?

   - Are you a part of any other parent's support system (e.g., baby-sitting co-op, car pool, etc.)?

   - What do you do with your child for quality time?

   - What are your thoughts about day care and/or early education? How did you resolve this issue?

   - How do you set limits for your child (or children)? When did you begin setting limits?

   Make up some of your own questions

3. During the interviews or soon afterward take some notes about your conversations. Reflect upon what these parents said and what you felt was valuable information.

4. Do you wish to emulate any part of their parenting style? Make a list headed *Useful Ideas*, based on what you learned in your interviews.

We all learn by imitating others, whether we do it intentionally or not. It can be very helpful to reflect upon parenting you have seen and wanted to emulate. In the next exercise you'll be doing just that: looking at role models. Again, it's a good idea to do this exercise before the baby is born.

Inventory: *Positive Parent Role Models*

Materials: Journal and felt-tip pens
Purpose: To identify and articulate more clearly your role models for the style of parenting you prefer
Technique:

1. Think about some parents you've known who related to their children in a way that you really like. It could be your own or other people's parents. It could be parents in fiction or in history. With your dominant hand (on the left side of your page), list the names of these people.
2. Switch to your non-dominant hand. To the right of each name, jot down the qualities that you admire in your role model's parenting style.

As you research what others say and do about parenting, you can create your own road map. Exploring your own needs and those of your baby will lead you toward your own style of parenting. Developing your style is a question of trial and error. Don't think that you have to be experts on parenting to do a good job. What you need is the willingness to learn and wholehearted commitment to being the best parent that you can be.

As only children, Mary Ann and Rodney had not been around kids when they were growing up. Mary Ann had done a little baby-sitting in her teens, and Rodney had been a camp counselor one summer. That was the extent of their exposure to children before Mary Ann became pregnant for the first time. They both wanted a child very much and had a strong desire to be conscientious parents. They knew that they didn't know very much, but were not sure how to get more information. They read all the books they could find and they observed other parents interacting with children.

Then Mary Ann took a class entitled "Child, Family, and Community" that Lucia was teaching at a local community college. By the time she started the class, Mary Ann was six months' pregnant and totally confused. She confided to Lucia, "The more I read, the less confident I feel. All these experts seem to be saying different things. They expect *so much* from parents. It's as if you can't be human or be yourself anymore after you've had a baby."

In the class we created a support-group atmosphere with much sharing, individual research into community resources, and guest visitors. Speakers included a pediatrician, a nursery school teacher, a family lawyer, a family counselor, a pregnant mom, and several parents with small and large families. Mary Ann learned to relax and honor her own instincts and needs. She also encouraged Rodney to do the same. Several months after their little boy was born, Mary Ann brought the baby to class one night to say thank you. She talked about the help she had received in finding her own way as a parent. She addressed the class with the baby in her arms and encouraged the students to be true to themselves and to find the parenting style that fit them.

A young single mother, Penny made an astute observation: "After I thought about it for a while, I realized I had been raised to believe that parenting is supposed to be a totally selfless endeavor. The myth of the 'perfect parent' was in the back of my mind—you know, the infinitely patient mother who is never tired, always loving her perfectly behaved children in their immaculate household. Just like on TV. Pretty intimidating, huh? No wonder I was nervous about how I was raising my son. I've been constantly criticizing myself for not measuring up to this ideal."

In addition to the myth of the "perfect parent" that Penny described, we now have the phenomenon of "supermom" and "superdad." Both parents are supposed to be climbing the career ladder as fast as they can and being "perfect parents" at the same time. It's enough to drive any parent crazy!

Parent bashing seems to be one of America's favorite pastimes. Parents have been blamed for every flaw and defect in the human race. The feelings of inadequacy that result from all this pressure can be overwhelming. Perfectionism is enemy number one in parenting. If you are hard on yourself, you'll be hard on your kids. Unrealistic expectations cause tremendous stress for you and your children.

In order to combat the tendency toward self-criticism, it is important to understand exactly what your expectations for yourself are. Once you've identified the unrealistic ones, you can discard them and set more humane goals for yourself.

Inventory: *Beliefs and Realities About Parenting*

Materials: Journal and felt-tip pens

Purpose: To identify your unconscious expectations of yourself as a parent and to recognize your own values about parenting

Technique:

1. Divide the page in half lengthwise. Label the left column *Ideal Parent,* and the right column *Source.*
2. With your dominant hand, under *Ideal Parent,* write down all the things you were led to believe parents "should" do for their children. In other words what was the image of the "ideal parent" that was set forth for you by family, church, media, community?
3. Read over what you just wrote and reflect upon it. With your dominant hand, under *Source,* write down where each belief about the "ideal parent" came from.
4. Turn to a new page and divide it into two columns. One column is titled *Agree,* the other is *Disagree.* In each column write down the items that you agree or disagree with from the "ideal parent" profile.
5. On a separate page, with your dominant hand, write down your own values regarding parenting. What kind of relationship with your child do you want? What can you do to have this kind of relationship with your child?

As you learned in earlier chapters, we each have a Nurturing and Protective Parent Within. Hopefully these parts of yourself have been developed (in the service of your own Inner Child) and can show you how to nurture and protect your baby. There is another aspect of the Inner Parent that is just as powerful: the Critical Parent Within.

This is the voice in our head that tells us we are inadequate, are not measuring up, and will never be good enough. It berates us about everything imaginable: our hair, our body, our house, our bank account, our car, our marriage, and our children. The voice of the Critical Parent goes on and on and never stops.

When it is turned toward the self, the Critical Parent attacks our self-esteem on a regular basis. It shames and blames us and never lets us forget our errors. When we become parents, it can go on for days about how "you don't know what you are doing, you're going to ruin this child, who ever told you you could raise kids?" To add insult to injury, there may be a family member in your life who says pretty much the same things to you. Perhaps it is your own mother or father. It's like having the Critical Parent in stereophonic sound. In fact the Critical Parent Within usually learned its speeches from the authority figures who raised us: parents, teachers, uncles, aunts, and older siblings.

Unaware of the Critical Parent Within, we often deliver its put-down messages onto others, usually our spouses and children. When we shame and blame others (especially our own children), it is the Critical Parent in us that has taken over. We owe it to ourselves, our family, and our loved ones *to take responsibility for our own Critical Parent Within*. For more in-depth guidance on how to deal with the Critical Parent Within, we recommend:

Recovery of Your Inner Child, by Lucia Capacchione, Ph.D.

Inner Dialogue: *Standing Up for Yourself*

Materials: Journal and felt-tip pens
Purpose: To identify your Inner Critical Parent's put-down messages. To assert yourself against destructive self-criticism.
Technique:

1. With your dominant hand write down all the self-critical messages that your Inner Critical Parent says to you about how you are parenting your child.
Example:

- Your baby cries too much. You're a terrible parent.

- Since the baby came, you've let the housework go. What kind of an example are you setting for your child?

- Whatever made you think you could raise a child?

- You don't have a clue about what you're doing.

As you make your list, write as quickly as you can. Do not stop to think about what you are writing.

2. With your non-dominant hand allow yourself to answer back to what the Critical Parent just told you. Think of yourself as a bratty three-year-old sassing back to the Critic Within. Say whatever you feel and use four-letter words if you wish. Have fun!!

Fathers

Just as mothers experience postpartum depression, a father can also have unresolved feelings after the birth of his baby. He can become extremely self-critical, and the perfectionistic voice inside can run rampant. Men have been trained by our culture to close themselves off from feelings of vulnerability. When these feelings arise, the Inner Critic goes into action with statements like "Shape up, you've got to be in charge here. You can't afford to let your fear show. Get a grip on yourself. You're responsible for the family, and don't forget it. They're counting on you."

The new father may turn away from physical and emotional contact with his wife and child. Fathers often feel abandoned and left out of the early parenting process. The mother is intimately involved with the baby's every need, especially if she is breast-feeding. Fathers often feel awkward and spend less time with the baby than the mother does. They may also have less skill and practice in caring for a baby. It is important for parents to talk with each other about these feelings and to problem-solve when necessary.

Another challenge for fathers, especially those who are the sole bread-winner, is the struggle of meeting heavier financial responsibilities. Under emotional stress at home, men often preoccupy themselves with work or career goals. This is easy to justify, but is often an escape from emotional stress at home. Men usually feel more competent in the work sphere than they do in the realm of feelings. Fortunately this pattern is changing. More and more men are participating actively during pregnancy, birth, and early parenting.

It is important for fathers to nurture themselves throughout the stages of parenting from conception onward. This can be done with the help of the exercises presented earlier in the book, especially the ones involving the Inner Child and the baby in the womb.

Inner Child Chat: *How Do You Feel?*

See Chapter Three, page 76.

Awakening Joy, Creativity, and Inner Guidance

Parenting is a sacred trust and one of the most important gifts we will ever receive. We learned this once again at a recent candlelight reunion for parents and babies who had "graduated" from Co-Creations classes. About thirty-five babies and their parents attended. It was truly a beautiful gathering. Several observers noted the feeling of happiness and joy that all these little ones expressed. There was momentary fussing, but very little crying. One woman (who knew nothing about Co-Creations) said, "I'm absolutely amazed at how joyful these babies are. They actually look happy to be here, as if they are excited to see one another." Experiencing this celebration told us that our approach to birth really does work. These babies were full of joy, and so were their parents.

May parenting awaken in you creativity and inner guidance. Have a Joyful Birth!

Glossary of Terms

Cesarean section—Sometimes called C-section. Surgical birth of the baby, involving major abdominal surgery for the mother.

Conception—The moment when the egg joins the sperm.

Crowning—The period during pushing when the baby's head comes out of the vagina.

Endorphins—Comes from *endogenous* ("coming from within") and *morphine* (strongest painkilling drug known). Refers to painkillers created by one's own body. Your body constantly releases endorphins, especially during movement.

Engagement—The firm placement of the baby's head in the pelvis just prior to birth.

Episiotomy—Surgical cut in the perineum to widen the vaginal opening during delivery.

Hyperventilation—Breathing that is too fast. Deprives the mother and the unborn baby of oxygen.

Intrauterine—Refers to whatever takes place within the uterus, such as some kinds of testing. Also applies to the activity and development of the baby.

In utero—The period of time when the baby is still in the uterus (womb).

Lamaze—A form of childbirth education originally taught in the late fifties and early sixties. It was popularized during the seventies and focused mainly on physical and intellectual preparation for childbirth. ASPO/Lamaze today strives to broaden that focus to incorporate more emphasis on the emotional and relationship awareness of childbirth education. It is an active organization of parents and professionals who work toward family-centered birth education.

Leboyer birth routine—Involves gentle birthing practices, such as low lights and soft music or even complete quiet during and immediately following birth;

waiting until the baby's umbilical cord stops pulsating with blood before it is cut; immediate skin-to-skin contact of the baby with the mother and allowing breast-feeding immediately; a warm-water bath for the baby at the bedside of the mother within the first hours following birth.

Neonatal—Refers to the newborn.

Nerve receptors—Nerve endings (receptors), which exist throughout the body and which receive information through your five senses.

Oxytocin—Naturally produced hormone in a woman's body that causes the contraction pattern of labor.

Phobia—An irrational, excessive, or persistent fear of a thing or a situation.

Pitocin—Synthetically produced form of oxytocin that induces the woman's body to create the same results as oxytocin.

Sonogram—Also called ultrasound. A form of X ray.

VBAC—Vaginal birth after prior cesarean. Commonly done following previous cesarean if C-section was for reasons such as fetal distress and had nothing to do with shape and size of pelvis. Check with caregiver for further information regarding this procedure.

Womb—Another term for the uterus.

Phases of Labor

Latent—Refers to early stages of labor: contraction pattern becomes longer, stronger, and closer together. Physical movements such as walking or rocking are useful during the latent phase (1–4 cm dilation). See the Friedman Curve (page 170) for corresponding emotional signs.

Active—Full attention is on each contraction and labor. The woman is actively engaged in breathing, focusing, and relaxation patterns. If it is hospital or birth-center delivery, the woman transfers to place of birth during this phase (4–7 cm dilation).

Transition—Contractions are intense; the woman requires constant physical and emotional love and support (7–10 cm dilation).

Appendix A

Questions to Ask When Choosing a Midwife

Note: Your midwife will be responsible for complete prenatal care, will see you through your labor, and will be available for a time after the baby is born. A midwife provides a communication link between you and your doctor when necessary. She will explain hospital procedures and care for you emotionally during the labor. She is an assistant who provides an emotional and practical service.

- What is your background, training, and experience? How long have you been a midwife? How many births have you attended since the completion of your training?

- What is your philosophy about birth? (Your concerns might include the midwife's attitude about the father's participation, doctor intervention, hospital versus home birth, what happens to the placenta, etc.)

- Explain your role before, during, and after the birth of my baby. What do you do exactly? What do you expect me, my partner, and the support team to do during labor and birth?

- Will you explain hospital procedure if we must transfer to the hospital? Is there a particular doctor or hospital you work with? Which hospital do you go to for tranfers? Can you still help take care of me there?

- Are you available twenty-four hours a day? How do we contact you when we need you?

- How many births do you attend each month? What happens if two births occur simultaneously? Have you ever missed a birth?

- Will you have an assistant or partner at this birth? What happens during medical emergencies if either I or the baby (or both) need immediate care?

- Do you provide postpartum visits after the birth? If so, how often will you visit? How long am I entitled postpartum care? Will there be a check-up at six weeks postpartum?

- What equipment do you carry with you for normal births and for emergencies? What procedures do you insist on?

- Is your CPR (cardiopulmonary resuscitation) certification current? How do you handle emergencies (hemorrhage, cord around baby's neck, baby not breathing spontaneously, cord prolapse)?

- Can I choose my own physician? What about a pediatrician?

- What is your attitude about breast-feeding? Will you help me learn how to do it, or can you refer me to a breast-feeding consultant?

- What is your fee and what services do you provide for this amount? What tests are included, and what extra costs are we likely to incur? (*Note:* It is advisable to research basic hospital charges in your area, including normal and cesarean birth.) What happens if we have to go to the hospital after all? Will our insurance plan reimburse you?

After talking with your prospective midwife, assess your feelings through journaling. Do you like her? Are you comfortable with her attitudes, what she expects of you? Can you be truthful with her? Do you feel free to make your own decisions?

Appendix B

Questions to Ask When Choosing a Doula or Childbirth Assistant

Note: Your doula will see you through your labor and will be available for a time after the baby is born. A doula provides a communication link between you and your doctor when necessary. She cares for you emotionally during the labor, providing a feeling of safety, reassurance, and practicality.

Statistics show that a trained childbirth assistant in attendance at the birth greatly reduces the need for medical intervention. Cesarean sections are reduced by 50 percent; the need for pain medication by 60 percent; labor is shortened by 25 percent. Your baby also has an easier, more gentle birth. An experienced, caring doula can be your greatest ally during the birth!

• What is your background, training, and experience? How long have you been a doula? How many births have you attended since the completion of your training?

• What is your philosophy about birth? (Your concerns might include your doula's attitude about family participation.) What is your attitude about laboring at home prior to hospital delivery?

• Explain your role before, during, and after the birth of my baby. What do you do exactly? What do you expect me, my support person, and my birth team to do? Will you explain hospital procedure before we go and while we're there?

• Are you available twenty-four hours a day? How do we contact you when we need you?

• How many births do you attend each month? What happens if two births occur simultaneously? Have you ever missed a birth?

• Will you have an assistant or partner at this birth? What happens during medical emergencies if either I or the baby (or both) need immediate care?

- Do you provide postpartum visits after the birth? If so, how often will you visit? How long am I entitled postpartum care?

- What is your procedure if I have an emergency delivery at home or on the way to the hospital?

- Is your CPR (cardiopulmonary resuscitation) certification current? Do you know how to perform emergency delivery and early postpartum care?

- Is there a particular doctor or hospital you work with?

- What is your attitude about breast-feeding? Will you help me learn how to do it, or can you refer me to a breast-feeding consultant?

- What is your fee and what services do you provide for this amount? Will our insurance plan reimburse you?

(*Note:* It is advisable to research basic hospital charges in your area. Ask about costs of normal vaginal birth and cesarean birth fees. Next call your personal insurance company and check on your coverage plan. They may already provide coverage for your childbirth-assistant fees. However, if they don't yet provide this service, you can explain the statistical value of the doula and the cost-effectiveness of her work. By repetitively asking about coverage, you will help bring about changes in insurance companies' policies.)

After talking with your prospective doula, assess your feelings through journaling. Do you like her? Are you comfortable with her attitudes, what she expects of you? Can you be truthful with her? Do you feel free to make your own decisions?

Appendix C

Child Care

LOOKING FOR CHILD CARE

There are three basic types of child care parents are looking for:

1. Ongoing day care
2. Baby-sitting
3. Full-time live-in care (nanny)

Note: Many women work shifts and are seeking care providers for evenings or nights as well.

These options require one or more of the following:

- A baby-sitter or nanny in your own home

- A day-care arrangement in someone else's home, usually with other children

- A day-care or play group offered through an institution or corporation

We offer the following suggestions to aid you in your search. First ask for referrals from:

- Your pediatrician

- Your friends

- A local women's organization or club

- Your childbirth educator

- The human resources department of your company

When you have a list of potential candidates, begin your interview process. Just as you searched for a health care provider during pregnancy, you can begin the screening process with a phone interview. Consider asking some of the following questions:

BABY-SITTING (SHORT-TERM)

1. Does the baby-sitter have prior experience? If so, with what age group? Does she or he have any certified training, such as CPR for infants?

2. Ask for three personal references if you don't know this person well.

3. Be certain that she does not smoke if nonsmoking is important to you.

4. Ask if she has her own transportation. Will you be driving her home later?

5. Have the baby-sitter come to your house a few days before you are going out so that you can all become accustomed to one another without the pressure of having to leave in a few minutes.

6. If you ask the baby-sitter to come to your home at least one-half hour before you need to leave, you can do (some of) the following:

- Finish getting ready to go out

- Show him or her where all your child's necessary items are

- Allow the baby-sitter and your child to get accustomed to each other while you're still there. This way the child is not scared to be left alone with a complete stranger, and you have had the chance to see how the baby-sitter relates to your child

7. Make sure the baby-sitter knows how to reach you while you are gone.

8. Take a few minutes to talk to your baby-sitter when you greet her and when you come home. Listen to what she has to say about your child. Over time if this baby-sitter works out for you and your child, her input will be invaluable. She deserves your praise and helpful suggestions.

9. Tell her your rules and expectations. Don't assume she will just know how you want things done.

LONG-TERM DAY CARE

Following your phone interview visit the day-care establishment whether it is in a home or a building. While you're there, observe how the children behave. Do they smile, play, interact with one another, run around? Is the place clean, comfortable, and safe for children, or is it a mess, uncontrolled and disorderly? You can determine a lot about an establishment just by looking around.

1. The day-care center might not take children of a certain age. Find out if they will take babies. Some age limits start with children who are already toilet trained.

2. If it is day care out of a private home, does the provider smoke, or have a smoker in the home? Do not assume your child will be only with the day-care provider. There might be other people at home during the day, or visiting.

3. If the day-care operation is being run as a business, find out about the operator's insurance coverage. Find out what it includes. Make sure your day-care provider has enough insurance to cover herself in case of an emergency.

4. Ask for references and follow up on checking into them. Confirm the specifics of the image of services you are paying for. What is the breakdown of your weekly or monthly payment?

5. Ask how long the day-care provider has been in business. Ask how long each of the staff has worked as day-care providers and if they are certified. Are staff members screened for criminal records at time of employment? If the day-care provider is in business for herself, ask if she is dedicated to this profession as a career. Is she doing this work because she loves it or because it is something to do while her own children grow up?

6. Ask whether they regulate how many vacation days you are allowed (you will not have to pay for these days). You may also be allowed a specific number of sick days. Some day-care centers state that any time you take your child out of day care beyond these limits requires payment. A good day-care provider will give you plenty of notice of her vacation time. She will also have a backup provider available when she is sick.

7. What is the daily routine of the day care? Are there planned activities? Is a rest period planned? Do children have a place to play? If the day-care provider is in her own home, check to see if the outdoor play area is safe.

8. Does this day-care provider show concern for you and your child's special needs? For instance, if your child is allergic to certain foods, will your day-care provider adhere to your instructions and give added attention to that matter?

9. Be prepared to be flexible. Your child is about to be socialized with many other children. Not all of her needs will be met in the same way they would if you were with her all the time. However, she will develop socially and learn how to share with other children.

10. Expect illnesses. Now that your child is in day care with other children, there is no way to protect her from colds. Make sure your child has had all her required inoculations before sending her to day care. Keep up with those inoculations—it is the only real protection against childhood illnesses such as mumps, measles, and chicken pox.

FULL-TIME LIVE-IN CARE (NANNY OR AU PAIR)

If you decide upon a caregiver who works in her own home, remember that this is a business arrangement. Treat your day-care provider as a businessperson, because that's what she is. Show her respect. Do not abuse the personal relationship. Do not make unreasonable personal demands "because she is at home all day." Her primary job is taking care of your child.

If you solicit references through an agency, get names and conduct phone interviews. Ask the following questions:

1. Do you have prior experience? If so, with what age group? Do you have any certified training, such as CPR for infants?

2. Ask for three personal and business references.

3. Be certain that she does not smoke if nonsmoking is important to you.

4. What is her philosophy about child rearing?

5. Your daily communication with this person is crucial. Having a nanny live in your home is a unique experience. It can be a marvelous opportunity to get to know your child through the eyes of another loving caregiver. It is crucial that you listen to what she has to say about your child. She needs your praise and suggestions and must have your respect if the relationship is to continue.

6. You will need to know her plans for the future. This can be extremely important if you are looking for permanency and she wants to leave after one or two years.

7. What are her religious or spiritual beliefs? Are they compatible with your own?

8. What is her lifestyle? Her habits in regard to smoking, drinking, diet, and general health? Are they compatible with yours? Find out if she has a record of criminal arrests. (You may need to do this on your own through city or county agencies.)

It cannot be said too often that you will *never* be replaced by your day-care provider. Your child may love and enjoy someone who takes good care of her, but that will never replace your love. Just as with your own work situation, though you may enjoy and love the people you spend all day with, your primary relationships are with your family. The same will be true for your child.

It is okay to encourage the bond of love and respect to grow between your child and a day-care provider, for they will see a lot of each other in times to come. Remember, your relationship with your child comes first. If your child is happy and healthy at the end of the day, tired but still playing, your day-care situation is a good one.

Resource Guide

ORGANIZATIONS—INFORMATION AND REFERRAL

Alliance of Genetic Support Groups
(National coalition of support groups addressing the needs of individuals and families affected by genetic disorders.)

35 Wisconsin Circle, Suite 440
Chevy Chase, MD 20815
(800) 336-4363

American Academy of Husband-Coached Childbirth (AAHCC)
(Training and referral service for the Bradley method.)

P.O. Box 5224
Sherman Oaks, CA 91413-5224
(800) 423-2397
California: (800) 42-BIRTH

American Cleft Palate Foundation
(Gives parents information about feeding and dental care and referrals to local professionals. Call for a list of support groups.)

1218 Grandview Avenue
Pittsburgh, PA 15211
(800) 24-CLEFT

American College of Nurse Midwives (ACNM)
(The official professional organization for nurse-midwives in the United States. Publishes *Journal of Nurse-Midwifery*—available to members only.)

1522 K Street, N.W., Suite 1000
Washington, DC 20005

American College of Obstetricians and Gynecologists (ACOG)

(The official professional organization for American gynecologists and obstetricians.)

409 12th Street, S.W.
Washington, DC 20024
(800) 762-ACOG (customer-service line)

American Foundation for Maternal Child Health

(Supports research on the effect of the perinatal period on infant and child development.)

439 E. 51st Street
New York, NY 10022
(212) 759-5510

American Holistic Medical Association

(Organization of medical professionals and students practicing holistic medicine. Publishes *Holistic Medicine Quarterly*.)

4101 Lake Boone Trail, Suite 201
Raleigh, NC 27607
(919) 787-0116

American Holistic Nurses' Association

(Organization for professional nurses practicing holistic medicine. Publishes *Journal of Holistic Nursing*.)

4101 Lake Boone Trail, Suite 201
Raleigh, NC 27607
(919) 787-0116

ASPO/Lamaze (American Society for Psychoprophylaxis Obstetrics)

(Official organization for the psychoprophylaxis, or Lamaze, method. Publishes *Lamaze Parents' Magazine* and *Journal of Perinatal Education*.)

1101 Connecticut Avenue, N.W., Suite 700
Washington, DC 20036
(800) 368-4404

Association for Childhood Education International (ACEI)

11501 Georgia Avenue, Suite 315
Wheaton, MD 20902
(301) 942-2443

Association for Pre and Perinatal Psychology and Health

(Organization devoted to the study of the psychological effects of pregnancy and birth on both mothers and children. Publishes *Pre- and Perinatal Psychology Journal*.)

1600 Prince Strret, #500
Alexandria, VA 22314
(703) 548-2802
Fax (703) 548-2808

Birth and Life Bookstore

(Complete source of books, videotapes, and audiotapes about pregnancy, childbirth, and newborns. Mail order available.)

141 Commercial Street, N.E.
Salem, OR 97301
(503) 371-4445

Birth Resources

(A training program in prenatal counseling using visualization and imagery to help pregnant women prevent premature births and increase the likelihood for normal delivery.)

1749 Vine Street
Berkeley, CA 94703
(510) 526-5951

Boston Women's Health Book Collective

(Grassroots women's health organization; creators of *Our Bodies, Our Selves.*)

240A Elm Street
Davis Square
Somerville, MA 02144
(617) 625-0271

Cesarean Prevention Movement (CPM)

(Organization dedicated to lowering cesarean rate.)

P.O. Box 152
Syracuse, NY 13210
(315) 424-1942

Cesarean/Support, Education and Concern (C/SEC)

(Provides support and information on cesarean recovery and prevention.)

22 Forest Road
Framingham, MA 01701
(508) 877-8266

The Confinement Line

(Referral service providing support for expectant mothers confined to bed during pregnancy.)

P.O. Box 1609
Springfield, VA 22151
(703) 941-7183

Doulas of North America (DONA)

(Organization of childbirth assistants.)

1100 23rd Avenue East
Seattle, WA 98112
Fax: (206) 325-0472

Global Maternal Child Health Association

(Water-birth resource and referral service; publishes water-birth information book.)

P.O. Box 366
West Linn, OR 97068
(503) 682-3600; (800) 641-BABY
Fax: (503) 682-3434

Informed Homebirth/Informed Birth and Parenting (IH/IBP)

(Resource information center on alternative birthing methods.)

P.O. Box 3675
Ann Arbor, MI 48106
(313) 612-6857

International Association of Parents and Professionals for Safe Alternatives in Childbirth (NAPSAC)

(Information and resource organization dedicated to freedom of choice in childbearing. Publishes *NAPSAC News*—available to members only.)

P.O. Box 267
Marble Hill, MO 63764
(314) 238-2010

International Childbirth Education Association (ICEA)

(Network and resource organization for childbirth education. Publishes *International Journal of Childbirth Education*—available to members only—and *ICEA Publications Catalog*—see Mail Order Catalogs and Bookstores.)

P.O. Box 20048
Minneapolis, MN 55420-0048
(612) 854-8660

International Confederation of Midwives (ICM)

(International federation of midwife associations.)

10 Barley Mow Passage
Chiswick
London W4 4PH
United Kingdom

International Lactation Consultants Association (ILCA)

201 Brown Avenue
Evanston, IL 60202
(708) 260-8874
Fax: (708) 475-2523; (708) 260-8879

La Leche League International (LLLI)

(Resource and informational network on breast-feeding. Publishes *La Leche League International Catalog* and *La Leche League Brochure for Breast Feeding Reference Library and Database*—see Mail Order Catalogs and Bookstores.)

9616 Minneapolis Avenue
Franklin Park, IL 60131
(800) LA LECHE; (708) 455-7730

Maternity Center Association (MCA)

(Education center for maternity care and midwifery. Publishes *Special Delivery*—available to members only.)

48 East 92nd Street
New York, NY 10128
(212) 369-7300

Midwives Alliance of North America (MANA)

(Dedicated to promoting midwifery, cooperation among midwives, and midwife education. Publishes *MANA News*—available to members only.)

P.O. Box 1121
Bristol, VA 24203-5561

National Association of Childbearing Centers (NACC)

(Referral service for NACC-approved birthing centers; founded by the Maternity Center Association. Also see: Maternity Center Association.)

3123 Gottschall Road
Perkiomenville, PA 18074
(215) 234-8068

National Association of Childbirth Assistants (NACA)

(Organization of childbirth assistants. Publishes *The Childbirth Assistant*.)

205 Copco Lane
San Jose, CA 95123
(408) 225-9167
(800) 868-NACA

National Council for Adoption

1930 17th Street, N.W.
Washington, DC 20009
(202) 328-8072 (hot line); (202) 328-1200 (information)

National Down's Syndrome Congress

(Complete information and hot line.)

1605 Chantilly Drive, Suite 250
Atlanta, GA 30324
(800) 232-6372

National Organization of Circumcision Information Resource Centers (NOCIRC)
(Anticircumcision organization.)

P.O. Box 2512
San Anselmo, CA 94979-2512
(415) 488-9883

National Women's Health Network
(Informational clearinghouse and consumer-advocacy group on women's health issues. Publishes *Network News*—available to members only.)

1325 G Street, N.W.
Washington, DC 20005
(202) 347-1140

Parent Care International, Inc.
(Organization dedicated to improving intensive-care experience for babies, parents, and caregivers.)

9041 Colgate Street
Indianapolis, IN 46268
(317) 872-9913
Contact: Sarah Killian

Parent-to-Parent
(Formerly Parents of Premature and High-Risk Infants International.)

50 North Medical Drive, Rm 2553
University of Utah Hospital
Salt Lake City, UT 84132
(801) 581-2098

Positive Pregnancy and Parenting Fitness
(Organization devoted to training and certifying prenatal and postpartum fitness teachers. Publishes the PPPF newsletter that features holistic articles, books, tapes, and video reviews—$2.50 an issue.)

51 Saltrock Road
Baltic, CT 06330
(203) 822-8573
(800) 433-5523

Pregnancy and Infant Loss Center
(Organization offering support, resources, and education on infant death.)

1421 East Wayzata Boulevard, Suite 30
Wayzata, MN 55391
(612) 473-9372

Resolve Through Sharing

(Organization offering support, literature, and referral to counselors and support groups for parents who have lost children through miscarriage, stillbirth, or neonatal death.)

Lutheran Hospital–La Crosse
1910 South Avenue
La Crosse, WI 54601
(608) 785-0530, ext. 3675

Salvation Army

(Provides a variety of services to young families and parents.)

Check your local listings for the Salvation Army in your area.

Self-esteem Center

(Information and guidance concerning parenting and families.)

16535 9th Avenue North
Plymouth, MN 55447
(612) 473-1840

Sidelines National Support Network

(National nonprofit organization with hundreds of experienced volunteers who have had high-risk pregnancies. Peer-support telephone counseling; community referrals. Founding member of Women and Children First—coalition for positive birth outcome. Publishes newsletter, educational literature.)

P.O. Box 1808
Laguna Beach, CA 92651
(714) 497-2265

Sudden Infant Death Syndrome (SIDS) Alliance

(National nonprofit voluntary health organization dedicated to supporting SIDS families and SIDS research. Information and referrals available through twenty-four-hour nationwide toll-free hot line: 800-221-SIDS. Publishes free brochure on SIDS facts.)

10500 Little Patuxent Parkway, Suite 420
Columbia, MD 21044
(800) 221-7437

Vega Study Center: Macrobiotics

1511 Robinson Street
Oroville, CA 95965
(916) 533-7702
Fax: (916) 533-7908

PERIODICALS

Parents' Magazines

The Birth Gazette
(Quarterly publication on home birth. Editor: Ina May Gaskin, author of *Spiritual Midwifery.*)

42, The Farm
Summertown, TN 38483
(615) 964-3895

The Clarion
(Cesarean-prevention magazine.)

The Cesarean Prevention Movement (CPM)
P.O. Box 152
Syracuse, NY 13210

The Compleat Mother
(Canadian magazine on childbirth and child rearing.)

RR 2
Orangeville
Ontario L9L 2Y9, Canada

Growing Child
(Journal of child rearing with emphasis on newborns.)

P.O. Box 620
Lafayette, IN 47902-0620
(800) 860-2625

Lamaze Parents' Magazine
(Quarterly magazine of ASPO/Lamaze.)

Lamaze Publishing Company
372 Danbury Road
Wilton, CT 06897-2523
(203) 834-2711

Mothering Magazine
(Quarterly magazine covering all aspects of childbearing and child rearing. Also publishes *Midwifery and the Law*—see "Resource Publications.")

515 Don Gaspar
Santa Fe, NM 87501
(505) 984-8116

Professional Journals

Birth—Issues in Perinatal Care
(Interdisciplinary quarterly journal regarding childbirth education and perinatal care.)

> Blackwell Scientific Publications, Inc.
> 238 Main Street
> Cambridge, MA 02142
> (617) 876-7000

The Childbirth Assistant
(Quarterly publication of NACA.)

> National Association of Childbirth Assistants (NACA)
> 205 Copco Lane
> San Jose, CA 95123
> (408) 225-9167
> (800) 868-NACA

Childbirth Instructor Magazine
(Quarterly journal for childbirth educators.)

> P.O. Box 15612
> North Hollywood, CA 91615-5612
> (818) 760-8983

Holistic Medicine Quarterly
(Quarterly journal of holistic medicine for medical professionals and students.)

> American Holistic Medical Association
> 4104 Lake Boone Trail, Suite 201
> Raleigh, NC 27607
> (919) 787-0116

Journal of the Association for Pre and Perinatal Psychology and Health
(Journal of the Association for Pre- and Perinatal Psychology and Health. Also see "Organizations.")

> 1600 Prince Stret, #500
> Alexandria, VA 22314
> (703) 548-2802

Journal of Holistic Nursing
(Quarterly journal of holistic nursing.)

> Sage Publications, Inc.
> 2455 Teller Road
> Newbury Park, CA 91320
> (805) 499-0721

Journal of Nurse-Midwifery
(Bimonthly publication of the American College of Nurse-Midwives; includes articles on all aspects of childbirth.)

Elsevier Science Publications Co., Inc.
655 Avenue of the Americas
New York, NY 10010
(212) 989-5800

Journal of Perinatal Education
(Professional journal for ASPO/Lamaze practitioners.)

ASPO/Lamaze
1101 Connecticut Avenue, N.W., Suite 700
Washington, DC 20036
(800) 368-4404

Midwifery Today
(Professional journal for birth practitioners.)

P.O. Box 2672
Eugene, OR 97402
(503) 344-7438

MAIL ORDER CATALOGS
Be Healthy Catalog for Expectant and New Parents
(Fitness and informational books; instructional, musical, and children's audio-tapes, videos, and natural products. Mail order.)

51 Saltrock Road
Baltic, CT 06330
(203) 822-8573
(800) 433-5523

Bookmarks (ICEA Publications Catalog)
(Quarterly catalog of childbirth education materials. Also see "Organizations.")

International Childbirth Education Association (ICEA)
P.O. Box 20048
Minneapolis, MN 55420-0048
(612) 854-8660

Childbirth Graphics
(Childbirth and parent education materials.)

5045 Franklin
P.O. Box 21207
Waco, TX 76702-1207
(800) 299-3366
Fax: (817) 751-0221

Imprints Catalog
(Reviews books, videotapes, and audiotapes about pregnancy, childbirth, and newborns. Mail order available.)

141 Commercial Street, NE
Salem, OR 97301
(503) 371-4445
Orders: (800) 736-0631
Fax: (503) 371-5395

La Leche League International Catalog
La Leche League Breast-feeding Reference Library and Database Brochure
(Catalog of books and resources on breast-feeding; directory of articles and other materials available from the La Leche League Reference Library and Database.)

La Leche League International
9616 Minneapolis Avenue
Franklin Park, IL 60131
(800) LA LECHE; (708) 455-7730

Maternity Center Association Publications
(Catalog of publications and educational materials from the Maternity Center Association. Also see "Organizations.")

48 East 92nd Street
New York, NY 10128
(212) 369-7300

Midwifery and the Law
(Summary of state midwife laws for all fifty states; includes listing of regional and national alternative birth organizations and midwifery schools.)

Mothering Magazine
515 Don Gaspar
Santa Fe, NM 87501
(505) 984-8116

Naturpath
(Catalog of birthing supplies, midwifery kits, and newborn products.)

4308 N.W. 13th Street
Gainesville, FL 32609
(800) 542-4784

Optimal Family Health Catalog
(Catalog of books, tapes, and products for holistic health, pregnancy, and birth.)

P.O. Box 398-MT
Monroe, UT 84758

Parenting Video Resource Center Catalog
(Catalog of instructional videotapes.)

Consumer Vision
149 Fifth Avenue
New York, NY 10010

Videofarm
(Spiritual midwifery. Catalog of birthing videos created by publishers of *The Birth Gazette*.)

34, The Farm
Summertown, TN 38483
(615) 964-2472

SUPPORT GROUPS

There are many support groups for expectant and new parents throughout the United States. To find a support group near you, check your local alternative-health magazines or call one of the groups listed in the "Organizations" section of this Resource Guide. For a listing of regional organizations, contact *Mothering Magazine* to obtain a copy of its nationwide review of home and alternative birthing methods, *Midwifery and the Law* (see "Mail Order Catalogs"). You can also learn about local support groups through computer on-line services, such as Echo (see "Computer On-Line Resources").

Compassionate Friends

P.O. Box 3696
Oak Brook, IL 60522-3696
(708) 990-0010

Grief Recovery Helpline
(For any significant loss.)

(800) 445-4808

Resolve
(Pamphlets and information about infertility and pregnancy loss.)

Send SASE to:
1310 Broadway
Somerville, MA 02144-1731
(617) 623-1156; helpline: (617) 623-0744

SHARE

(Pregnancy and infant-loss support. Free newsletter to bereaved parents; fee for newsletter to others.)

Saint Joseph Health Center
National SHARE Office
300 First Capitol Drive
St. Charles, MO 63301-2893
(314) 947-6164

COMPUTER ON-LINE RESOURCES

Echo Communications Group

On-line computer network with 40 percent female subscribers (highest of any on-line service), featuring the following birth-related "conferences" and on-line support groups:

- Alternative Birth

- Having Children

- Motherhood and Friendship

For information or to become a subscriber, contact:
Stacey Horn, Director
Echo Communications Group
97 Perry Street, Suite 13
New York, NY 10014
(212) 255-3839

CompuServ

For information or to become a subscriber, contact:
Westbrook Corporate Park
2180 Wilson Road
Columbus, OH 43228
(800) 848-8199

Annotated Bibliography

GENERAL CHILDBIRTH INFORMATION

Armstrong, Penny, and Sheryl Feldman. *A Wise Birth: Bringing Together the Best of Natural Childbirth with Modern Medicine*. New York: William Morrow and Co., Inc., 1990.
- Offers ideas for planning a healthier, more emotionally satisfying birth.

Baldwin, Rahima. *Special Delivery: The Complete Guide to Informed Birth*. Berkeley, CA: Celestial Arts, 1986.
- A general guide to childbirth preparation, including practical information and emotional considerations. This book includes emphasis on home birth.

Eisenberg, Arlene, Sandee Hathaway, and Heidi E. Murkoff. *What to Expect When You're Expecting*. New York: Workman, 1991.
- A comprehensive guide for pregnancy.

Harper, Barbara. *Gentle Birth Choices*. Rochester, VT: Inner Traditions, 1994.
- An informative book to help women decide on birth options that provide a gentle birth transition.

Kitzinger, Sheila. *Your Baby, Your Way: Making Pregnancy Decisions and Birth Plans*. New York: Pantheon Books, 1987.
- A helpful guide to options for birthing.

———. *The Complete Book of Pregnancy and Childbirth*. New York: Alfred A. Knopf, 1980.
- A well-illustrated manual for childbirth preparation.

———. *Birth over Thirty*, revised edition. New York: Penguin Books, 1985.
- A practical, reassuring book about the joys and challenges of birth over thirty.

Korte, Diane, and Roberta Scaer. *A Good Birth, a Safe Birth*. New York: Bantam Books, 1984.
- Informs you of options available during pregnancy, labor, and birth.

Lieberman, Adrienne. *Easing Labor Pain: The Complete Guide to Achieving a*

More Comfortable and Rewarding Birth, second edition. Garden City, NY: Doubleday and Co. Inc., 1992.

McKay, Susan. *The Assertive Approach to Childbirth: The Future Parents' Guide to a Positive Pregnancy.* New York: Prentice Hall, 1983.

Simkin, Penny, Janet Whalley, and Anne Keppler. *Pregnancy, Childbirth and the Newborn: A Complete Guide for Expectant Parents.* Deephaven, MN: Meadowbrook Press, 1984.

- A comprehensive, well-written guide for expectant parents. This book includes information concerning early postpartum care of your newborn and yourself.

MIDWIVES AND THE DOULA

Gaskin, Ina Mae. *Spiritual Midwifery.* Summertown, TN: The Book Publishing Co., 1980.

- Birth stories of several women who delivered on a farm commune using midwives. Each story illustrates spiritual, emotional, and relationship aspects of labor and delivery. Offers emotional support.

Hallet, Elizabeth, and Karen Ehrlich. *Midwife Means with Woman: A Guide to Healthy Childbearing.* California Association of Midwives, 1991.

- Informative, useful booklet about midwifery.

Jones, Carl. *Alternative Birth: The Complete Guide.* Los Angeles: Jeremy P. Tarcher, Inc., 1991.

- A helpful guide to exploring birth options.

Klaus, Marshall H. *Mothering the Mother: How a Doula Can Help You Have a Shorter, Easier, Healthier Birth.* Redding, MA: Addison–Wesley 1993.

Perez, Paulina, and Cheryl Snedeker. *Special Women: The Role of the Professional Labor Assistant.* Seattle, WA: Pennypress, 1990.

EXERCISE

Bing, Elisabeth. *Elisabeth Bing's Guide to Moving Through Pregnancy.* New York: Farrar, Straus and Giroux, 1992.

- Exercises and helpful tips about how to make your pregnancy more comfortable at work and at home.

Noble, Elizabeth. *Essential Exercises for the Childbearing Years,* revised edition. Boston: Houghton Mifflin, 1982.

- Extensive, well-illustrated guide to exercises during pregnancy and after birth.

Olkin, Sylvia Klein. *Positive Pregnancy Fitness.* New York: Avery Publishers Group, Inc., 1987.

- Mental, spiritual, and physical preparation for childbirth through yoga, relaxation, and body exercises.

———. *Positive Parenting Fitness.* New York: Avery Publishers Group, Inc., 1992.

- A useful guide to exercises, nutrition, breast-feeding, baby massage, and acupressure for the entire new family.

Parvati-Baker, Jeannine. *Prenatal Yoga and Natural Birth.* Berkeley, CA: North Atlantic Books, 1986.

- Emphasis on spiritual aspects of yoga during pregnancy and natural birth.

JOURNALING

Baldwin, Rahima, and Terra Palmarini. *Pregnant Feelings: Developing Trust in Birth,* second edition. Berkeley, CA: Celestial Arts, 1990.
- A workbook about feelings during pregnancy for pregnant women and their partners.

Capacchione, Lucia. *The Creative Journal: The Art of Finding Yourself.* Athens, OH: Ohio University/Swallow Press, 1980.
- Guidelines for over fifty journal activities, illustrated with drawings and writings by the author's students and clients.

———. *The Well-Being Journal.* North Hollywood, CA: Newcastle, 1989.
- More journal activities, this time with a focus on health and healing.

———. *The Picture of Health: Healing Your Life with Art.* Carson, CA: Hay House, 1992.
- A guide to healing and health with art and writing therapy techniques. Includes collage, mandala-making, and creative journaling. Illustrated with client and student art.

———. *Recovery of Your Inner Child.* New York: Simon & Schuster, 1991.
- Features a step-by-step self-parenting guide for healing one's inner child through journal work, right/left hand drawing, inner dialogues, art, and movement.

———. *The Creative Journal for Children: A Guide for Parents, Teachers, and Counselors.* Boston: Shambhala Publications, 1989.
- Simple exercises in writing and drawing to foster your child's creativity, self-esteem, and learning skills. An excellent tool for older siblings (five- to fifteen-year-olds) to deal with their feelings about mom's pregnancy and the addition of a new family member.

———. *The Creative Journal for Teens,* revised edition. North Hollywood, CA: Newcastle Publishing Co., 1992.
- A journal-keeping guide addressed to teenagers. It is illustrated by high school students. Extremely valuable for pregnant teenagers and their partners or support persons.

———. *The Power of Your Other Hand.* North Hollywood, CA: Newcastle Publishing Co., 1988.
- A course in channeling the inner wisdom of the right brain through writing with the non-dominant hand and dialoguing with both hands.

Peterson, Gayle. *An Easier Childbirth: A Mother's Guide for Birthing Normally,* second edition. 1993. Shadow and Light Publications, 1749 Vine Street, Berkeley, CA 94703.
- A woman's workbook concerning emotional preparation for labor and birth.

PARENTING/CHILD DEVELOPMENT

Brazelton, T. Berry. *Families: Crisis and Caring.* Reading, MA: Addison-Wesley Publishing Co. Inc., 1989.

- Reassuring advice to parents concerning parenting during crisis.

Clarke-Illsley, Jean. *Self-Esteem: A Family Affair.* San Francisco: Harper & Row Publishers, 1978.
- Emotional ages and stages of development with affirmations designed for each developmental stage.

———. *Growing Up Again: Parenting Ourselves, Parenting Our Children.* San Francisco: Harper & Row Publishers, 1989.
- Supports reparenting yourself as you parent your children.

Crary, Elizabeth. *Without Spanking or Spoiling: A Practical Approach to Toddler and Preschool Guidance.* Seattle: Parenting Press, Inc. 1993.
- A useful guide to common early-childhood parenting issues.

Dreikurs, Rudolph, and Vicki Soltz. *Children: The Challenge.* New York: NAL-Dutton, 1987.
- A parenting classic that gives useful advice concerning effective parenting techniques.

Gordon, Thomas. *P.E.T.: Parent Effectiveness Training.* New York: The New American Library, Inc., 1975.
- A handbook of effective, tested ways to raise responsible children.

Jones, Sandy. *Crying Baby, Sleepless Nights: Why Your Baby Is Crying and What You Can Do About It.* Boston: Harvard Common Press, 1992.
- Self-nurturing for parents as well as information on nurturing your baby.

Leach, Penelope. *The First Six Months: Getting Together with Your Baby.* New York: Alfred A. Knopf, 1987.
- A guide to child care for your newborn.

———. *Your Baby and Child: From Birth to Age Five.* New York: Alfred A. Knopf, 1989.
- Revised and expanded paperback edition concerning child care. This new edition is sensitively written and well illustrated.

Samuels, Michael, and Nancy Samuels. *The Well Baby Book.* New York: Summit Books, 1979.
- A holistic approach to baby care.

Sears, William, M.D. *Keys to Caring and Preparing for Your New Baby.* Hauppauge, NY: Barron's Educational Series, Inc., 1991.
- Practical advice about prenatal and newborn care.

———. *The Fussy Baby: How to Bring Out the Best in Your High Need Child.* New York: NAL-Dutton, 1985.
- Support, tips, and loving, helpful advice for parents of fussy babies.

Sears, William, M.D., and Martha Sears. *The Baby Book: Everything You Need to Know About Your Baby—From Birth to Age Two.* Boston: Little, Brown & Co., 1993.
- Warm, practical guide to caring for your newborn. Large book but easy to read.

———. *Three Hundred Questions New Parents Ask: Answers About Pregnancy, Childbirth and Infant and Childcare.* New York: NAL-Dutton, 1991.
- Written in a question and answer format.

Thevenin, Tine. *The Family Bed.* Wayne, NJ: Avery Publishers Group, Inc., 1987.

- A discussion concerning the rediscovery of an age-old concept in child rearing: the family bed.

GRIEF AND UNEXPECTED OUTCOMES

Childs-Gowell, Elaine. *Good Grief Rituals, Tools for Healing.* Barrytown, NY: Station Hill Press, 1992.
- Useful ways to deal with past or present grief.

Davis, Deborah L. *Empty Cradle, Broken Heart.* Golden, CO: Fulcrum Publishing, Inc., 1991.
- Helpful information concerning the emotions surrounding the death of a baby.

English, Jane. *Different Doorway: Adventures of a Cesarean Born.* Mount Shasta, CA: Earth Heart, 1985.
- The true account of the author's experience of her cesarean birth and its impact on her life.

Harrison, Helen. *The Premature Baby Book: A Parent's Guide to Coping and Caring in the First Years.* New York: St. Martin, 1984.
- Well-illustrated and comprehensive data, with helpful emotional and medical advice for dealing with the birth of a premature baby.

Ilse, Sherokee, and Linda Burns. *Empty Arms: Coping After Miscarriage, Stillbirth and Infant Death,* revised edition. Minneapolis: Wintergreen Press, 1990.
- Practical support for decision-making during the grieving period.

Jason, Janine. *Parenting Your Premature Baby.* New York: Doubleday and Company, Inc., 1990.
- A realistic guide explaining the care of your premature baby. Offers supportive and loving advice.

Kübler-Ross, Elizabeth. *On Children and Death.* New York: Macmillan, 1993.
- Advice for parents concerning the death of a child or dealing with children's feelings about death. This book is written by a pioneer in the field of death and grief counseling.

Pacific Post Partum Support Group: *Post Partum Depression and Anxiety: A Self-Help Guide for Mothers.* British Columbia, Canada: University of British Columbia Press, 1988.
- A very helpful booklet concerning postpartum depression. A good tool for support groups after childbirth.

Schwiebert, Pat, and Paul Kirk, M.D. *When Hello Means Goodbye.* Portland, OR: University of Oregon Medical School, 1985.
- A sensitive guide for parents whose child dies before birth, at birth, or shortly after birth.

———. *Still to Be Born.* Portland, OR: University of Oregon Medical School, 1990.
- Guide to pregnancy after experiencing a miscarriage, stillbirth, or infant death.

Vissell, Barry, M.D., and Joyce Vissell. *Risk to be Healed: The Heart of Personal and Relationship Growth.* Borgro Press. 1989.

FOOD AND NUTRITION

Brewer, Gail Sforza. *Pregnant Vegetarian.* New York: Viking Penguin, 1994.
- Helpful suggestions for vegetarians during pregnancy.

Brewer, Gail Sforza, and Tom Brewer. *What Every Pregnant Woman Should Know: The Truth About Diets and Drugs in Pregnancy.* New York: Viking Penguin, 1986.
- Very useful information on the nutritional needs of pregnancy. Helpful advice about the relationship of toxemia and diet in pregnancy.

Elliott, Rose. *The Vegetarian Mother and Baby Book: A Complete Guide to Nutrition, Health and Diet During Pregnancy and After.* New York: Pantheon, 1986.
- Advice on vegetarian dietary needs. Includes recipes.

Kushi, Michio, and Aveline Kushi. *Macrobiotic Pregnancy and Care of the Newborn.* Briarcliff Manor, NY: Japan Publications Inc., 1983.
- Thorough and useful guide to a vegetarian diet during pregnancy and early childhood. This book includes dietary information concerning macrobiotics during and after childbirth.

Lappé-Moore, Frances. *Diet for a Small Planet.* New York: Ballantine Books, 1982.
- Valuable information on nutrition and supportive reasons for a vegetarian diet.

Robertson, Laurel, Carol Flinders, and Bronwen Godfrey. *Laurel's Kitchen: A Handbook for Vegetarian Cookery and Nutrition.* New York: Bantam Books, 1982.
- This book offers a section on nutrition during pregnancy, infancy, and early childhood.

BREAST-FEEDING

Huggins, Kathleen. *The Nursing Mother's Companion,* revised edition. Boston: Harvard Common Press, 1991.
- Helpful guide to problem-solving during breast-feeding.

La Leche League. *The Womanly Art of Breastfeeding.* Franklin Park, NY: Interstate Printers and Publishers, Inc., 1991.
- A breast-feeding classic with the latest information. An extremely useful resource.

Renfrew, Mary, Chloe Fisher, and Suzanne Arms: *Bestfeeding.* Berkeley, CA: Celestial Arts, 1990.
- A clear, accurate, and helpful breast-feeding resource.

TOUCH AND MASSAGE/RELAXATION

Benson, Herbert. *Relaxation Response.* Avenal, NJ: Outlet Book Co., Inc., 1993.
- General information about how the body achieves relaxation.

Heinl, Tina. *Baby Massage: Shared Growth Through the Hands.* Boston: Sigo Press, 1991.
- Beautifully illustrated book about infant massage.

McClure, Vimala Schneider. *Infant Massage: A Handbook for Loving Parents.* New York: Bantam Books, 1989.

- Reasons and instructions for infant massage. Fully illustrated.

Stillerman, Elaine. *Mother Massage: A Handbook for Relieving the Discomforts of Pregnancy.* New York: Bantam Doubleday Dell, 1992.
- Acupressure, effleurage, and massage techniques for mothers during and after pregnancy and delivery.

MIND/BODY CONNECTION

Bresler, David E., and Richard Trubo. *Free Yourself from Pain.* New York: Simon & Schuster, 1981.
- Useful guide to understanding how the brain interprets pain sensations.

Dick-Read Grantly, M.D. *Childbirth Without Fear: The Original Approach to Natural Childbirth,* revised edition. Helen Weisel and Harlan F. Ellis, eds. New York: HarperCollins, 1987.
- Valuable information concerning the mind-body connection in labor as it relates to the fear/pain cycle.

Grof, Stanislav. *Beyond the Brain: Birth, Death and Transcendence in Psychotherapy.* Albany, NY: University of New York Press, 1985.

————. *Realms of the Human Unconscious.* New York: Dutton, 1976.

Jones, Carl. *Mind Over Labor.* New York: Penguin Books, 1987.
- Very useful little book with helpful ideas presented clearly.

————. *Visualizations for an Easier Childbirth.* Deephaven, MN: Meadowbrook, 1988.
- Exercises in visualization to help with relaxation during labor and following birth.

Robbins, Anthony. *Awaken the Giant Within.* New York: Simon & Schuster, 1991.
- A useful guide to personal growth. Information about how the mind affects the body's response and how you can feel in control of your own decisions.

THE UNBORN CHILD

Chamberlain, David. *Babies Remember Birth: And Other Scientific Discoveries About the Mind and Personality of Your Newborn.* New York: Ballantine Books, 1990.
- Latest information about the capabilities of newborn babies, including consciousness and memory.

Gabriel, Michael, and Marie Gabriel. *Voices from the Womb.* Lower Lake, CA: Aslan Publishing, 1992.
- A hypnotherapist relates countless stories of adults who have relived their memories of prebirth experiences.

Leboyer, Frederick. *Birth Without Violence.* New York: Fawcett Columbine, 1990.
- Newly translated, a classic in childbirth preparation. A sensitive look at infants, with useful ideas to prepare a pleasant, peaceful birth for your child.

Nathanielsz, Peter W. *Life Before Birth and a Time to Be Born.* Ithaca, NY: Promethian Press, 1992.

- Documented scientific research concerning the unborn child.

Nilsson, Lennart. *A Child Is Born*. New York: Delacorte Press, 1990.
- Outstanding photographic review of fetal development and birth.

Verny, Thomas, M.D., with John Kelly. *The Secret Life of the Unborn Child*. New York: Dell, 1986.
- Groundbreaking book in prenatal psychology. Explores the influence of prebirth environment on the unborn child.

Verny, Thomas, M.D., and Pamela Weintraub. *Nurturing the Unborn Child: A Nine-Month Program for Soothing, Stimulating, and Communicating with Your Baby*. New York: Bantam Doubleday Dell, 1991.
- A rich, multifaceted program of stimulation and bonding with your unborn baby.

HISTORY/SOCIOLOGY OF PREGNANCY

Dunham, Carroll, and The Body Shop Team. *Mamatoto: A Celebration of Birth*. New York: Penguin Books Inc., 1991.
- Visually stunning guide to lore and legends about childbirth. Good ideas for planning birth.

Edwards, Margot, and Mary Waldorf. *Reclaiming Birth: History and Heroines of American Childbirth Reform*. Trumansburg, NY: The Crossing Press, 1984.
- An inspirational treatise on women's rights in birth.

Mitford, Jessica. *The American Way of Birth*. New York: Penguin Inc., 1992.
- Hard-hitting and well-researched survey of the economics and politics of the multibillion-dollar birth industry in America today. Includes historical background, examples of healthy, empowering (for parents and babies) approaches as well as common atrocities perpetrated by professionals, organizations, and institutions.

PHILOSOPHICAL

Gibran, Kahlil. *The Prophet*. New York: Alfred A. Knopf, 1956.
- Beautiful, philosophical advice on love, marriage, children, and many more subjects.

Panuthos, Claudia. *Transformation Through Birth: A Woman's Guide*. New York: Bergin & Garvey, 1984.
- Philosophical discussion of psychological preparation for birth, and its potential for a woman's empowerment and transformation.

Peterson, Gayle. *Birthing Normally: A Personal Growth Approach to Childbirth*, second edition. Berkeley, CA: Shadow and Light Publications, 1984.
- Philosophical discussion about how a woman's beliefs, lifestyle, behavior, and environment affect childbirth.

COUPLES/PARTNERS

Hendricks, Harville. *Getting the Love You Want: A Guide for Couples*. New York: Harper Perennial, 1988.
- Useful self-help information and exercises for couples to stimulate communication and interaction.

Jones, Carl. *Sharing Birth: A Father's Guide to Giving Support During Labor.* Granby, MA: Bergin & Garvey Publishers, Inc., 1989.
- Helpful suggestions concerning how to guide a woman through birth.

Jones, Carl, and Jan Jones. *The Birth Partner's Handbook.* Deephaven, MN: Meadowbrook, 1989.
- Short, concise guide to preparing for labor.

Ray, Sondra, and Bob Mandel. *Birth and Relationship: How Your Birth Affects Your Relationships.* Berkeley, CA: Celestial Arts, 1987.
- This book provides information concerning effects of birth on the adult.

Schwartz, Leni. *Bonding Before Birth: A Guide to Becoming a Family.* Boston: Sigo Press, 1991.
- One of the first guidebooks, now updated. For couples preparing mentally and emotionally for birth.

Simkin, Penny. *The Birth Partner: Everything You Need to Know to Help a Woman Through Childbirth.* Boston: Harvard Common Press, 1989.
- Very complete and useful information to guide a birth-support person in role preparation.

Stone, Hal, and Sidra Winkelman. *Embracing Each Other: Relationship as Teacher, Healer and Guide.* Marina Del Rey, CA: DeVorss and Co., 1985.
- How to work on your relationship.

Vissell, Barry, M.D., and Joyce Vissell. *The Shared Heart: Relationship, Initiations and Celebration.* Oakland, CA: Ramira Publishing, 1984.

VIDEOTAPES

Most of the following videotapes can be ordered through Birth & Life Bookstore, (800) 736-0631

Baldwin, Rahima. *Special Delivery.* (42 min.).
- Detailed exploration of three births. Helpful labor and birth options given.

Driscoll, Jeanne. *Diapers and Delirium.* (27 min.).
- Excellent video about early parenting.

Harper, Barbara. *Gentle Birth Choices.* (46 min.). 1993.
- A video showing several birth choices. Good discussion of birth options in America today.

Hathaway, Jay. *Children at Birth.* (48 min.).
- Shows four natural, unmedicated births at home, hospital, and birth center. All births are with children present.

———. *Dr. Brewer's Pregnancy Nutrition Program.* (17 min.).
- The role of good nutrition for a healthy, low-risk birth.

Kidvidz. *Hey, What About Me?* (25 min.).
- Action-packed video of songs, games, and rhymes for the older sibling. This video helps with adjustment after birth.

Lehman, Richard, and Kittie Frantz. *Delivery Self-Attachment.* (6 min.) 1992.
- Visual verification of babies' self-attachment to the breast. Shows three babies and the effect of medication on breast-feeding attachment.

Netherlands Association of Midwives. *Home Birth in Holland.* (60 min.).

- A film about home deliveries.

Noble, Elizabeth. *Baby Joy.* (68 min.). 1989.
- Exercises and activities for parents and infants.

Paciornik, Claudio and Moyses. *Birth in the Squatting Position.* (10 min.).
- Classic film of South American women giving birth in the squatting position. Each birth is done with ease.

Peterson, Gayle. *Body-Centered Hypnosis for Childbirth.* Shadow and Light Productions, 1749 Vine Street, Berkeley, CA 94703.
- A training tape of Gayle Peterson's techniques for resolving emotional fears and concerns during childbirth. Uses imagery and visualization techniques.

Schmidt, Tracy. *Every Mom's Prenatal Exercise and Relaxation Video.* (60 min.).
- Healthy prenatal exercise program.

Smith, Linda. *A Healthier Baby by Breast-feeding.* (20 min.). 1991.
- Excellent tips and helpful suggestions about breast-feeding.

St. Charles, Elise. *Modern Moves for Pregnancy Fitness.* (60 min.). 1990.
- Exercises appropriate for a woman's health during pregnancy.

Taylor, Ron. *Heart to Heart.* (15 min.)
- Caring and helpful film on the techniques of infant massage.

Uplinger, Laura. *A Gift for the Unborn.* (28 min.)
- Ways creative interaction enhances well-being and learning in your unborn baby.

Wilbert, Dennis. *The Circumcision Question.* (15 min.). 1991.
- A clear discussion concerning the pros and cons of circumcision.

AUDIO RECORDINGS

The following tapes may be ordered through the three bookcenters for childbirth and parenting.

ASPO/LAMAZE National Bookstore
2931 S. Sepulveda Blvd., Suite F.
Los Angeles, CA 90064
(800) 650-0818

Birth and Life Bookstore, a division of Cascade HealthCare Products
141 Commercial St., N.E.
Salem, OR 97301
(800) 736-0631 or (503) 371-4445

ICEA Bookcenter
P.O. Box 20048
Minneapolis, MN 55420
(800) 624-4934

Relaxation

Dream Images. Search for Serenity
The Healer's Touch. Search for Serenity
Lullabies. Marcia Berman
Dolphin Dreams. Jonathan Goldman
Rain Dance. Philip Elcano
Music to Be Born By. Mickey Hart
Transitions: Womb Sounds for Mother and Child. Transitions Music
Transitions 2: Music to Help Baby Sleep. Transitions Music
Relax with the Classics. The Lind Institute
Ritual Songs. Colorado Midwives Association
Pachelbel's Canon in D Minor: With Nature's Ocean Sounds
Love Chords: Music for the Pregnant Mother and her Unborn Child. Compiled by
   Thomas Verny.

Soothing *"popular"* music
Your favorite *religious* music

Rhythmic

Medicine Music. Bobby McFerrin

Imagery

The Picture of Health. Lucia Capacchione. Hay House.
The Wisdom of Your Other Hand. Lucia Capacchione. Sounds True.
   • A set of five tapes: "The Body as Storyteller," "The Inner Family,"
      "Meaningful Work," "The Relationship Dance," and "Art Therapy
      and the Creative Journal."
Birth Cave Imagery: Relax in Your "Special Place." Sandra Bardsley. Co-Creations.
   (P.O. Box 3204, Ashland, OR 97520 (503) 488-3446).
   • Guided imagery set to music. Designed to help you find your "special
      place" and the "birth cave."
*The Child Within: Six Meditations for Expectant Couples. Relax and Enjoy Your
   Baby Within.* Sylvia Klein Olkin.
Pregnancy, Birth, and Bonding. Shadow and Light Productions, 1749 Vine Street,
   Berkeley, CA 94703.
   • An audiotape for pregnant women. Side one: relaxation and bonding
      with the unborn child. Side two: visualization and body-centered hyp-
      nosis for giving birth.

PAMPHLETS AND CATALOGS

ASPO/LAMAZE National Bookstore
2931 S. Sepulveda Blvd., Suite F.
Los Angeles, CA 90064
(800) 650-0818

Birth and Life Bookstore, a division of Cascade HealthCare Products
141 Commercial Street, N.E.
Salem, OR 97301
(800) 736-0631 or (503) 371-4445

ICEA Bookcenter
P.O. Box 20048
Minneapolis, MN 55420
(800) 624-4934

Index

massage:
  abdominal, postpartum bleeding and, 193
  of infants, 243–45
  perineal, 184–87
  sources on, 244–45, 292–293
maternity clothes, 44
medical care, see health care
medical interventions:
  Birth Plan and, 151–52
  routine, in hospital births, 129, 131, 132
Merry, Teri A., 104
midwives, 51, 52, 59
  choosing, 265–66
  sources on, 288
mind/body connection, 200
  sources on, 293
Mirror Work:
  Body Image/Self-image exercise, 45
  Standing Tall exercise, 46–47
miscarriages, 200
  delayed mourning for, 81
Mitford, Jessica, 208
"Mom, Just Say No" exercise, 123–25
mourning, see grieving
movement:
  during labor, 171, 181
  during pregnancy, 46
Moving into Place exercise, 190–91
music, 30
  baby's response to, 179–80
  during labor, 178–79

nannies, 272
negative beliefs:
  changing of, 23
  about pregnancy and birth, 21
negative expectations, 86

negative imagery, 26
negative thoughts:
  letting go of, 86, 87–88
  questions asked of oneself and, 142–44
  verbal affirmations and, 93
  worry and, 89
neglect, 249
  see also abuse
non-dominant hand:
  dialogues between dominant hand and, 25
  drawing and writing with, 25–26
non-stress test, 66–67
nursery care, Birth Plan and, 153
nursing, see breast-feeding
Nurturing Parent Within, 101–103
nurturing yourself, see self-nurturing
nutrition, 115–25
  baby's needs and, 123–25
  calcium and, 120–21
  carbohydrates and, 121–22
  cravings and, 117–18, 119
  Eats and Treats exercise and, 118
  fats and, 122
  iron and, 121
  "Mom, Just Say No" exercise and, 123–25
  paying attention to eating and, 118–19
  protein and, 121
  sources on, 119–20, 292
  toxins and, 123
  unhealthy foods and, 122
  water and, 120
  weight gain and, 116–17

office interviews, with health care providers, 55, 57–59